GRAZING ACROSS TEXAS

For Charles —
Tosca B.

GRAZING ACROSS

TEXAS

Rod, Gun & Ranch Cooking

Photography and Commentary by
Tosh Brown

Collectors Covey
DALLAS

© 2007 Collectors Covey

Photography and commentary © 2007 Tosh Brown

All rights reserved. No portion of this book may be reproduced—mechanically, electronically, or by any means, including photocopying—without prior written permission of the publisher.

ISBN 1-892505-06-1

Published in 2007 by Collectors Covey

Gallery at Inwood Village
5550 West Lovers Lane, Suite 160
Dallas, Texas 75209

www.collectorscovey.com

Collectors Covey gratefully acknowledges the publishers that have granted permission to reprint the following recipes:

Perini Ranch Steak Rub, Wild Turkey Pie, Roasted Garlic–Horseradish Cream Sauce, Texas Caviar, and Cowboy Potatoes (pages 78, 79, 80, 81, 82, 83) from *Texas Cowboy Cooking* by Tom Perini. Copyright © 2000 by Tom Perini. Reprinted with permission of Comanche Moon Publishing.

Rattlesnake Cakes in a Pistacho Nut Crust, Duck Breast with Red Chili Glaze, Quail and Spinach Salad with Honey Mustard and Bacon Dressing, and Wild Boar Schnitzel (pages 112, 113, 114, 158, 159) from *Cooking Fearlessly: Recipes and Other Adventures from Hudson's on the Bend* by Jeff Blank, Jay Moore, and Deborah Harter. Copyright © 1999 by Fearless Press. Reprinted with permission.

Reata Grill Blend, Grilled Venison Backstrap with Apricot Glaze, Cheese and Bacon Grits, and Cajeta Pound Cake (pages 140, 141) from *A Cowboy in the Kitchen: Recipes from Reata and Texas West of the Pecos* by Grady Spears and Rob Walsh. Copyright © 1998 by Grady Spears and Robb Walsh. Reprinted with permission of Ten Speed Press.

Green Chili and Mexican Crème Smashed Potatoes, Espresso-Rubbed Venison Backstrap with Shiner Bock Beer Blanc, and Grilled Peaches with Spicy Lemon Honey (pages 115, 156) from *Fired Up: More Adventures & Recipes from Hudson's on the Bend* by Jeff Blank and Sara Courington. Copyright © 2005 by Laurentius Press. Reprinted with permission.

Venison Cortadillo, Venison Tampiqueña, and Flan (pages 237, 238, 239) from *Dishes from the Wild Horse Desert: Norteño Cooking of South Texas* by Melissa Guerra. Copyright © 2006 by Melissa Guerra. Reprinted with permission of Wiley Publishing Inc., a subsidiary of John Wiley & Sons, Inc.

Printed and bound through Asia Pacific Offset Ltd.

Printed in China

For my mother, Carolyn Brown, a valiant and accomplished broiler, roaster, baker, and fryer of (nearly) everything we've dragged into her kitchen

CONTENTS

Preface 12

Acknowledgments 14

Publisher's Note 15

Plains and Panhandle 18
    First Shot Outfitters 25
    U Ranch 40
    Stasney's Cook Ranch 51
    Tule Ranch Hunts 58
    Pitchfork Land and Cattle Company 65
    Perini Ranch Steakhouse 75
    Winging It on the High Plains 85

Trans-Pecos 96
    Wildlife Systems 103
    Ocotillo Restaurant 108
    Gage Hotel 116
    Longfellow Ranch 124
    CF Ranch 131
    Reata Restaurant 136

Hill Country 142
    YO Ranch 149
    Hudson's on the Bend 152
    Broken Arrow Ranch 160
    Executive Outfitters 169
    Joshua Creek Ranch 174
    Rough Creek Lodge & Resort 185

Brush Country 192
    Hindes Ranch 198
    Perlitz Ranch 204
    Salado Seco Ranch 210
    Sandy Oaks Ranch 220
    La Bandera Ranch 229
    McAllen Ranch 234

Gulf Coast 240
    Gaido's Restaurant 246
    Bucksnag Hunting Club 252
    Bayflats Lodge 258
    Redfish Lodge 264
    Port "A" Seafood Company 272
    Shells Pasta & Seafood 278
    Lisabella's Bistro 284
    Port Bay Hunting & Fishing Club 290
    Lodge on the Arroyo 296

East Texas 302
    Coon Creek Club 308
    The Big Woods 314
    Sartin's Seafood 322
    Upland Bird Country 326
    East Texas à la Carte 334

Contact Information 343

Index 344

PREFACE

I wish I could have recorded the expressions and statements of courteous befuddlement during the spring of 2005 as word spread among my friends and family members that I was working on a cookbook.

The blank stare would typically come first, and then I would hear: "No kidding? A *cookbook*?"

"Yes, a game and fish cookbook."

"That's great, Tosh. Are they *your* recipes?"

I hate to use a New Millennium cliché here, but I guess you could call these folks my "inner circle"; they obviously know me very well. I've never had any training as a chef—or even a cook. I do love to eat (as my inner circle will also affirm), and during my time on this earth I've probably consumed an entire wild animal park worth of game and fish cooking.

When it comes to mealtime, I'm not a fussy person. Since I'm not much of a cook, I hold firmly to the axiom that beggars should not be choosers. When invited to a potluck affair, I usually volunteer to bring the drinks and the ice, and before I leave I'll make sure that I fuss and fawn over the folks who did the actual cooking. If backed into a corner where I actually have to prepare a meal, you can bet it will be something that shows evidence of hook or bullet trauma. I typically choose recipes with fewer than four ingredients (one of them bacon) that don't require a dedicated trip to the grocery store.

Now, before you slam this book shut and start digging for your receipt, let me explain why I considered myself qualified to swindle my way into such an ambitious project.

From 1989 to 1999, I owned an outfitting company that arranged angling and shooting trips with lodges and outfitters from Alaska to the Amazon. What I learned during that decade of expedition is that the typical sportsman can repeatedly take it on the chin from Mother Nature as long as he is comfortable, well fed, and treated with respect. If it rains for a solid week and the birds don't fly or the fish don't bite, he may still rebook for next year if his bed was cozy and his meals were memorable. But if the weather is awful, the critters don't cooperate, and our sport chokes down garfish and Cheetos for a solid week, there's a good chance that he'll take his business elsewhere.

I have enjoyed a lot of spontaneous shoreline, tailgate, and transom meals, and I've dined with a view in some of the world's finest remote venues. I've eaten a lot of great game and fish cooking with every imaginable spice and regional influence, and I've also picked my way around a few dishes that were entirely indigestible. I am a worldly and practiced diner, a dimly evolved carnivore with a passport and sensible luggage. If my arms appear short, it's because there's an obscure kink in my DNA helix that links me back to *Tyrannosaurus rex*.

In the following pages, you will find a diverse collection of Texas sporting and dining opportunities. My plan with this book was to seek out and present the places where hunters and anglers congregate within our great state: the lodges, ranches, private sporting clubs, and restaurants that indulge the traveling sportsmen. I've also included a few individual entries (entrées) from guides and plain ole good cooks who love to hunt and fish.

With respect to the actual game and fish species, I've included recipes for all of our state's indigenous favorites and a few imports that deserve recognition. Obviously, some may disagree on which species should qualify as a "favorite," so I took the liberty of establishing a set of criteria for inclusion—an editorial sniff test, of sorts.

First off, if John Cowan has ever painted it, it definitely made the book. If it's a species that the average civilized sport prefers not to clean, then it did not make the cut. If the animal sustains itself by grazing and browsing, I was proud to feature it. If it slinks around in the dark and eats out of trash cans, sorry, no recipes for that set.

In some of these pages you'll find lavish facilities with salaried chefs who prepare our various game and fish species with unimaginable ingenuity. And in some cases I've interviewed a guide or camp cook with a hand-welded grill or a propane fryer that prefers to keep it simple: home-style cooking for big appetites.

From Hereford to Harlingen, our state represents a wide spectrum of culinary tastes, cultural influences, and creativity. Each dish, and each personality, has its place among the fields, waters, and timbers that we frequent.

Tosh Brown
Austin
January 27, 2007

ACKNOWLEDGMENTS

I would like to thank the many contributors—chefs, camp cooks, guides, outfitters, ranch owners, and restaurateurs—that you'll find represented in these pages. Visit their restaurants and book their hunts and charters. They're among the best in the business.

I would also like to acknowledge my publisher, Bubba Wood, and his crew at Collectors Covey for taking multiple chances on a small-towner with no formal photography training and absolutely no recall of how to properly diagram a sentence.

A huge thanks to my sister Ellen McKeown for her months of organizing, formatting, and testing all of the recipes that we've published, and dozens more that space could not accommodate.

Thanks to my accountant, Mary Ann Kilgore, for reminding me to log the 9,172.6 Texas road miles that I tallied while gathering material for this book.

Finally, I extend my sincere appreciation to the award-winning editorial and design team of Alison Tartt and Barbara Jezek of Austin. If people only knew what my words and images looked like before this book rolled off the press . . . .

PUBLISHER'S NOTE

State and federal laws prohibit the sale of birds, fish, and animals that are designated as game species; it is therefore illegal for restaurants, clubs, and lodges to serve (sell) them to their patrons. When you see venison listed on a restaurant menu, it is typically an exotic species, such as axis, fallow, or sika deer. The same goes for quail, duck, and pheasant; the restaurants buy those birds from farm-raised stock. With respect to fish, the same laws apply to speckled trout, redfish, bass, crappie, and so on. Flounder, along with most offshore species such as wahoo, tuna, snapper, and dolphin, are not protected as game fish; therefore, they are legal to sell.

This book is a celebration of wild game and fish cooking in Texas. By including recipes that feature designated game species, we are in no way implying that the establishments which furnished the recipes actually serve those dishes to their clientele, or that you may request them when you go there to dine, hunt, or fish.

PLAINS AND PANHANDLE

I **DIDN'T KNOW MUCH ABOUT THE REGION OF TEXAS KNOWN AS THE ROLLING PLAINS**
before I started nosing around in that area and looking for quail leases back in the mid-nineties. At the time I was the proud owner of a string of pointers, a generator on wheels, and a collection of tents and trailers that made up an itinerant little bird hunting lodge on wheels. I was a quail outfitter with gypsy-nomadic inclinations. What I found, during five seasons of leasing ranches and hosting hunters north and west of Abilene, is that just about everything out there can be described with a single adjective.

Big.

Big ranches. Big wind. Big freezes. Big heat. *Huge* thunderstorms. Big country.

One season, on the Foster Ranch near Guthrie, I met a ranch hand named Delbert Ellis, who described the land where he worked quite nicely: "I ain't ever been in a place where a feller can be up to his ass in mud and still have sand blowin' in his eyes."

Officially, the Rolling Plains of Texas is the region sandwiched between the Hill Country, the Cross Timbers, and the High Plains—which is the flat country above the Caprock. To save space and avoid splitting hairs, I'm going to lump the Rolling Plains and the Panhandle into one section. When it's cold in Borger, it's usually cold in Big Spring. When the dust starts blowing sideways in Amarillo, it'll be doing the same in Aspermont a few hours later. There's a distinctive difference in terrain between the two regions (flat as a fritter versus steep and crumbly), but beyond that comparison there's not much reason to split them apart.

It's all big.

From a culinary perspective, there's not much in the way of exotic or foreign influence in the cooking that you'll find in the upper left corner of Texas. Sorry, Oklahoma: some might consider you a bit foreign, but you're not at all exotic. So if I could categorize the cooking that you'll typically find on a Rolling Plains or Panhandle ranch, then I guess I'd describe it as simple, hearty, home-style dishes in large quantities.

Big food for big appetites.

The hunting, up north and out west, is typically done a bit differently than in other parts of the state. You'll find a few tower blinds, top-drive trucks, and tricked-out ATVs, but many hunters in the Plains and Panhandle prefer to go at it on foot. For whitetails and muleys, it's spot-and-stalk hunting using cedar clumps and rimrock as a blind. For quail, there's no need to wait until late season for cold weather and fewer snakes; you can hit the ground running on opening day without much risk of your dogs succumbing to heatstroke, or worse. And then there's the pheasant, the well-decorated import from China that prefers sprinting over flying. In good hatch years you can road-hunt them in the bar ditches with a pellet gun, if you're so inclined, but most people prefer hoofing it through the CRP and the grainfields with several dozen of their best friends and a couple of big-running retrievers.

Sturdy boot leather, however, is not a requirement for all Plains and Panhandle species. In December of 2005, I signed on to a goose hunt near Lubbock that involved a fleet of pickups and Suburbans. We

didn't actually shoot geese out of the vehicles, but that's where we hunkered and shivered and bartered hand-warmer packets while we waited for the geese to start flying. It was 2 degrees that morning, with a sustained wind from the Arctic Circle at about 20 knots. When the geese finally left their roost pond with rings of ice clinging to their breast feathers, there was nothing we could do to keep them out of the corn stubble field where we were set up.

As we were picking up the birds and chipping pack ice from our nostrils after the hunt, one of the guys in our party turned toward the north, squinted into the stinging wind, and polled the group: "Anybody catch the forecast for Anchorage this morning on the Weather Channel?"

If anyone did, they were apparently in too much pain to respond.

"Low 23 and a high of 42," he said.

FIRST SHOT OUTFITTERS

⊞ **Coleman**

Occasionally, you'll find a husband and wife business team that almost seems predestined for success.

Mike Wyatt grew up in Midland and spent his youth raising bird dogs and chasing quail across West Texas. After building a successful pest control business in San Angelo, he sold out to a national chain in 1998 to pursue a career as an outfitter.

Monica Mize grew up in Hico, where her father, Mike, operated Honey Creek Sporting Clays, one of the first clay courses and shooting preserves in the state. At fifteen, Monica applied for a job as a waitress at the Koffee Kup restaurant; she didn't get that job, but they did hire her as a cook.

Today Mike and Monica and their four children live adjacent to their spacious log-built hunting lodge on a small piece of land between Coleman and Abilene. Within twenty-five miles of the lodge, they have leased access to over 50,000 acres of prime Rolling Plains hunting habitat. If dry conditions warrant a change of venue, they also have gate keys to another 60,000 acres farther north and west. Mike oversees the dogs and the hunting and Monica presides over the kitchen and the books. Ask anyone who has seen these two in action, and you'll probably hear a consensus description: boundless energy, enthusiasm, and Texas-style hospitality.

In less than ten years, the Wyatts have built a phenomenally loyal clientele. Hunting purely wild quail over fine dogs, Mike and his guides run basically nonstop from opening day until the closing bell. Mike

Opposite: A determined pointer leading the charge
Right: Mike and Monica Wyatt's new lodge between Coleman and Abilene

Above: Loading up for a morning quail hunt   Below: Classic pointer technique: head down, tail up, nose into the wind

Above: Could be a single, could be another covey . . .   Below: Close to a limit at lunchtime

doesn't believe in clock-watching, and if he finds a big concentration of birds just before noon, then lunch will just have to wait.

In addition to quail hunting, First Shot also runs fully outfitted dove, deer, and spring turkey hunts. A duck/quail combo can be arranged during the winter months, and ranch pond bass fishing is available year-round.

On a blazing hot April afternoon, I followed Mike, belly-crawling and knee-walking, through 100 yards of prickly pear and mesquite to get us within calling range of five big gobblers and a harem of hens. After we seduced and bagged the dominant bird in the bunch, Mike admitted his basic theory of success. "Some people get into this business because they like to hunt and fish," he said. "I do this every day because I love to guide."

After sampling Monica's expertise in the kitchen, I'm convinced that she feels the same about her cooking.

Opposite: Mike Wyatt takes a bird from two of his compadres.
Below: Break time for a tired pointer

QUAIL POPPERS

••

Yield: 12 pieces

6 fresh jalapeño peppers
6 quail breasts, filleted (12 pieces)
Cheddar cheese
6 slices bacon, cut in half
1 bottle (10-ounce) soy sauce
1 bottle (10-ounce) Worcestershire sauce

Preheat oven to 350 degrees. Slice jalapeños down the middle lengthwise and remove seeds. Cut cheese into chunks approximately ¼ inch thick, ¼ inch wide, and 1 inch long. Stuff each pepper with a piece of cheese and a quail breast fillet; wrap each stuffed pepper with one piece of bacon, securing with a toothpick. Place peppers in a baking dish. Combine soy sauce and Worcestershire sauce in a bowl. Pour over peppers to cover. Bake for 40 minutes. Remove from oven and drain juices. Return to oven and cook an additional 15 minutes, or until bacon is crisp. Serve warm.

—Monica Wyatt

Preceding page: I fired one frame—from the hip—when Ben Novack stepped into the middle of this covey.
Right: A hen bobwhite in the bag

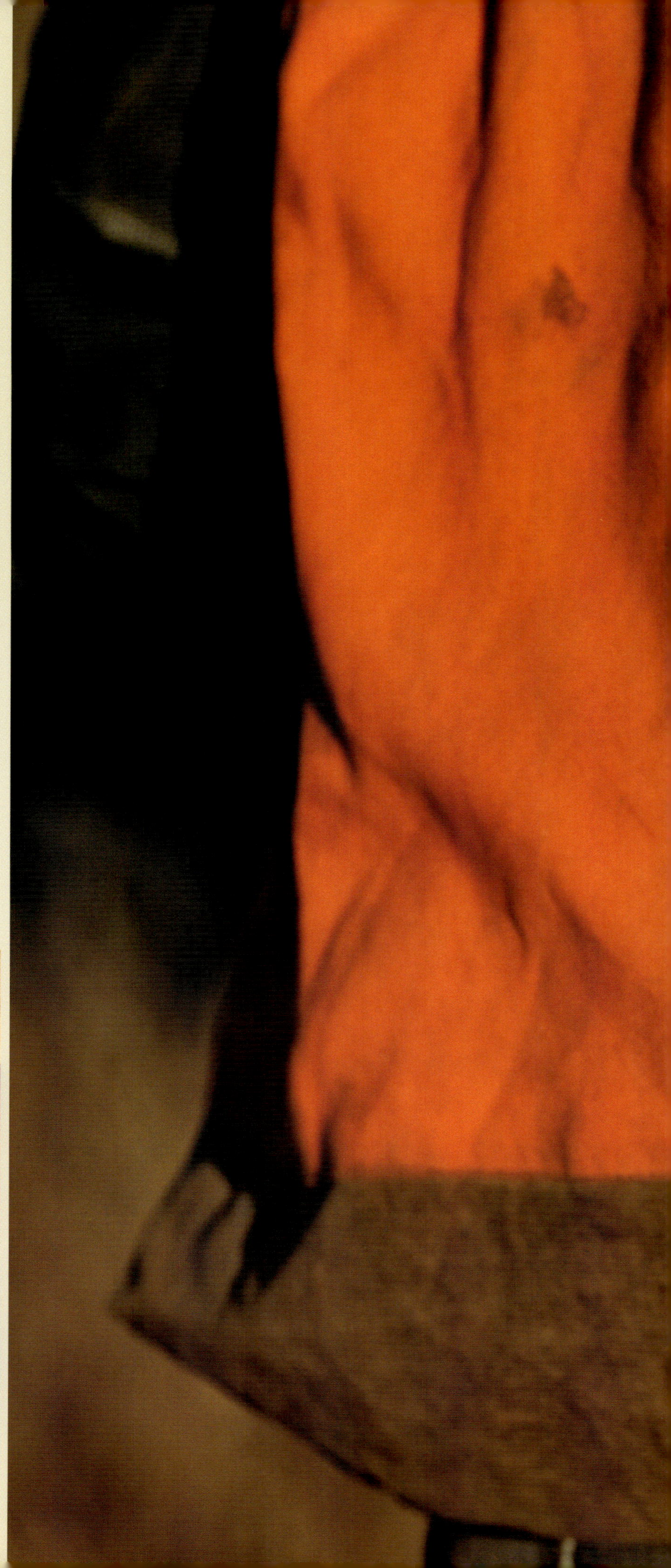

FRIED QUAIL

2 or 3 quail per person
Seasoned salt
Flour
Salt and pepper to taste
2 eggs
4 cups milk
Vegetable oil for frying

Generously season quail with seasoned salt. Mix flour, salt, and pepper and set aside. In a medium bowl, whisk eggs and milk together. Add ¼ to ½ inch oil to a large deep skillet and heat over medium-high heat. When oil is hot, dredge quail in seasoned flour, dip in milk mixture, and then dredge again in flour. Fry until golden brown.

—Monica Wyatt

VENISON STEW

Serves 8

1 pound venison, cut into 1-inch cubes
¼ cup flour
3 tablespoons olive oil
1 cup chopped onion
6 cloves garlic, chopped
2 tablespoons Italian seasoning
2 teaspoons salt
1 tablespoon sugar
1 cup sliced carrots
1 pound small pearl onions, peeled and trimmed
3 cups beef broth
2 cups dry red wine
1 can (14-ounce) diced tomatoes
12 fresh mushrooms, cleaned and sliced

Lightly coat venison with flour. In a large pot, heat oil over medium-high heat. Add onion and garlic and stir to flavor the oil. Add venison cubes to onion and garlic mixture. Cook, stirring, for 5 to 7 minutes, or until meat is browned. Reduce heat to medium and add Italian seasoning, salt, sugar, carrots, onions, broth, and wine. Bring to a boil and add tomatoes and mushrooms. Reduce heat to low and cook for 2 hours, or until meat is tender. Adjust seasonings and serve.

—Monica Wyatt

Brent Bodecker (left) and Mike Wyatt with an April gobbler
Opposite: Mike tending the grill

BEER BREAD WITH HONEY BUTTER

This bread is quick and easy with great homemade flavor. It is also good toasted.

>   2 cups flour
>   2 tablespoons sugar
>   1½ teaspoons baking powder
>   ½ teaspoon baking soda
>   ½ teaspoon salt
>   1 can (12-ounce) beer
>   ½ cup butter, softened
>   ½ cup honey
>   ½ teaspoon cinnamon
>   1 tablespoon sugar

Preheat oven to 375 degrees. Generously grease an 8 × 4 × 2-inch loaf pan. In a large bowl, stir together flour, sugar, baking powder, baking soda, and salt. Pour beer over dry ingredients and stir just until combined; the mixture will be lumpy. Pour into prepared pan and bake for 35 to 40 minutes.

Meanwhile, beat butter and honey until smooth. Add cinnamon and sugar and mix well. Serve with warm bread.

—Monica Wyatt

A Coleman County gobbler duped by the Pretty Boy decoy

TURTLE CHEESECAKE

Serves 16

3 packages (8-ounce) cream cheese, softened
1 can (14-ounce) sweetened condensed milk
4 eggs
2½ tablespoons fresh lime juice
½ cup sugar
2 teaspoons vanilla extract
1 cup milk chocolate chips
2 chocolate graham cracker pie crusts
Chocolate syrup
Caramel syrup
½ cup chopped pecans
½ cup semisweet chocolate mini-chips

Preheat oven to 300 degrees. Beat cream cheese and condensed milk in large mixing bowl until smooth. Add eggs and mix well. Add lime juice, sugar, and vanilla and mix until blended. Pour milk chocolate chips into medium bowl and microwave until melted, stirring frequently. Add 1 cup of the cream cheese mixture to the melted chocolate and mix well. Add 2 more cups of the cream cheese mixture and stir until completely blended. Fill each pie shell with one-fourth of the remaining white cream cheese mixture, and then pour half of the chocolate mixture into each pie. Top each with the remaining white cream cheese mixture, divided evenly. Bake for 1 hour and 15 minutes, or just until the center starts to crack. Cool completely on a rack. Drizzle each pie with chocolate and caramel syrups. Sprinkle with pecans and chocolate mini-chips. Refrigerate before serving.

—*Monica Wyatt*

Almond Bread Pudding with Amaretto Cream Sauce

ALMOND BREAD PUDDING WITH AMARETTO CREAM SAUCE

Almond filling can be found in most major grocery stores; it is usually shelved with pie fillings.

1 loaf (16-ounce) Honey White bread
2 packages (8-ounce) cream cheese, softened
13 large eggs
¼ cup sugar
3 teaspoons vanilla extract
1 can (12.5-ounce) almond filling (about 1¼ cups plus 2 tablespoons reserved for topping)
2 cups butter, melted
2½ cups half-and-half
Dash of salt

Topping

2 tablespoons almond filling
2 tablespoons sugar
1 egg yolk
¼ cup slivered almonds

Amaretto Cream Sauce

1 cup amaretto liqueur
2 tablespoons cornstarch
1½ cups whipping cream
½ cup sugar

Generously spray a 9 ×13-inch pan with vegetable spray. Arrange 4½ bread slices in pan, cutting slices to fit. Beat together cream cheese, 1 of the eggs, sugar, and 1 teaspoon of the vanilla until smooth. Spread half of this mixture over bread. In a small bowl, whisk together 1¼ cups of the almond filling and 1½ cups of the melted butter; spread half of this mixture over the cream cheese layer. Beginning with 4½ slices of bread, repeat layers one more time.

Cut the remaining bread slices into 1-inch cubes and sprinkle evenly over almond mixture. Whisk together the remaining 12 eggs, the remaining 2 teaspoons vanilla, half-and-half, and salt. Pour over bread cubes. Cover and chill for 30 minutes, or until most of the egg mixture is absorbed.

Preheat oven to 325 degrees. Whisk together the remaining ½ cup of butter and all topping ingredients except almonds. Remove bread pudding from refrigerator and drizzle topping evenly over bread cubes. Sprinkle with slivered almonds. Bake for 1 hour, or until set.

Meanwhile, make the Amaretto Cream Sauce. Whisk together amaretto liqueur and cornstarch until smooth. In a heavy saucepan, heat cream over medium heat just until bubbles appear, stirring often. Gradually stir in amaretto mixture and mix well. Bring sauce to a boil, stirring constantly for 30 seconds. Remove from heat, stir in sugar, and cool completely.

Serve bread pudding warm or chilled with Amaretto Cream Sauce.

—*Monica Wyatt*

U RANCH

⊞ **Sterling City**

William Randolph McEntire first saw the Concho Valley in the 1870s when West Texas was sparsely settled and Indian raids were still a threat. The Comanches and Apaches were largely on the run in those days, but they still made time for stealing horses, slaughtering cattle, and plundering the white settlements that were creeping westward at a steady pace. Fort Concho was fully staffed near San Angelo during those years, but the soldiers couldn't offer much protection for families that chose to settle farther west.

After serving in the Civil War, McEntire had moved from his home state of Georgia to Dallas, where he had established himself as a cotton merchant. He was also an avid outdoorsman, and while hunting deer and antelope out west of San Angelo, he recognized the Concho Valley's potential for a large-scale cattle operation.

In the spring of 1880, McEntire struck a deal with cattleman M. B. Stephenson to purchase his herd bearing the U brand. In those days you didn't have to own land to be a cattle rancher; all you needed were cows. For several years McEntire grazed his cattle on the open range until barbed wire and land disputes finally forced him to make a claim and establish boundaries on a piece of land west of Sterling City.

Today the U Ranch consists of 23,000 acres and is owned by McEntire's great-granddaughter, Ruth, and her husband, Lee Caldwell. Inside their main ranch house, originally built in 1934, is a small museum of correspondence and ledgers chronicling the history of the U Ranch. They also have a significant collection of Indian artifacts that they've found on the ranch, and

Lining up the shot from a ground blind on the U Ranch
Opposite: A nice Sterling County buck

cavalry leavings that they've unearthed from the footprint of Camp Elizabeth, an army outpost on the ranch that once served as a satellite facility to Fort Concho.

Cattle, sheep, farming, and minerals have always been the primary interests for the Caldwells, but like many Texas ranch families, they've recently tapped into the substantial conduit of hunting revenue that flows through the state of Texas each fall and winter. In 1990 the Caldwells partnered with Kent Carpenter, an outfitter from Silverton who was looking to expand his deer-hunting operation. Each year Kent brings out a big group of deer hunters after Thanksgiving for a three-day hunt. Many of them have been coming to hunt the U Ranch for several years, and the Caldwells treat them like immediate family.

After college, the Caldwells' son, Cliff, moved home with his wife, Lauren, to raise a family and manage the day-to-day operations on the ranch. Healthy livestock, big-racked deer, flowing water, and brush control are Cliff's enduring concerns. Indian raids, thankfully, are no longer a problem.

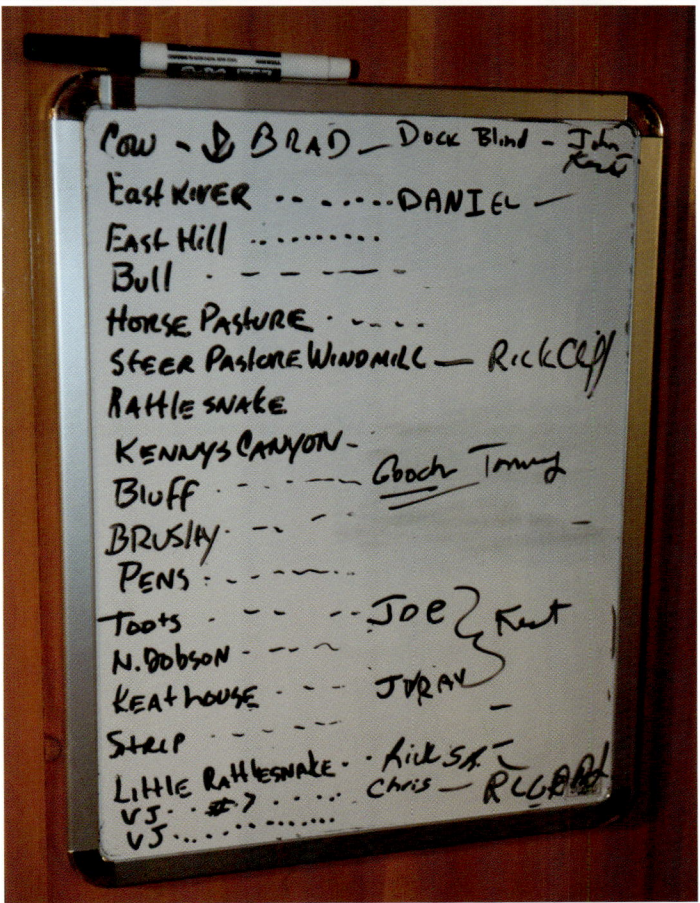

Opposite, clockwise from top: Dinnertime at the U Ranch. The U Ranch headquarters, built in 1934. Ranch accommodations for hunters.

Above: Mike Colbert and Dale Land tending to one of their army field ovens

Below: Morning blind assignments

Plains and Panhandle • 43

VENISON POSOLE

Serves 12–14

Posole is a dish that is indigenous to New Mexico and northern Mexico. Garnish with shredded cabbage, sliced radishes, and limes for an authentic taste.

> Bacon drippings or vegetable oil
> 2½ pounds venison, cut into ½-inch cubes
> 7 stalks celery, chopped
> 3 medium onions, chopped
> 8 cloves garlic, chopped
> 1 can (14-ounce) chopped tomatoes with juice
> 2 tablespoons oregano
> 2 teaspoons cumin
> 1 tablespoon paprika
> 1½ teaspoons salt
> 2 cans (4-ounce) chopped green chilies
> 4 cups low-sodium beef broth
> 2 cups water
> 2 cans (30-ounce) white hominy, drained and rinsed
> 2 cans (30-ounce) yellow hominy, drained and rinsed

In a large Dutch oven, heat bacon drippings or vegetable oil until hot; brown venison on all sides. Add celery, onions, garlic, tomatoes, seasonings, and chilies and sauté for 1 minute. Add broth and water and bring to a boil. Reduce heat, cover, and cook for 1½ hours over low heat. Add hominy and simmer for an additional 30 minutes.

—*Mike Colbert, contract cook*

Opposite above: Cliff Caldwell (left) and Kent Carpenter: no rest for the weary during deer season
Opposite below: Kicking back before the afternoon hunt
Cliff putting an edge on his skinning blade

Plains and Panhandle

FRIED WILD TURKEY FINGERS
....

2 eggs
2 cups buttermilk
2 teaspoons baking soda
1 cup flour
3 packages (1-ounce) ranch dressing mix
Salt and pepper to taste
Vegetable oil for frying
2½ pounds wild turkey breasts, cut into strips

Whisk together eggs and buttermilk in a shallow bowl. In another shallow dish, combine baking soda, flour, ranch dressing mix, salt, and pepper. Heat oil in a skillet until hot, dip turkey strips into the buttermilk mixture, and then dredge in the flour mixture. Fry in batches until golden brown.

—Mike Colbert, contract cook

Cooks Mike (left) and Dale pulling ribs from the smoker
True confessions on the wall of the cleaning shed

46 • GRAZING ACROSS TEXAS

PEACH COBBLER

Serves 16

This recipe can easily be halved and baked in a 9 × 9-inch baking pan.

> 1 package (5-pound) frozen sliced peaches (10 cups), thawed
> ⅔ cup butter, melted
> ¼ cup flour
> 2 teaspoons vanilla
> 3 cups sugar
> 1 teaspoon cinnamon
> ½ teaspoon nutmeg
> 1 dash whiskey, optional

Crust

> 4 cups flour
> 1 teaspoon salt
> 1 tablespoon sugar
> 1¾ cups shortening
> ½ cup cold water
> 1 tablespoon apple cider vinegar
> 1 egg, lightly beaten
> 2 tablespoons butter, melted
> Sugar and cinnamon

Preheat oven to 400 degrees. In a large bowl, mix peaches, melted butter, flour, vanilla, sugar, cinnamon, nutmeg, and whiskey until well combined. Spread into a large baking dish and set aside.

To make the crust, mix dry ingredients together in a large bowl. Add shortening and cut into flour until mixture is crumbly. Add water, vinegar, and egg and mix well. Place dough on a floured surface and roll thin. Cut into strips and layer over peach mixture. Brush with melted butter and sprinkle with sugar and cinnamon. Bake about 50 to 55 minutes, or until crust begins to brown.

—*Mike Colbert, contract cook*

"A spontaneous non-sanctioned wagering contest among good friends"

STASNEY'S COOK RANCH

⬖ **Albany**

I doubt that James H. Nail was the originator of the saying "Never do business with family," but I'll bet that he was one of the first in Texas to mull it over.

In April of 1897, Nail and his sister, Matilda "Dude" Nail Cook, bought a 17,000-acre ranch in Shackelford County, just a few miles from Fort Griffin, the decommissioned army outpost that played a vital role in the Indian battles of the 1870s. By 1899 the partners were squabbling over the ranch, and James Nail finally agreed to sell out to his sister. Disgruntled because she wouldn't sell out to *him*, he bragged that he had just sold Dude the sorriest piece of land in Shackelford County and that she would be broke within a year.

In 1929 the first oil well was drilled on the Cook Ranch. The firm of Roeser and Pendleton punched into a massive pool at only 1,240 feet, and the first rig produced a respectable 1,000 barrels a day. Within three years the Cook Field was producing ten times that amount from the largest shallow field in the country. The Cook Ranch remained in the family's estate until the termination of the trust in 1989, when it was sold to Eska Gage Stasney of Albany. Ten years later, she bought the mineral rights and standing production on the ranch. The Cook Field is still producing oil today.

Nowadays Stasney's Cook Ranch is owned by Dr. Dick Stasney and managed by Albany natives Johnny and Debbe Hudman. Over the past few years the Stasneys and Hudmans have built a number of significant improvements that surround the original, century-old Cook Ranch house. Most notable is their impound-

Opposite: Long brow tines are a genetic trademark of many Rolling Plains whitetails.

Ranch guests can stay in wonderfully detailed replicas of Forts Griffin and Concho.

A fitting tribute to the ranch's remarkable oil legacy
A sign of spring in Shackelford County 

ment of Taylor Creek into a substantial lake located just below the ranch headquarters. A modern and spacious main lodge fronts the new lake, and meticulous replicas of Forts Griffin and Concho have been built for additional guest lodging.

The Stasney's Cook currently totals 25,000 acres with leased access to another 15,000 acres next door. Whitetail hunting is the ranch's biggest draw, and each year it produces a number of respectable, free-ranging trophy bucks. Shackelford County wasn't really known as a big buck destination until the early 1990s, when a few ranchers around Albany got serious about deer management. According to Johnny Hudman,

their success has largely been a result of selective culling and their maintenance of a proper deer density.

In addition to deer, the ranch has a thriving population of Rio Grande turkeys that are hunted in the spring and feral hog numbers that require no flashy adjectives or exaggeration. Quail are hunted over dogs in years when the hatches are big, and dove hunts can also be arranged around tanks and sunflower fields.

Even though the ranch itself stands as a model of success and innovation in the oil, cattle, and hunting industries, its record of philanthropy may ultimately define its legacy. In 1929 Matilda Cook dedicated a portion of her oil royalties to build a fifty-five-bed hospital in Fort Worth. During the polio epidemic of 1952, the hospital expanded its bed capacity and changed its mission to care exclusively for the needs of children. That hospital today is known as the Cook Children's Medical Center, a renowned care facility that has touched the lives of countless children and their families worldwide.

And to think it all started with a "sorry" piece of Shackelford County ranchland.

Locked down in deep grass

A bobwhite's wing plumage will indicate its age, valuable information for managing the annual quail harvest.

Opposite, clockwise from top: Big Mama and her brood breaking for cover. Front porch of the new main lodge. Autographs from hunting celebrities in the historic Cook ranch house.

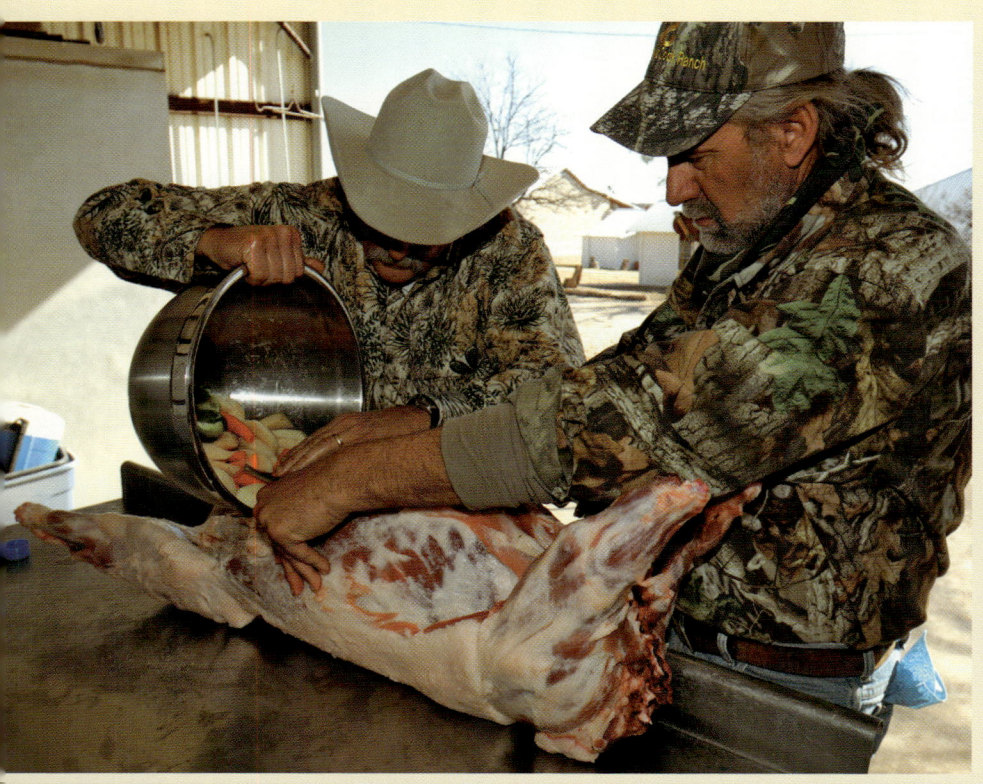

PIG IN THE GROUND

Serves 10–12

In the Cajun vernacular, a small suckling pig cooked whole is called Cochon de Lait, literally "pig in milk." In Hawaii a pig wrapped in banana leaves and roasted in a pit full of hot stones is known as a Kalua Pig. Smaller feral pigs are the best eating, and a 40- to 50-pounder will feed a group of ten to twelve people. This version turns out a full meal with meat and vegetables.

Plenty of oak or mesquite wood
Potatoes
Sweet potatoes
Carrots
Onions
Bell peppers
1 small (40- to 50-pound) feral pig, cleaned and skinned, with head and feet removed
Cooking oil
Any dry rub mixture (black pepper, cayenne, garlic powder, Cajun, etc.)
Heavy needle and 3 feet of twine, optional
Heavy foil, enough to wrap the pig in several layers
Fire grate or piece of expanded metal, with heavy wire handles attached

Dig a pit that is long enough to accommodate the pig placed on its side. It should be deep enough to allow a good bed of coals beneath the pig and on top of it after burying it. Fill the pit with firewood and light.

While the fire is burning down, slice vegetables into halves or quarters and mix together in a large bowl. You will need enough vegetables to completely fill the body cavity of the pig. Lay the pig out on a large work surface and completely coat the carcass inside and out with cooking oil. Season liberally, inside and out, with your favorite dry seasoning rub. Fill the body cavity with vegetables and use large pieces to plug obvious openings. Sew the cavity shut with a heavy needle and twine. Wrap the entire carcass tightly in at least four or five layers of heavy foil, alternating between lengthwise and crosswise layers. Make sure there are no openings large enough for dirt and ash to enter or for juices to leak out. Place the wrapped carcass on a fire grate.

When the fire has burned down to a bed of hot coals, use a shovel to remove about three-fourths of the coals (wear gloves as a safety precaution). Set excess coals aside next to the pit. Spread the remaining coals across the bottom of the pit to create an even layer. Set the grate and the pig on top of the coals. Make sure that the wire handles are upright, and begin shoveling the excess coals back into the pit. Surround the pig with coals along the sides and on top. When the pig is covered with coals, shovel enough dirt on top to completely seal the pit—at least 6 to 8 inches deep. Go hunting or watch football.

Cook at least 5 to 6 hours. (Larger pigs might require a full day.) When you're ready to eat, dig up the pig. Using gloves, grasp the wire handles and lift the pig and grate from the pit. Remove the layers of foil, one by one, and press them down around the pig to form a foil dam for containing the juices. If the pig is properly cooked, the meat will easily fall away from the bones. Serve with the vegetables from inside the carcass.

—*Johnny Hudman*

Opposite, clockwise from top left: Johnny Hudman (left) and guide Joe Barrington prepping a pig for the pit. Stoking the fire. Six hours later: digging up dinner.

TULE RANCH HUNTS

◈ Silverton

One would presume that if a person had exclusive access to a large portion of our state's best mule deer habitat, he could earn a persistent and comfortable living running guided hunts. According to rancher and outfitter Kent Carpenter, that's not exactly true, especially in the Texas Panhandle.

The Tule Ranch is located southeast of Amarillo at the confluence of the Tule and Palo Duro canyons. Founded in 1953 by D. M. Cogdell of Snyder, the ranch has grown from an initial purchase of 27,000 acres to its present footprint of over 175,000. Today the Tule Ranch is owned by Cogdell's grandchildren, including Penny Cogdell Carpenter, Kent's wife.

Kent has managed the hunting on the Tule Ranch since 1991, and he'll admit that he's still scratching his head over the best way to utilize the habitat. "We've got about 10,000 acres of flat land up on top, and the rest of the ranch is canyon country," Kent explained. "If these deer would just stay put down in the canyons, we wouldn't have a management problem, but they move around a lot up here, and that's why we have to be really conservative with our harvest."

According to Kent, wheat farming along the rim of the canyon draws a large number of mulies out of the rough country and into the wide open during deer season. He has been a longtime promoter of a permit system in the Texas Panhandle whereby mule deer tags would be issued on the basis of acreage or habitat quality. What he's trying to curb is the harvest of dozens of trophy mule deer each season that migrate from the canyon country onto small farm plots during the winter.

Opposite: An early-fall mule deer using the rough country for cover
A nice pronghorn buck on a Tule Ranch lease west of Hereford

Prime Panhandle mule deer habitat north of Silverton

In the early years Kent ran guided hunts on the Tule, but recently he's been leasing it out to a small group of hunters with strict harvest criteria in place. Since he has no control over the number of Tule Ranch mulies that migrate into the farm country and meet their end, he allows his lease hunters to harvest only five bucks per year. He explains that mule deer are much more difficult to manage on open range than whitetails; therefore, a smaller percentage of bucks will reach trophy status in a given year. According to Texas Parks and Wildlife surveys, the Texas mule deer population in the Panhandle and the Trans-Pecos can vary from 150,000 animals during drought times to as many as 250,000 in the wetter years.

To hedge his bets on the home ranch and to extend his outfitting season, Kent also runs guided aoudad sheep hunts on the Tule and pronghorn antelope hunts on leased country west of Hereford. During whitetail season he guides hunters on the U Ranch near Sterling City as well as a couple of smaller ranches in the Hill Country.

Over the past few years Kent has experimented with a small captive mule deer herd (fully permitted) in an enclosure next to his home. His goal is to find out if mule deer will respond as well to intensive management as whitetails do. Kent feels that mule deer are, unfortunately, the forgotten game animal in the Texas Panhandle. He's hoping to change that, though, by promoting his basic theory that little mulies can grown into big mulies if the population is better managed.

VENISON STEAK WITH MUSHROOM GRAVY

Serves 2

Any cut of venison can be used for this recipe. Pounding the meat thin and slow-cooking it produces a very tender dish.

> Garlic salt
> Seasoned salt
> 1 cup flour
> 2 tablespoons butter
> 1 pound venison, sliced thin and pounded to a thickness of ¼ inch
> ¼ cup warm water
> 1 can (10-ounce) cream of mushroom soup
> ¾ cup milk

Add seasonings to flour. In a large skillet, melt butter. Dredge venison pieces in seasoned flour and then add to skillet. Cook in batches until nicely browned on both sides. Remove meat from skillet and place on paper towels to drain. Remove skillet from heat and add warm water. Using a wooden spoon, scrape browned bits from bottom of pan and stir to dissolve in the water. Mix the soup and milk together and add to skillet. Return the venison to the skillet, bring to a gentle boil, reduce heat to simmer, and cover. Cook over low heat for 45 minutes to 1 hour, or until meat is tender. If sauce becomes too thick, add a little warm water to thin.

—*Penny Carpenter*

TULE RANCH CORN BREAD

Serves 6–8

A quick and easy bread to serve with pinto beans, black-eyed peas, chili, or stew.

> 2 boxes (8.5-ounce) corn bread mix
> 1 can (4-ounce) chopped green chilies
> 1 can (14.75-ounce) cream-style corn
> 2 cups grated cheese
> 2 eggs, beaten

Preheat oven to 400 degrees. Lightly grease an 8 ×11-inch baking dish. In a large mixing bowl, combine all ingredients and mix well. Pour into prepared dish and bake for 20 minutes, or until lightly browned. Serve warm.

—*Penny Carpenter*

VENISON SAUSAGE DIP

Serves 12–14

This is a great hunting-camp appetizer. It can be made ahead and reheated in a microwave or slow-cooker.

> 1 pound venison sausage
> 1 pound lean ground beef
> 1 onion, diced
> 2 pounds Velveeta cheese, cubed
> 1 can (10-ounce) Rotel tomatoes
> 1 teaspoon garlic powder

Brown sausage and ground beef with the onion; drain. In a large saucepan over low heat, heat cheese, tomatoes, and garlic powder until the cheese is melted. Add meat mixture and mix well. Serve hot with tortilla chips.

—*Penny Carpenter*

Opposite: A small mulie out in plain view during the hunting season. Mule deer does and fawns grazing on wheat above the canyon rim.

PITCHFORK LAND AND CATTLE COMPANY

⊞ **Guthrie**

Over the past eighteen years of outfitting and photographing across our state, I've had the pleasure of visiting, and occasionally hunting, a number of remarkable ranches. Some of those trips lasted only an hour or two, some a couple of days. During my years as a lodge operator, though, I was often allowed to move in for several weeks at a time to run guided dove, quail, and spring turkey hunts.

For two seasons, in 1998 and 1999, I had access to one of the premier quail-hunting ranches in the Rolling Plains. The Pitchfork Ranch originated from a cattle herd that bore a pitchfork brand and grazed the open range in King and Dickens counties back in 1881. In 1883 Eugene F. Williams and A. P. Bush Jr. of St. Louis bought the Pitchfork herd and began amassing their landholdings. By 1928 the ranch totaled 115,000 acres with 9,000 head of cattle and over 500 horses. Today the Pitchfork stands at 165,000 acres; it is widely known for its quality beef cattle, its signature "Pitchfork Gray" horses, and some of the finest hunting in our state.

Some ranches in Texas will consistently produce huntable numbers of native quail, but their difficult terrain or heavy brush cover make for exasperating hunting. Not so on the Pitchfork. There are a couple of rough pastures on the southwest side (great mule deer habitat), but most of the ranch offers wide-open shooting across miles of rolling grass and sparse mesquite brush. Quail densities on the Pitchfork are a function of rainfall, just like any other ranch in Texas, but what

Opposite: Pick out a bird and stay with it.
Jay Gates with one of the Pitchfork's crowning accomplishments: a big whitetail on low-fenced range

Plains and Panhandle • 65

often sets the ranch apart is its grazing management. With the ability to move cattle onto wheat for winter grazing, the Pitchfork can leave more native pasture grasses for spring nesting and summer brooding cover. The Pitchfork typically has huntable numbers of birds when many of its neighbors don't, and in the big hatch years the ranch turns up covey counts that a cynical quail hunter would dismiss as overstated campfire talk.

Deer hunts on the Pitchfork employ a combination of driving, walking, and glassing the ranch's draws, canyons, and sidehills. Both the whitetails and mule deer are free-rangers that produce substantial racks on the native browse that the ranch provides. While King and Dickens counties aren't traditionally named as big-buck producers in Texas, they may soon join a notable list if the Pitchfork continues producing trophy bucks without high fences or supplemental feeding.

Just as its cattle and horse operations reflect the nostalgia of the Texas cowboy culture, the Pitchfork Ranch also promotes a quality, authentic experience for its hunting guests. There aren't too many places left in our state where you can stand on a hilltop at the end of a hunting day and gaze for miles in every direction without spotting a highway, a porch light, or a distant hint of civilization.

Above: A fine view from the best seat on the ranch

Below: Outfitter James Stephens with one of his big-running pointers

Opposite: The historic cookshack where Pitchfork cowboys and ranch guests have dined for decades

Plains and Panhandle • 67

BAKED DOVES

This is a great recipe for doves that will ensure a juicy, tender meal. For a spicier taste, add a strip of fresh jalapeño before wrapping with bacon. Serve with cheese grits or mashed potatoes.

> 2 or 3 doves per person
> Garlic powder
> Salt and pepper to taste
> Smoked Cheddar or Gouda cheese
> 1 strip bacon per dove
> Chicken broth

Preheat oven to 375 degrees. Generously season doves with garlic powder, salt, and pepper. Slice cheese into thin strips. Place a strip of cheese into the cavity of each dove; wrap with a strip of bacon, securing with a toothpick. Place doves in a shallow baking dish. Add enough chicken broth to reach a depth of 1 inch in the dish. Bake for 45 minutes to 1 hour, or until bacon is crisp and doves are tender.

—*Cheryl Bouher, ranch cook*

SMASHED RANCH POTATOES

Serves 6–8

> 2 pounds red-skinned potatoes, scrubbed
> ½ cup (1 stick) butter
> ½ cup buttermilk plus additional as needed
> 1 package (1-ounce) ranch dressing mix
> Salt and pepper to taste

Place potatoes in a large pot with salted water to cover. Bring to a boil and cook until tender. Drain potatoes. Place in a large bowl, add butter, and mash thoroughly. Add buttermilk and dressing mix. Mix until smooth with a hand mixer. If potatoes are too thick, add more buttermilk. Season to taste.

—*Cheryl Bouher, ranch cook*

Dogs that will reliably hunt singles are worth their weight in . . . quail?

SMOTHERED QUAIL

A great quail dish that goes well with rice or mashed potatoes.

> 1 cup flour
> Salt and pepper to taste
> Garlic powder to taste
> Cooking oil for frying
> 2 or 3 quail per person
> 1 onion, sliced
> 1 can (14-ounce) chicken broth
> 1 can (10-ounce) cream of mushroom soup

Mix flour with seasonings. Heat a small amount of oil in a deep skillet or Dutch oven with a lid. Rinse and dry quail, dredge in seasoned flour, and brown. Remove birds from skillet and drain on paper towels. Add onions to skillet and cook until translucent. Add 1 tablespoon of the seasoned flour and cook, stirring, until brown. Whisk together broth and soup and add to skillet, scraping up browned bits from bottom and stirring until smooth. Return quail to skillet and bring sauce to a boil. Reduce heat to simmer, cover, and cook until quail are tender, about 45 minutes.

—*Cheryl Bouher, ranch cook*

HOT COCOA CAKE

> 1 cup brewed coffee or water
> 3 tablespoons cocoa powder
> 1 cup (2 sticks) butter
> 1 teaspoon baking soda
> ½ cup buttermilk
> 2 cups flour
> 2 cups sugar
> 1 teaspoon cinnamon
> 2 eggs, beaten
> 1 teaspoon vanilla

Icing

> ½ cup (1 stick) butter
> 4 tablespoons cocoa powder
> ½ cup milk
> 1 box (16-ounce) powdered sugar, sifted
> 1 teaspoon vanilla

Preheat oven to 400 degrees. Grease and flour a 9 × 13-inch baking pan. In a medium saucepan, bring coffee, cocoa, and butter to a boil. Stir until butter is melted; remove from heat and set aside. Dissolve baking soda in buttermilk. In a large mixing bowl, mix together flour, sugar, and cinnamon. Beat eggs and vanilla together and add to dry ingredients. Stir in cocoa mixture and mix well. Pour batter into prepared pan and bake for 20 minutes.

Meanwhile, make the icing. Combine butter, cocoa, and milk in a saucepan and bring to a boil; remove from heat. Stir in powdered sugar and vanilla and whisk until smooth. Pour over hot cake. Allow cake to cool before slicing.

—*Cheryl Bouher, ranch cook*

Left: Guide Paul Hamilton praising one of his dogs for a job well done

Opposite: The Pitchfork has a few blue quail, but bobwhites make up the majority of the annual hatch. Headquarters gate between Dickens and Guthrie.

PERINI RANCH STEAKHOUSE

◈ Buffalo Gap

Tom Perini wanted to be a cattle rancher when he moved back home to Abilene in 1965, but it eventually took a small measure of respected advice to change his career path. In the early 1970s Tom was running cattle on leased country around Abilene when he started cooking from a refurbished chuck wagon that he could haul from pasture to pasture to prepare meals for the ranch hands. As he continued to wrestle with the cattle business over the next several years, word of his cowboy cooking talents began to spread among the ranching communities of North and West Texas.

While Tom was catering an event at the Lambshead Ranch, family friend and ranching legend Watt Matthews made a suggestion that changed his perspective. "Demand for beef was down, and I wasn't doing very well in the cattle business," Tom explained. "Watt told me that I could do more for the beef industry by cooking it than raising it."

In 1983 Tom converted an old barn into a restaurant on his family's land near Buffalo Gap, south of Abilene. "I had been in ranch cookshacks all over the state, and I wanted this place to have that type of rustic and nostalgic feel," Tom said. With only a small sign erected near his gate on a quiet country highway, the advertising debut for the Perini Ranch Steakhouse didn't exactly fit the accepted protocol for a successful start-up in the restaurant business.

To look back now at Tom Perini's list of awards, accomplishments, and appearances over the past

Preceding pages: Masters of camouflage
Opposite: Serving real Texas food in Buffalo Gap since 1983 (above). No pretensions here, just great West Texas cooking (below).
The watering hole at Perini's

Tripods don't provide much protection from the winds of January in West Texas.

twenty-five years, it's hard to imagine how he was able to fit it all in. He's been recognized by *Texas Monthly, Texas Highways, Southern Living,* and *Gourmet* magazines. He's appeared on *Good Morning America, The Early Show,* PBS, the Outdoor Channel, and the Food Network. With his chuck wagon and a load of mesquite wood in tow, he traveled to Japan for the U.S. Beef Promotional Tour and later to Russia and Poland for the Texas Beef Council. In 1995 he offered his famous Mesquite-Smoked Peppered Beef Tenderloin as a mail-order item, and he has since sold thousands of them via his website, the Williams-Sonoma catalog, and the first-class cabins of Northwest and KLM airlines. In 2000 Time-Life published a collection of Tom's favorite recipes titled *Texas Cowboy Cooking.* The book is now in its fourth printing with over 50,000 copies sold.

When I interviewed Tom Perini for this book in December of 2006, he offered his cooking philosophy in a concise disclosure: "The food we serve has to look good and taste good," he stated, "and we also want you to recognize what you're eating. We don't stack food into little towers on your plate, and we don't use fancy garnishes. If your plate arrives from the kitchen with some type of vegetation on it, then send it back because it's not supposed to be there."

When I asked him about local hero Colt McCoy, UT's emerging star quarterback, Tom laughed and explained that Colt is actually from Tuscola (seven miles down the road), but he figures that Buffalo Gap must sound better to the commentators on ESPN.

"Colt signed his scholarship papers with Mack Brown right here in the restaurant," he remembered. "He's a great kid, and my wife, Lisa, gives me a hard time about Colt stealing my thunder around here."

With all that Tom Perini has accomplished, he admitted that one of his most memorable moments involved a catered event that was abruptly canceled: "We were set up on the south lawn of the White House to cook for over a thousand people on the morning of September 11, 2001, when the planes came in." He recalled the chaos when the Secret Service poured from the building and yelled for everyone to run for cover as they tracked American Airlines' Flight 77 on its eventual collision course with the Pentagon.

While Tom Perini's cooking fame has emerged largely from his allegiance to our cattle and ranching heritage, he also has a few wild game recipes on file that he was happy to share with me. He still doesn't advertise, and any increase in traffic on Farm Road 89 heading west out of Buffalo Gap over the past two decades is probably a result of his steady restaurant patronage. So if you're driving south of Abilene someday and you're looking for a good place to eat, pull off the beaten path and ask for directions to "Perini's." All the locals know where it is, and reservations are suggested.

Buffalo Gap was named for the spot where great herds of bison once migrated through a wide break in the Callahan Divide.

PERINI RANCH STEAK RUB

Yield: ½ cup

This is a great dry rub for beef or game cuts.

- 1 tablespoon cornstarch or flour
- 2 tablespoons salt
- 4 teaspoons coarse-ground black pepper
- 1 teaspoon dried oregano
- 4 teaspoons garlic powder
- 1 teaspoon paprika
- 1 teaspoon granulated beef stock base

Mix all ingredients together and store in an airtight container.

—Perini Ranch Steakhouse

Tom Perini combined his two passions—ranch life and cooking—into one hugely successful enterprise (photo courtesy of Perini Ranch Steakhouse).

Tom's chuck wagon has racked up significant mileage in the last thirty years: multiple trips across Texas; a couple of cross-country spins, and a tour of Japan.

WILD TURKEY PIE

Serves 6–8

1½ cups sliced carrots

1 large onion, chopped

1 pound mushrooms, sliced

2 stalks celery, diced

4 tablespoons butter

¼ cup flour

3 cups turkey or chicken broth

Salt and pepper to taste

4 cups cooked turkey meat, cut in small pieces

4 hard-boiled eggs, peeled and quartered

1 unbaked piecrust for a 9-inch pie

Sauté carrots, onion, mushrooms, and celery in the butter until the onion is translucent. Sprinkle vegetables with the flour and stir to combine. Slowly add the broth, stirring constantly, and cook until thickened. Season to taste and stir in turkey meat just until mixed. Add the eggs and pour into a deep 3-quart baking dish.

Preheat oven to 400 degrees. Roll out piecrust and lay over top of baking dish. Moisten edges and press to the edges of the dish. Prick the crust decoratively in the center. Bake for 30 minutes, or until crust is golden brown.

—*Perini Ranch Steakhouse*

Spring turkey hunters at sunset

VENISON BACKSTRAP WITH ROASTED GARLIC–HORSERADISH CREAM SAUCE

Serves 2–3

This is an adaptation of Tom Perini's beef tenderloin recipe.

Venison backstrap, white muscle sheath removed
Olive oil
Perini Ranch Steak Rub (page 78)

Roasted Garlic–Horseradish Cream Sauce
 1 head garlic
 1 teaspoon olive oil
 Salt to taste
 2 cups heavy cream
 ¼ cup prepared horseradish
 ⅛ teaspoon freshly ground white pepper

Prepare the Roasted Garlic–Horseradish Cream Sauce. Preheat oven to 400 degrees. Place the head of garlic in the center of a piece of aluminum foil, coat with olive oil, and season with salt. Wrap the foil around the garlic and bake until soft and brown, about 1 hour. Cool to room temperature.

In a saucepan over medium-low heat, bring the cream to just under a boil, taking care that it does not boil over. Reduce heat and simmer until reduced by one-third, about 15 to 20 minutes. Remove from heat and refrigerate at least 20 minutes.

With a serrated knife, cut the garlic in half horizontally and squeeze the paste into a bowl. Mix in the horseradish and pepper to form a smooth paste, then add the cooled cream and stir until smooth. Adjust seasonings. Refrigerate at least 15 minutes before serving.

Meanwhile, cut the backstrap in half and lay the pieces alongside each other. Tie the halves together with three or four pieces of string, the same way that a butcher ties a beef tenderloin. (This will result in a thicker cut of meat that will cook more uniformly.) Coat the backstrap in olive oil and cover liberally with Perini Ranch Steak Rub. Allow the meat to rest until it comes to room temperature.

Preheat grill to its highest setting. Sear the backstrap on one side for 4 minutes, then turn and sear for an additional 3 minutes. With an instant-read thermometer, test the internal temperature (it should be 135 to 140 degrees for medium rare). Cook a bit longer if needed. Remove the backstrap from the grill and let it rest 5 to 10 minutes. Slice and serve at once with the chilled Roasted Garlic–Horseradish Cream Sauce.

—*Perini Ranch Steakhouse*

Gnarled antlers are a sign of old age or injury during the velvet stage; this one might be past his prime.

TEXAS CAVIAR

Serves 10–12

A Texas tradition, this can be served as a side dish or as a dip with tortilla chips.

> 2 pounds shelled black-eyed peas, cooked (about 4 cups)
> ½ cup chopped green onions, tops and bottoms
> ½ cup diced red onion
> 1 cup diced fresh tomato
> 2 cloves garlic, minced
> 1 medium jalapeño pepper, seeded and diced
> ¾ cup vegetable oil
> ¼ cup cider vinegar
> 1 teaspoon chopped fresh oregano
> 1 teaspoon chopped fresh basil
> ½ teaspoon salt
> ½ teaspoon freshly ground black pepper

Rinse and drain black-eyed peas. Add onions, tomato, garlic, and jalapeño. In a separate bowl, whisk together oil, vinegar, and seasonings; pour over peas and mix thoroughly. Refrigerate for at least 6 hours, stirring occasionally. Drain and serve chilled.

—*Perini Ranch Steakhouse*

COWBOY POTATOES

Serves 8–10

A wonderful alternative to mashed potatoes. This dish is quick and easy to assemble (the potatoes are left unpeeled) and is delicious with any grilled meat. Quantities are easily adjusted to feed a crowd of any size.

> 4 to 5 pounds red-skinned potatoes, cut into wedges
> ½ cup (1 stick) butter, melted
> 1 medium white onion, sliced
> 1 to 2 cloves garlic, finely minced
> 1 teaspoon salt
> 1 teaspoon ground black pepper
> ½ teaspoon ground dried oregano

Preheat oven to 350 degrees. Coat potatoes in butter, toss with onion and garlic, and sprinkle generously with salt, pepper, and oregano. Place in a baking dish, cover with aluminum foil, and bake for 1 hour, stirring occasionally. Remove the foil and continue cooking for an additional 30 minutes, or until potatoes are nicely browned.

—*Perini Ranch Steakhouse*

Texas Caviar

WINGING IT ON THE HIGH PLAINS

The Texas Panhandle offers some of the finest upland bird and waterfowl hunting in the country, yet many of the top wingshooting outfitters up there are running their hunts on a pay-per-day basis without meals or lodging. There's certainly nothing wrong with that program; it's a viable business model that works anywhere there's a huntable population of birds within a short drive of a Best Western and a Denny's. For purposes of filling out a cookbook, though, this section required a bit of cutting and pasting to represent the game bird species of Northwest Texas.

Even though Texas Parks and Wildlife has recently extended the pheasant season in the Panhandle, that sport is not exactly a maker or breaker of the region's hunting economy. It's a mystery to me—and quite a few pheasant guides as well—why many Texas hunters prefer buying airline tickets to the Dakotas instead of Lubbock or Amarillo when our daily bag limits are the same as theirs: three roosters per day. We've got some darn good pheasant hunting in our state; go check it out.

For the waterfowl hunter, the Plains and Panhandle offer a unique combination of pursuits. Most Texans consider the rice country along the coast as our qualified nexus of duck and goose hunting, but in recent years the Panhandle has established itself as an intriguing second option. From November through January, any open-water source within flight distance of a grain field will be standing room only for a quack-

Opposite: Pass-shooting sandhill cranes near Floydada
Rolling out the welcome mat in Plainview

Plains and Panhandle • 85

ing, honking, and trilling hodgepodge of ducks, geese, and sandhill cranes.

In the following pages you'll find a collection of recipes from a few guides and hunters who keep the birds moving and the dollars flowing through the Plains and Panhandle economies. Book the motels that they suggest and pick a good chain buffet for breakfast; they're all benefactors of our sport, and they provide services that allow a bunch of great guides to make a living without the overhead risk.

A vigilant yellow Lab
Pintails and widgeons on a High Plains playa lake

MAPLE SYRUP AND APPLE CIDER BRINED DUCK

Ducks are frequent visitors to the corn, wheat, and peanut fields of the Plains and Panhandle, but most avid duck hunters prefer to hunt them over decoys on the playa lakes. The brining technique in this recipe from Erik Guggenheim is great for removing the gamey taste from ducks. Use dabbling ducks (mallards, pintails, teal, widgeon) for best results. Be careful not to overcook the ducks; they are best medium-rare to medium. Allow two days to prepare this dish.

Erik runs guided hunts for geese, sandhill cranes, and ducks in the peanut country between Haskell and Seymour. As you will probably surmise, he also counts cooking as one of his more addictive hobbies.

2 or 3 whole ducks, cleaned
1 orange, peeled and segmented
1 apple, cut into quarters
1 can (14-ounce) vegetable stock or chicken broth plus additional as needed
4 cloves garlic, finely chopped
4 sage sprigs, finely chopped
4 thyme sprigs, finely chopped
4 parsley sprigs, finely chopped
1 medium onion, quartered
4 tablespoons unsalted butter, melted
Salt and pepper to taste

Brine

1 cup maple syrup
7 cups apple cider
⅔ cup brown sugar
⅔ cup sea salt or kosher salt
1 tablespoon ground black pepper
6 whole cloves
1 tablespoon ground allspice
8 slices fresh ginger, peeled
3 bay leaves
2 oranges, peeled and segmented

Gravy

3 cups pan juices, or add enough additional broth to equal 3 cups
Pan drippings from the roasted duck
½ cup chopped celery
½ cup chopped carrots

Prepare the brine by combining all brine ingredients in a large saucepan. Bring to a boil and cook for 5 minutes, or until sugar and salt are dissolved. Remove from heat, cool to room temperature, and refrigerate until completely chilled.

Stuff body cavity of each duck with equal portions of orange and apple pieces. Place ducks in a stock pot and pour chilled brine over the ducks. Refrigerate 18 to 24 hours, stirring mixture every 6 to 8 hours.

To roast the ducks, remove ducks from brine and

discard liquid. Rinse ducks with cold water and pat dry. Preheat oven to 500 degrees. Combine stock, garlic, sage, thyme, parsley, and onion in the bottom of a roasting pan. Place a roasting rack in the pan. Arrange ducks, breast side down, on rack; brush with butter and season with salt and pepper. Bake for 30 minutes, or until ducks begin to brown. Reduce oven temperature to 350 degrees and turn ducks breast side up. Brush again with the butter and season with salt and pepper. Bake for an additional 1 hour, or until an instant-read thermometer registers 140 degrees. (Start checking after 40 minutes to avoid overcooking.)

Remove pan from oven and let ducks rest 20 minutes before slicing. Reserve pan juices for gravy.

Meanwhile, make the gravy. Pour juices from the roasting pan into a measuring cup, adding stock, if necessary, to equal 3 cups; set aside. Add some of the rendered fat from the roasting pan to a saucepan and heat over medium heat. When hot, sauté celery and carrots until tender. Add the 3 cups of stock and bring to a boil. Cook over medium-high heat until reduced by half. Strain mixture, pressing on vegetables to extract all of the juices. Adjust seasonings and serve over sliced duck meat.

—*Erik Guggenheim, outfitter*

Duck hunter slinging decoys at dawn

BAKED PHEASANT

Serves 2

The Chinese ring-necked pheasant was originally imported from Manchuria to Oregon's Willamette Valley in the late 1800s. Additional stockings in the Dakotas, Nebraska, and Kansas after the turn of the century established the pheasant as an upland emblem of the Midwest prairies. State biologists believe that pheasants first snuck into Texas from western Oklahoma in the 1930s. State-sponsored stockings through 1970 assisted their proliferation throughout the Texas Panhandle. In Texas, pheasants are recognized by a number of applicable monikers: disco chickens, pasture peacocks, ditch parrots, and sorry-running-sonsabitches by those relegated to hunting them on the last weekend of the season.

Pheasant tends to dry out quickly if overcooked. This recipe keeps them tender and juicy; it also works well with quail.

2 pheasants, skinned
4 tomatoes, diced
2 cups fresh sliced mushrooms
1 cup chicken broth
½ teaspoon onion powder
½ teaspoon garlic powder
½ teaspoon dried oregano
2 bay leaves

Preheat oven to 350 degrees. Place pheasants in a 9 × 13-inch baking dish. In a bowl, combine the remaining ingredients and pour over the pheasants. Cover dish with foil and bake for 1 hour; check for tenderness. Cook longer if needed.

—*Bob Adamson, bird hunter*

GOOSE BREAST IN COGNAC GRAVY

Serves 2

The geese in the Texas Panhandle are mostly lesser Canadas, mixed in with a few specklebellies and snows. With relatively little hunting pressure on the High Plains, they offer consistent close-range shots with their necks craned and their wings cupped over the decoys. There are no boggy rice fields, no fire ants, and no plausible reasons for sky-busting at passing white specks that are smarter than the average decoy manufacturer.

In the early 1990s this was a favorite dish among the guests at Barry Batsell's El Tejón lodge in the northern Mexican state of Tamaulipas.

2 goose breasts, filleted (4 pieces)
1 cup heavy cream
1 cup cognac
Flour
Butter
Salt and pepper to taste

Slice each breast fillet lengthwise into 1-inch-thick strips. Using a tenderizing mallet, pound to a thickness of ½ inch. Dust each strip in flour seasoned with salt and pepper. Brown quickly in butter, turning when the juices begin to appear. Remove meat from skillet and set aside on paper towels to drain.

Reduce heat to low and add cognac to the pan drippings. Ignite the cognac (be careful) and stir slowly with a long-handled spoon until the alcohol burns off completely and the flame dies out. (Any alcohol remaining in the skillet will curdle the gravy when the cream is added.) Slowly pour the cream into the skillet while stirring with a wire whisk. Whisk until smooth; add flour a pinch at a time for desired thickness. Return goose strips to the skillet and allow to simmer in the gravy for 5 to 7 minutes.

—*Barry Batsell, outfitter*

Opposite: A cock pheasant and a fine shotgun (above). Pheasant hunting is typically a cooperative effort (below).

SANDHILL CRANE IN PORT CREAM SAUCE

Serves 4

The gangly and intellectual sandhill crane is the fine-eating (non-endangered) cousin of the whooping crane. If you've never seen them lined up in squadrons and approaching a decoy spread, then you owe yourself that opportunity at some point in your hunting career. Sandhills can spot movement and poorly planned camouflage at incredible distances. When they look like they're flying slowly, they're definitely not. And when you think you're perfectly hidden, you're usually not. Physically they resemble something out of a Dr. Seuss sketchbook, but there's not a more agile and vigilant waterfowl species on this continent.

2 sandhill crane breasts, filleted (4 pieces)
½ teaspoon finely chopped fresh rosemary
½ teaspoon kosher salt
½ teaspoon crushed peppercorn medley
2 cloves garlic, chopped
1 tablespoon olive oil

Port Cream Sauce
2 shallots, finely chopped
2 thin slices prosciutto, chopped, or bacon
1 tablespoon chopped fresh rosemary
¾ cup port
¼ cup water
½ cup heavy cream

Preheat oven to 350 degrees. Place breast pieces between two pieces of plastic wrap and pound to a uniform thickness of about ½ inch. In a small dish, mix rosemary, salt, pepper, garlic, and olive oil. Arrange fillets in a lightly greased baking dish and generously brush meat with the olive oil mixture. Cover with foil and bake until an instant-read thermometer registers 135 to 140 degrees for medium rare. Do not overcook. Remove from oven and keep warm.

To make the Port Cream Sauce, heat a small saucepan over medium heat; add shallots, prosciutto, and rosemary and cook until shallots are soft and prosciutto is crisp. Add port and water and bring to a boil. Reduce heat and simmer until mixture is reduced and thickened enough to coat the back of a spoon, about 12 to 15 minutes. Add cream and cook 3 to 5 minutes longer, or until cream thickens slightly. Spoon over fillets and serve.

—*Erik Guggenheim, outfitter*

Preceding page: Peanut-field action near Lubbock

Opposite: Sandhill cranes erupting from a milo field near Lockney (above). Fluttering flags look like landing geese to flocks approaching in the distance (below).

TRANS-PECOS

IF YOU WERE TO TAKE OFF DRIVING NORTH FROM AUSTIN and then pull over when the odometer read 550 miles, you would be parked just south of Wichita, Kansas. Heading south from our capital city for 550 miles would put you somewhere in the vicinity of Aguas Calientes, Mexico. On the perpendicular axis, an eastward drive of 550 miles would drop you just shy of Gulfport, Mississippi. And where would an Austinite wind up if he took off driving due west for 550 miles?

West Texas.

The arid and rugged far corner of our state known as the Trans-Pecos is a long way from a lot of places. El Paso, in case you were wondering, is closer to San Diego than it is to Beaumont. In fact, on my first trip out to gather material for this book, I racked up 1,482 miles on my truck and never swung within 250 miles of our westernmost city.

If you're driving out there for a hunting trip and you've never seen West Texas, then the incredible

scenery alone will probably keep you from nodding off on the outbound leg. But if the same mountains, canyons, and cactus viewed from the reverse angle aren't that exciting to you, then let me offer a few must-see stops and side bets for your drive home that might add a nice cultural patina to your hunting experience.

In Langtry, just west of Del Rio, be sure and check out the spot where Paul Newman shot Bad Bob the Albino (Stacy Keach) in the back as he drank boiling coffee from a tin pot yanked right out of the fire. In Marfa, stop and ask if anyone was best friends with James Dean, Rock Hudson, and Elizabeth Taylor during the summer of 1955 when they argued about cows versus oil in front of a giant faux mansion on the prairie outside of town. If you're pining for your old college days, try tracing Kevin Costner's *Fandango* route through West Texas as he and his Groovers trekked from UT to Big Bend to dig up a bottle of champagne and stave off their inductions to Vietnam. In Fort Stockton, have your picture made with Paisano Pete, the eleven by twenty-two-foot roadrunner recently featured in the documentary *World's Largest*.

And finally, as you're edging closer to the Hill Country, stop north of Bracketville where you can pay a token entry fee and see the spot where John Wayne, Richard Widmark, and Frankie Avalon held off Santa Anna's formidable army of extras back in 1960.

West Texas is a true gem, and I'd be willing to bet that fewer than one Texan in ten has ever experienced its grandeur firsthand. That old adage "If you don't like the weather, wait five minutes" is trumpeted statewide, but there's not another place in our state where you can say "drive five minutes" and convey the same message. West Texas is a land of microclimates. On a fall afternoon in the Chisos Mountains the temperature might not top 70 degrees, while the desert floor, just a few miles away, is sweltering in the upper 90s. Those lowland hardpan and creosote flats rarely receive any rain, but they do produce extreme heat that rises against the nearby mountains and causes rain to fall in buckets across their craggy peaks.

With respect to the hunting in West Texas, there's one difference you'll notice right away as you drive and scan the vistas and valleys of the Trans-Pecos: no deer stands and no feeders. Those icons of Texas

hunting have their place in the thick brush where slipping up on wary game is next to impossible, but not out here. West Texas is spot-and-stalk country in its purest form. Even though whitetails are starting to encroach in areas once considered inhospitable for their kind, the desert mule deer will always be king in West Texas, with the pronghorn running a close second. Bring your shotgun and your running shoes in case you tag out early; blue quail tend to covey up in populous road gangs in years when the grass is tall.

Much of the cooking in West Texas can be traced back to the early Spanish settlers and the Anasazi Indians; green chilies, masa, and pinto beans were their staples. In addition to this selection of ranches and lodges offering guided hunts in the Trans-Pecos, I've also mixed in a few restaurants and celebrated chefs that are serving wild game in grand fashion. Drop in, sample their fare, and keep an eye out for screen legends. With no more than ten folks per square mile out there, the odds of a star encounter are in your favor.

WILDLIFE SYSTEMS

◈ **Based in San Angelo**

Greg Simons grew up hunting the river bottoms and sloughs near his northeast Texas home of Kaufman. That's a considerable distance from where I tracked him down in October of 2006 as he hosted a group of antelope hunters on the sprawling Catto Gage Ranch near Marathon.

These days, a big ranch in East Texas might tape out at around 2,000 acres, and you'd have to shinny up a pretty tall tree to view more than a third of it at a time. Out where Greg works, though, it's not unusual to find several thousand acres between the game you've located with a spotting scope and the mountain ridge or patch of prairie that you're standing on.

After graduating from Texas A&M in 1987 with a degree in wildlife management, Greg's first stop was the Rolling Plains, near Albany, where he had done some intern work during college. His plan was simple: contact the ranchers that he already knew in the area and offer his expertise as a degreed range and wildlife consultant. As the habitat improved on the ranches that Greg was managing, the number of quality animals on those ranches also grew at an exponential rate. So what's a rancher to do with all of those excess management bucks and trophies that his family and friends don't have time or tags to harvest? The logical choice would be to hire a guide like Greg to bring in hunters and convert those animals into a naturally renewing revenue source.

As time passed and the ranches around Albany began to change hands and shrink in size, Greg found himself spending more time in West and South Texas

Opposite:. A trophy buck and a broadside shot
Glassing the flats for antelope near Marfa

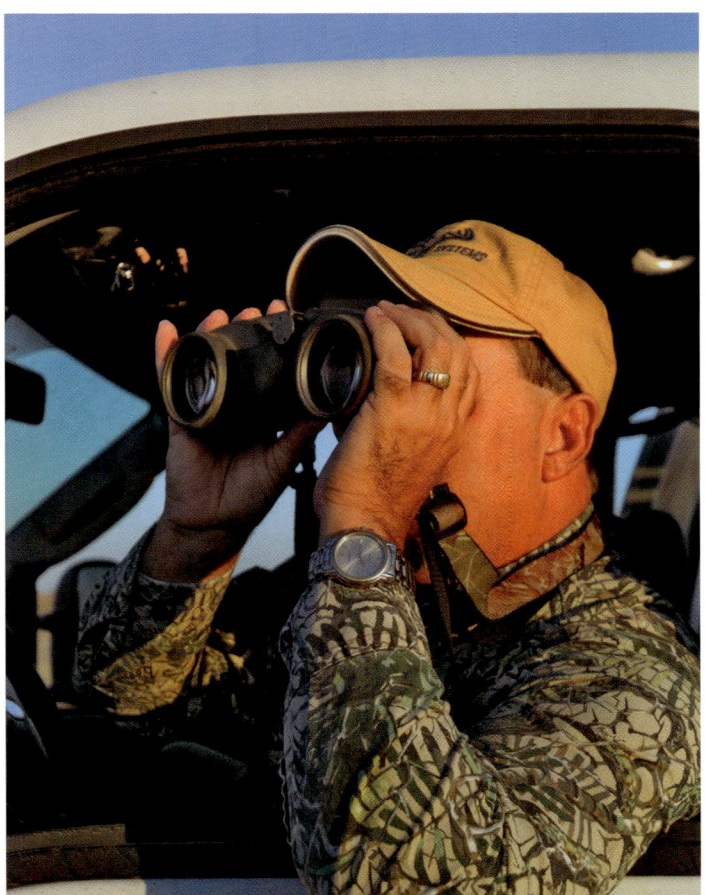

managing larger spreads with more animals per client. Greg and his family now live in San Angelo, and from that base of operation his crew of guides and cooks can efficiently work the thousands of acres that they manage and hunt between McAllen and Marfa.

Greg's hunters harvest more whitetail deer than any other species, but Wildlife Systems also has a steady stream of clients looking for pronghorns, mule deer, exotics, nilgai, and spring turkeys. In a typical year, he and his crew will guide over 300 hunters, and roughly 90 percent of them will come in from out of state. When I asked Greg about the dynamics of his company's success over the past twenty years, he readily credited their mobility and the quality of his support staff. Their land expenses are normally paid by the acre, the animal, or the hunter, and they typically use the accommodations that are already in place on each ranch that they manage and hunt. "It's a system that's worked well for us," he explained. "More than anything, it allows us to quickly put a crew of hunters and guides in place and take advantage of a good opportunity when it comes along."

STUFFED ANTELOPE TENDERLOIN

Instead of antelope tenderloins, whitetail or mule deer tenderloins can be used in this recipe. The tenderloins are located alongside the spine on the inside of the body cavity, just above the rear leg joints. If fresh green chilies aren't available, you can substitute fresh jalapeños with stems and seeds removed.

> *2 antelope tenderloins*
> *Balsamic vinegar*
> *2 fresh green chilies, with stems and seeds removed, cut into strips*
> *½ onion, julienned*
> *6 sun-dried tomatoes, cut into strips*
> *l package (8-ounce) cream cheese*
> *Seasoned salt to taste*
> *Thin-sliced bacon*

Butterfly each tenderloin lengthwise to form a pocket for stuffing. Place in a bowl, cover with balsamic vinegar, and marinate for 30 minutes. Remove from marinade, lay flat, and stuff each piece with strips of pepper, onion, and tomato. Place slivers of cream cheese on top and sprinkle with seasoned salt. Wrap each stuffed tenderloin with enough bacon slices to cover its entire length. Secure with toothpicks. Grill over hot coals until the bacon begins to crisp. To prevent flare-ups, grill in an open foil boat to catch the bacon and cheese drippings.

—*Trey Cowan, contract cook*

VENISON SAUSAGE AND WILD RICE CASSEROLE

Serves 12

This is a hearty casserole that will feed a hungry crowd. Perfect for a cold winter night.

2 boxes (6-ounce) long-grain and wild rice
2 cans (14-ounce) chicken broth
2 pounds venison pan sausage
1 pound sliced fresh mushrooms
2 large onions, chopped
¼ cup flour
½ cup heavy cream
¼ teaspoon dried oregano
¼ teaspoon dried thyme
¼ teaspoon dried marjoram
1 teaspoon salt
¼ teaspoon freshly ground black pepper
Dash of Tabasco sauce

Preheat oven to 350 degrees. Cook rice according to package directions, substituting the chicken broth for water; set aside. In a large skillet, cook sausage until well browned, remove sausage from skillet, and reserve drippings. Sauté onions and mushrooms in sausage drippings until onions are soft; remove from skillet and set aside. Reduce heat to low, add flour and cream, and whisk until smooth. Return sausage, onions, and mushrooms to skillet, add spices and seasonings, and cook until thickened. In a large bowl, combine sausage mixture, rice, and Tabasco, mixing thoroughly. Pour mixture into a large casserole dish. Bake for 30 minutes. Serve warm.

—*Trey Cowan, contract cook*

Opposite and above, left to right: Moving bush to bush to get within shooting range. Jim Gustafson (front) and Greg Simons lining up the shot. Snapping a few photos for Greg's Web site. Heavy bases, good prongs, and plenty of length (right)

FRIED CORN AND PEPPERS

Serves 4

1 tablespoon olive oil

2 cups fresh corn kernels (scraped from 4 ears of corn), or 1 package (16-ounce) frozen corn kernels, thawed

1 onion, chopped

1 red bell pepper, chopped

1 jalapeño pepper or green chili pepper, seeded and chopped

Seasoned salt

Black pepper

Heat oil in a large skillet over medium-high heat. Add corn, onion, and peppers and sauté until corn begins to brown and crisp. Season vegetables to taste with seasoned salt and pepper. Serve immediately.

—*Trey Cowan, contract cook*

GREEN CHILI TWICE-BAKED POTATOES

Serves 6

The amount of onion, green chilies, cheese, and sour cream can be varied according to taste. Use less if more potato flavor is preferred, or the full amount for a richer-tasting dish.

6 large baking potatoes

6 slices bacon, fried and crumbled

Bacon drippings

1 cup diced onion

1 cup diced green chilies

½ to 1 cup grated cheese

½ to 1 cup sour cream

Seasoned salt

Black pepper

Preheat oven to 400 degrees. Wash and pierce each potato with a fork, then wrap with foil. Bake potatoes for 1 hour, or until done. Remove potatoes from foil and allow to cool for 15 minutes. Reduce oven temperature to 350 degrees. Sauté onion and chilies in bacon drippings until onion is translucent. Slice potatoes in half lengthwise and scoop out the flesh, taking care not to tear the skin; set skins aside. Place potato flesh in a large bowl; add onion, chilies, cheese, and sour cream and mix thoroughly. Season to taste. Carefully spoon mixture back into the potato skins and bake for 20 to 30 minutes, or until heated through.

—*Trey Cowan, contract cook*

PEPPER AND CHEESE BEER BREAD

This bread is excellent with all game dishes, especially chili and stews. Be creative with the combination of peppers and cheese. Mild green chilies and Cheddar or roasted red bell pepper and Pepper Jack are good choices. Although this bread is not too sweet, the sugar can be omitted if even less sweetness is preferred. This results in a drier loaf with a coarser texture.

3 cups self-rising flour

¼ cup sugar, optional

½ cup diced bell pepper or chili pepper

½ cup grated cheese

1 can (12-ounce) regular beer

Preheat oven to 350 degrees. In a large bowl, mix flour, sugar, pepper, and cheese until evenly distributed. Add beer to dry mixture and stir just until combined; mixture will be lumpy. Pour into a greased loaf pan and bake for 1 hour, or until top of loaf is a light golden brown. Cool 10 minutes before slicing.

—*Trey Cowan, contract cook*

Opposite: Breakfast at the Catto-Gage Ranch

OCOTILLO RESTAURANT

⊞ Lajitas

Blas Gonzalez grew up in the Mexican state of San Luis Potosí and moved to Texas in the mid-1980s. He wasn't really sure what he wanted to do when he arrived in Austin, but he never guessed that he'd one day be recognized as one of the top chefs in the state.

His first official job title in Texas was "kitchen helper" when Jeff Blank hired him at Hudson's on the Bend restaurant in 1987. With no formal culinary or business training, Blas learned the restaurant industry, literally, from the bottom up. After a brief stint at the dishwasher, Blas was entrusted with the salad prep, where he demonstrated his enthusiasm for cooking and his attention to detail. From there, Blas was gradually worked into the starting lineup at Hudson's, where he integrated some of the flavors from his mother's kitchen back in San Luis Potosí. One of Blas's more celebrated contributions was his family's mole sauce, which Jeff Blank, to this day, refers to as "Blas's Holy Mole."

After seventeen years at Hudson's on the Bend, Blas was offered an opportunity that he couldn't pass up. Austin resident Steve Smith had recently purchased the town of Lajitas in far West Texas and transformed the dusty little outpost into a multimillion-dollar golf resort. He needed an accomplished chef and businessman to run the resort's Ocotillo Restaurant, and Blas was exactly the person he was looking for.

Having cooked at Hudson's on the Bend for so many years, wild game cooking, by default, has become one of Chef Blas's favorite pursuits. When I first spoke with him by phone before my road trip to Lajitas, he asked me about the species of West Texas game that I already had lined up for this book. I told

The Ocotillo Restaurant at Lajitas Resort
Opposite: A blue quail using an allthorn bush for a morning calling perch

him I was pretty well stocked up with deer, quail, and antelope recipes and that I would be open for suggestions. "How about a rattlesnake?" Blas asked before we hung up. "Have you ever tried one with chipotle sauce?"

After two days of driving and photographing on my way to Lajitas (I unfortunately missed the Terlingua World Chili Championships by three days), I was pleasantly surprised when I pulled into the Ocotillo and found Blas heating up his grill in a tricked-out kitchen that was larger than many of the fine dining rooms I've visited.

After shooting some photos and sampling Blas's renowned rattlesnake cakes, I asked him about his more memorable moments during his culinary career. He told me about the dinner at the Governor's Mansion where he and Jeff Blank cooked for Governor Rick Perry and President Vicente Fox of Mexico, and he also recounted the day that Tommy Lee Jones called him at the Ocotillo and asked if he could bring a group down during a break in filming for his current movie project.

"We closed down the Ocotillo and had a big private party with Mr. Jones and all of his cast and crew," Blas explained. "I served them venison and quail and many other dishes, and Mr. Jones introduced me as the best chef in Texas. It was a great evening!"

Gas station relic in Terlingua
The Rio Grande near Santa Elena Canyon
Opposite: View across the river from the Ocotillo bar and lounge area
Rock burial cairns at the Terlingua Cemetery east of Lajitas

RATTLESNAKE CAKES IN A PISTACHIO NUT CRUST

These cakes are very versatile; try using crab or pheasant if rattlesnake is unavailable. You can also purchase canned or fresh rattlesnake meat from purveyors of exotic and specialty meats. The cakes can be made a day ahead, breaded, and refrigerated. The sauce can be made earlier in the day.

- 3- to 4-foot rattlesnake (about 5 to 7 pounds, live weight)
- 3 quarts water
- 1 cup white wine
- 1 onion, quartered
- Juice from 4 lemons
- 2 tablespoons Tabasco sauce
- 4 cloves garlic
- 2 tablespoons salt

Cakes

- 1 pound diced, cooked rattlesnake meat
- ¾ cup diced celery
- 1 tablespoon minced garlic
- ½ cup mayonnaise
- 2 egg yolks, beaten
- 2 tablespoons Creole or spicy mustard
- 2 tablespoons chopped cilantro leaves
- 1 tablespoon chopped basil
- 2 jalapeños, seeded and minced
- ¼ cup bread crumbs
- 1 tablespoon salt

Pistachio Nut Crust

- 1 cup shelled pistachio nuts
- ½ cup bread crumbs
- Salt and pepper
- ⅓ cup olive oil

Chipotle Sauce

- 2 cups rich chicken stock
- 3 cloves shallots, minced
- 2 large chipotle peppers
- 4 dashes of Tabasco sauce

3 cloves garlic, minced
¼ cup sun-dried tomatoes
1 tablespoon Worcestershire sauce
¼ cup brown sugar, packed
2 teaspoons salt
½ cup heavy cream
1 bunch cilantro, leaves only

Make the Chipotle Sauce. Pour stock into a large saucepan and add shallots, peppers, Tabasco, garlic, tomatoes, Worcestershire sauce, and brown sugar; simmer for 15 minutes. Purée in a food processor. Add salt. Stir in cream and cilantro and mix well. Set aside.

Carefully cut the head and tail from the rattlesnake. Split the snake's skin; starting at the neck, peel the skin toward the tail and pull it off in one quick motion. Remove all entrails and wash thoroughly. Cut into 6-inch pieces.

In a 5-quart Dutch oven, combine water, wine, onion, lemon juice, Tabasco, garlic, and salt; bring to a boil. Add snake meat and cook for at least 30 minutes, adding water as necessary. When tender, remove meat from cooking liquid, discarding liquid. Cool meat slightly and pull meat from bones. (The easiest meat to remove from the bones will be the "backstraps" from each side of the spine; the rest comes from between the ribs.) Dice the meat until it has the consistency of crabmeat.

To make the cakes, combine rattlesnake meat with remaining ingredients in a large mixing bowl; blend well and set aside.

Make the Pistachio Nut Crust. In a food processor, combine pistachios, bread crumbs, salt, and pepper and pulse until coarsely chopped. Form balls of the rattlesnake mix (about the size of a golf ball) and drop into the nut crust mix. Press the nut mixture into the meat, forming 2-inch patties. In a large sauté pan heat oil over medium-high heat until it shimmers (about 325 to 350 degrees). Sauté patties about 2 minutes per side, or until golden brown. Remove from pan, pat off excess oil, and keep warm.

Return the Chipotle Sauce to the saucepan and bring to a simmer to reheat. Serve the cakes on top of the Chipotle Sauce.

—*Blas Gonzalez, chef*

Opposite: Tastes like chicken . . . well, sort of. Chef Blas Gonzalez at work in the Ocotillo kitchen.

DUCK BREAST WITH RED CHILI GLAZE

Serves 4–6

The glaze in this dish is also good with chicken, pork, quail, and other game birds. The glaze can be made up to two days in advance.

4 duck breasts with skin on, filleted (8 pieces)

Salt and pepper

Red Chili Glaze

1 cup champagne vinegar

1 to 1½ tablespoons red chili flakes, depending on amount of heat desired

1 tablespoon minced garlic

2 tablespoons minced onion

2 cups light brown sugar, packed

2 tablespoons tomato paste

½ cup soy sauce

1 teaspoon salt

½ cup unsalted butter, cut into 8 to 10 pieces

Make the Red Chili Glaze. In a heavy saucepan, simmer vinegar, chili flakes, garlic, and onion until reduced by half. Add brown sugar, tomato paste, soy sauce, and salt; return to a simmer and cook 3 minutes, stirring constantly (this glaze can burn easily). Remove from heat and whisk in butter pieces, one at a time. Set aside.

To cook the duck breasts, prepare a hot charcoal or hardwood fire. Score the skin and fat layer of each duck breast with a sharp knife in a crosshatch pattern. Lightly season with salt and pepper. Place the duck breasts, skin side down, over the fire. Watch for flare-ups and cook for about 6 minutes, depending on the heat of the fire. Turn breasts over and grill for an additional 2 minutes at the most. (Duck is best served medium rare to medium.) Slice the duck breasts and fan out on a serving plate. Serve topped with Red Chili Glaze.

—Blas Gonzalez, chef

TAMALE CHEESE AND QUAIL PIE WITH CHIPOTLE MEXICAN CRÈME

Serves 6

Here's a quiche with a Southwest twist. Any smoked meat can be substituted for the quail. The Chipotle Mexican Crème should be started at least one day in advance.

Crust

- 1 cup masa
- 1 tablespoon chili powder
- 1 teaspoon salt
- 2 tablespoons chilled butter, cubed
- 1 cup water

Filling

- 4 eggs
- 1 cup heavy cream
- 1 tablespoon minced garlic
- 1 cup diced red onion
- 1 poblano pepper, seeded and diced
- 2 smoked quail (about 8 ounces each), diced
- 2 tablespoons chili powder
- 1½ teaspoons salt
- ½ cup grated Pepper Jack cheese
- ½ cup grated Cheddar cheese

Chipotle Mexican Crème

- 6 ancho peppers
- 2 cups warm water
- 2 cups heavy cream
- ½ cup buttermilk, not ultra-pasteurized

Start the Chipotle Mexican Crème. Mix the cream and buttermilk together in a glass bowl. Cover with plastic wrap and let sit at room temperature overnight.

When ready to prepare the pie, soak the ancho peppers in water for 30 minutes, or until soft. Drain and purée in a blender, adding a small amount of the water used for soaking. (The purée should equal ½ cup.) Add the ancho purée to the cream mixture; mix and set aside.

Preheat oven to 325 degrees. To make the crust, mix together masa, chili powder, and salt. Add butter and cut it into the mixture with a fork or pulse in a food processor until butter is pea-sized. Add water and mix to form a dough. Press into a 9-inch pie pan and bake for 15 minutes. Set aside to cool.

Increase oven temperature to 350 degrees. To make the filling, whisk together eggs and cream. Stir in the garlic, onion, poblano pepper, quail meat, chili powder, and salt. Sprinkle cheeses into the baked pie shell. Pour egg mixture over cheese and bake 50 minutes. Let the pie rest 10 minutes. Serve with Chipotle Mexican Crème.

—Blas Gonzalez, chef

GREEN CHILI AND MEXICAN CRÈME SMASHED POTATOES

Serves 8

Mexican crème can be purchased in the dairy section of major grocery stores. If it is unavailable, make your own using the recipe below. It needs to sit overnight, so start it the day before you want to make the potatoes. The potatoes are delicious with any game meat, especially chicken-fried venison with gravy.

- 1 bottle (12-ounce) Shiner bock beer
- 6 large baking potatoes, peeled
- 1 cup Hatch green chilies, roasted and peeled, or canned or frozen green chilies
- 1 bunch fresh cilantro, chopped
- 1 cup Mexican crème at room temperature (see note)
- ½ pound (2 sticks) butter, softened
- Salt and pepper to taste

Pour the beer into a small saucepan and cook over medium heat until reduced to ½ cup. Keep warm. Bring a large pot of salted water to a boil and add the potatoes; cook until tender. Drain potatoes, discarding liquid. Cook over medium heat for an additional 1 minute to remove excess moisture. Mash potatoes. Add green chilies, cilantro, Mexican crème, reduced beer, and butter; mix together. Season with salt and pepper. Keep warm until served.

NOTE: To make your own Mexican crème, mix 1 cup heavy cream and ¼ cup buttermilk (not ultra-pasteurized) in a glass bowl. Cover with plastic wrap and let the mixture sit at room temperature overnight.

—Blas Gonzalez, chef

GAGE HOTEL

⌖ **Marathon**

Alfred Gage was only eighteen years old when he arrived in West Texas looking for work as a cowhand. Having grown up in the Northeast among deep conifer forests, sparkling lakes, and landholdings measured in square feet, one can only imagine his shock when he arrived in Marathon and found that rainfall was a celebrated event and that Brewster County was nearly as large as his home state of Vermont.

After a few years of apprentice ranch work, Gage bought a piece of land near McKinney Springs and recruited his two brothers to form a business partnership. By 1920, their Alpine Cattle Company had grown to over 500,000 acres and Alfred Gage had moved to San Antonio, where his reputation had preceded him as a shrewd dealer and proprietor of land and cattle.

As Gage made frequent trips between San Antonio and Brewster County to check on his landholdings during those years, he eventually recognized the need for a fine accommodation in Marathon that he could use as a base of operation. Aspiring to build a functional and modern facility, Gage hired the architectural firm of Trost & Trost to design a hotel of the same quality and tradition as El Paisano in Marfa and El Capitan in Van Horn. Ponford & Sons, a prominent contractor from El Paso, was hired to build the two-story brick facility.

The Gage Hotel opened on U.S. Highway 90 in Marathon in 1927 and enjoyed a brisk business among travelers, ranchers, and miners passing through West Texas. Alfred Gage, however, was never able to fully utilize or enjoy his vision; he died soon after the hotel opened. Over the next fifty years, there were numerous attempts to revitalize the hotel, but the Gage eventually foundered due to neglect and lack of steady patronage.

In 1978, the original Gage Hotel building was

The historic Gage Hotel in Marathon, a fine accommodation for hunters and travelers since 1927

Opposite, clockwise from left: Fireplace adornments in Café Cenizo. Symbols of our frontier heritage. The focal point of the White Buffalo Bar.

purchased by J. P. and Mary Jon Bryan of Houston. Through extensive renovations and marketing, the Bryans have restored the Gage Hotel as a landmark accommodation in West Texas.

Today the historic Gage has expanded to occupy two city blocks, and the facility enjoys consistent bookings from deer, quail, and antelope hunters in the fall as well as a year-round stream of hikers, bikers, and rafters who stop in on their way to Big Bend National Park. The original accommodations remain largely unchanged with quaint rooms and baths down the hall. For guests who prefer a full-service room, there are more spacious facilities available in the newer Los Portales addition that fronts the pool and courtyard just west of the original building.

With tourism and real estate purchases for retirement at an all-time high in West Texas, the Gage Hotel has reestablished itself to cash in on the flow. There aren't too many busy intersections in Brewster County, but the Gage sits near one of them, and it's hard to pass through Marathon without pulling in for a look.

Los Portales courtyard at the Gage

Sunset view through the Window in Big Bend National Park

ANTELOPE MEDALLIONS WITH MUSHROOM DEMI-GLACE

....

Serves 4

Whitetail or mule deer can also be used for this dish. Serve with Potato-Mushroom Hash.

>8 (3-ounce) antelope medallions, cut from loin or backstrap
>Salt and pepper to taste
>1 tablespoon olive oil
>1 tablespoon unsalted butter

Mushroom Demi-Glace
>2 tablespoons olive oil
>2 cups sliced fresh cremini mushrooms
>2 cups good-quality red wine
>3 cups rich, low-sodium beef stock
>Cornstarch and water for slurry

Make the Mushroom Demi-Glace. In a 2-quart saucepan, heat oil over medium-high heat. Add mushrooms and sauté just until tender. Add red wine and deglaze pan, scraping up any browned bits. Cook until wine is reduced by half. Add stock, lower heat, and simmer until reduced by three-fourths, about 10 to 12 minutes. Thicken with slurry if a thicker sauce is desired. To make a slurry, mix together equal parts cornstarch and water and add to sauce, stirring until thickened. Set aside and keep warm.

Lightly pound the medallions to a thickness of about ½ inch. Season both sides with salt and pepper. Heat a large cast-iron skillet until very hot. Add olive oil and then butter. When butter has melted, add antelope and sear on one side for 2 minutes. Turn and continue cooking for an additional 2 to 2½ minutes, or until medium rare. Serve with Mushroom Demi-Glace.

—*Paul Petersen, chef*

Opposite: A promising pronghorn buck west of Marathon. Fine dining in the Texas Trans-Pecos.

CHICKEN-FRIED VENISON WITH WILD BOAR SAUSAGE GRAVY

Serves 4

Panko bread crumbs are found in the Asian section of major supermarkets.

4 (5-ounce) venison medallions, preferably from backstrap
4 cups flour
4 large eggs, beaten
1 cup buttermilk
2 cups panko bread crumbs
1½ tablespoons kosher salt
2 tablespoons ground black pepper
2 cups vegetable oil

Wild Boar Sausage Gravy

2 tablespoons vegetable oil
½ pound wild boar sausage, casings removed
1 red onion, finely diced
2 poblano peppers, roasted, peeled, and diced
½ pound (2 sticks) unsalted butter
½ cup flour
1 quart dark chicken stock or low-sodium chicken broth
Kosher salt and freshly ground pepper to taste

Make the Wild Boar Sausage Gravy. In a 2½-quart sauté pan, heat oil over medium-high heat for about 1 minute. Crumble sausage into pan; stir to coat with oil and break up large pieces. When sausage is almost cooked through, add onion and cook until onion is soft. Add poblano peppers and stir just to combine. Add butter and melt completely. Slowly sprinkle the flour over the mixture, stirring constantly. Cook for 1 minute, stirring. Whisking constantly, slowly add stock and stir until smooth. Bring to a gentle boil, then reduce heat and simmer about 15 minutes, stirring occasionally. If gravy becomes too thick, add a small amount of stock. Keep warm while preparing venison.

Place venison medallions between layers of plastic wrap and pound to a thickness of ¼ inch. Remove plastic and lightly pound with the tenderizing side of the meat mallet, being careful not to cut through the meat.

Place 2 cups of the flour in a shallow dish. In a separate bowl, beat together eggs and buttermilk. In another shallow dish, combine the remaining 2 cups flour, bread crumbs, salt, and pepper. Heat the oil in a large skillet over medium or medium-high heat until oil is glistening. Dredge the venison medallions in the flour, dip into the egg mixture, and then heavily coat both sides in the flour and bread crumb mixture, pressing mixture into the meat to make it adhere. Fry the venison 2 to 2½ minutes per side, or until crisp and golden brown on both sides. Drain on paper towels. Serve with Wild Boar Sausage Gravy.

—*Paul Petersen, chef*

POTATO-MUSHROOM HASH

Serves 6

A wonderful side dish that complements any grilled game.

12 fingerling potatoes
Salt and pepper to taste
2 leeks, ends removed, washed, and cut in half
2 cups fresh oyster mushrooms
1½ tablespoons olive oil plus additional as needed
1 tablespoon unsalted butter
1 cup heavy cream
2 tablespoons Asiago cheese

Preheat oven to 350 degrees. Scrub potatoes, toss with a small amount of oil, and place on greased baking sheet. Season with salt and pepper and roast until tender, about 15 minutes. Set aside to cool.

Grill leeks or roast in hot oven until cooked. Cool, slice, and set aside. Sauté mushrooms in a hot skillet with a bit of olive oil until cooked. Season with salt and pepper and set aside to cool.

Heat olive oil in a large sauté pan and add butter. Slice cooled potatoes in half lengthwise and add to skillet, cut side down. Cook until golden brown. Add leeks and mushrooms and mix with potatoes; cook 2 minutes. Add cream and cook, stirring, until cream is thickened and reduced by half. Add cheese and mix well. Continue to cook until mixture has thickened, about 2 to 3 minutes. Be careful not to let the mixture burn.

—*Paul Petersen, chef*

The main lobby at the Gage

LONGFELLOW RANCH

⊞ **Fort Stockton**

The steam locomotives that traversed our country in the late 1800s required regular water stops to keep their big engines chugging along. And like most consumers of water in West Texas—resident or transient—those locomotives needed big refills at regular intervals.

In 1881 the Galveston, Harrisburg, and San Antonio Railroad built a pumping facility sixteen miles west of Sanderson and named it after the poet Henry Wadsworth Longfellow. There's no written record as to why this name was chosen; perhaps he wrote an obscure, unpublished verse about dust, or scorpions, or prickly pear that was favored among the rail workers during that time.

By 1890, the Longfellow rail stop had become a bustling, working depot with postal and telegraph offices, loading chutes for cattle, a ballast quarry, and a vein of silver ore running beneath the town. Sadly, though, like many railroad stops that eventually found a highway running through them, the town of Longfellow ultimately went the way of the steam engine when U.S. 90 was paved westward through Del Rio, Dryden, Langtry, and Sanderson.

Today you can still see remains of the old pump station, located not too far from the southern entrance to the Longfellow Ranch. The ranch was originally formed around the time of World War I by cattleman Buck Pyle and James Marion West Jr., an eccentric lawyer and oilman from Houston known as "Silver Dollar Jim." The West-Pyle Cattle Company operated the ranch until 1959, when it was eventually split up among the proprietor's heirs. In 1995 the Longfellow

The main lodge at the Longfellow Ranch
Opposite: Mule deer bucks using a brushy draw for cover

was bought by Malone Mitchell, an oil and gas producer who had grown up just south of the current headquarters on Big Canyon. Energy and cattle are still the ranch's strongholds, but Mitchell has also developed an extensive wildlife management program and a wonderful facility for hunters and ranch guests.

Says Pat Peacock, the thirty-year manager of the Longfellow, "We've got a few whitetails on the ranch, but mule deer will always be our biggest draw." The Longfellow also has a thriving elk herd, plenty of blue quail in the wet years, and a growing population of Rio Grande turkeys. Peacock explains that the Longfellow Ranch is not really promoting trophy animals. It's selling a safe, quality hunting experience on an authentic working ranch.

With a maximum of twelve guns per hunt on a ranch spanning 400 sections, it's doubtful that overharvest will ever be an issue on the Longfellow.

The historic saloon at Langtry where Judge Roy Bean doled out whiskey, justice, and contempt to the laborers who built the rail stops at Pumpville, Dryden, Longfellow, and points west during the late 1880s

The Pecos River gorge from the U.S. 90 bridge east of the Longfellow Ranch

SUGAR-CURED SMOKED VENISON HAM

Morton's Sugar Cure can be ordered online at www.mortonsalt.com.

> 1 venison ham
> 2 cups Morton's Sugar Cure
> 5 gallons cold water
> Bacon, cut into small pieces
> Garlic cloves, peeled and cut into slivers
> Salt and pepper to taste

Thoroughly dissolve curing mix in cold water (a small ice chest works well). Submerge the venison ham in the water mixture for 24 hours, periodically adding ice to keep the water cool.

Remove ham from the curing brine. Using a sharp knife, cut 1-inch-deep slits into the thickest part of the ham. Space the slits evenly, making sure not to cut all the way through the ham. Roll slivers of garlic inside bacon pieces and insert into the slits.

Slow-cook in a smoker or grill using an aromatic wood, such as mesquite or hickory. Be sure to place a pan of water beneath the meat and take care not to overcook.

—Harold Stokes, ranch cook

VENISON JERKY

> 1 pound dark brown sugar
> ½ cup table salt
> ¼ cup coarsely ground black pepper
> 1 teaspoon garlic powder
> 10 pounds venison (ham, shoulder, or backstrap), cut into ⅜-inch-thick strips

Mix dry ingredients together and pour into a large, flat pan. Roll each strip of meat in the spice mixture until completely coated, shaking off excess. Layer the meat in a separate pan and refrigerate, covered, for 3 or 4 days. Arrange strips on smoker grate so that they do not touch. Smoke at 150 degrees for 9 to 10 hours, or until meat is firm and chewy.

—Harold Stokes, ranch cook

OATMEAL APPLE CRISP

Granny Smith or any other crisp, tart apple works best for this recipe.

> 6 cups sliced and peeled apples (about 7 medium apples)
> 1½ cups sugar
> ¾ cup plus 1 tablespoon flour
> 2 teaspoons cinnamon
> Dash of salt
> ¾ cup packed light brown sugar
> ¾ cups rolled oats (not instant)
> ¼ teaspoon baking soda
> ¼ teaspoon baking powder
> ⅓ cup melted butter or margarine

Preheat oven to 350 degrees. Lightly grease an 8 × 11-inch baking dish. In a mixing bowl, combine apples, sugar, 1 tablespoon flour of the flour, cinnamon, and salt. Arrange apple mixture in prepared baking dish. In a separate bowl, combine brown sugar, oats, the remaining ¾ cup flour, baking soda, and baking powder. Add melted butter and mix thoroughly. Sprinkle evenly over apples and bake for 45 minutes to 1 hour.

—Pat Stokes, ranch cook

Opposite: The patio and grill overlooking Big Canyon. Venison Jerky. Mule deer track in a caliche creek bed

CF RANCH

▣ **Alpine**

The first blast of cold air rocked my cabin at around 3:00 a.m. on the last morning of my visit to the CF Ranch near Alpine. The wall heater next to my bed, thankfully, kicked on a few minutes later. It was plenty warm in my cabin when my alarm went off at 5:30, but I could hear sleet pellets blasting against the window as I dug through my duffle, hoping that the long-handles I hadn't packed five days before had miraculously appeared overnight.

By the time I pulled up to the ranch kitchen at 6:00 a.m., it was snowing sideways and the green LED readout on my rearview mirror was intermittently flashing 22°... ICE... 22°... ICE. The previous afternoon I was photographing mule deer hunters under sunny skies and temperatures in the low 70s.

With the Weather Channel droning winter storm warnings in the background, I loaded up on bacon, eggs, and coffee while CF Ranch owner Al Micallef explained the origin and operation of his remarkably diverse business interests in West Texas.

"I started buying ranches in the early 1990s," Al explained. "At one point we owned over 150,000 acres in Texas and New Mexico, but we've since scaled it back."

Today the CF Ranch consists of the 9,000-acre headquarters division north of town and another 11,000 acres on the south side of Alpine. Cattle, horses, and hunting are a significant portion of the ranch's revenue, but Al and his son, Mike, fully understand the importance of diversification in the ranching business. They also own the renowned Reata restaurants in Alpine and Fort Worth, and they've formed an income stream between the ranch and Hollywood with two on-site movie sets. Their western town and

Franklin Hoet Jr. with a classic 5 × 5 from the Davis Mountains (photo courtesy of CF Ranch).

Opposite: Glassing for mule deer on the CF Ranch

Spanish mission replicas have served as backdrops in a Brooks & Dunn video, a Chevy Truck commercial, and several full-length movie productions, including *Dead Man's Walk*, *The Good Old Boys*, *Streets of Laredo*, and *Rough Riders*. Mike and Al are also avid polo players, and in the summer of 2006 they hosted their first tournament at the newly constructed Reata Polo Club near the ranch headquarters.

Mule deer are the ranch's primary hunting draw, but the CF also hosts a few hunters each year who are looking for a shot at an aoudad ram or one of the ranch's free-range trophy elk. The CF manages its wildlife under a State of Texas MLD (Managed Lands Deer) permit, and a combination of selective culling, supplemental feeding, and habitat management has paid off generously.

"We brought the elk in six or seven years ago, and they've done incredibly well," Al explained. "Our biggest bull so far, killed by a bowhunter, was a huge 7 × 7 that grossed 455 B&C."

After breakfast I was standing in the driving snow next to my rented mid-size squirrel cage and wondering if its diminutive street tires would get me back to the airport in Midland. My predicament, though, seemed fairly benign when hunters Brad Urbanczyk and James Zipprian emerged from their rooms walking like camouflaged cadavers wearing every stitch of clothing they had packed. The afternoon before, I had relentlessly ribbed James about passing up a nice buck that I was hoping to photograph. As I was loading my gear, he stopped next to my car to shake hands. "Well, I doubt we'll see that buck again in these conditions," James laughed.

I heard later on that he shot one on the last afternoon of his hunt that was considerably bigger.

Sunrise view south of Alpine
Main façade of the Spanish-style mission movie set on the CF Ranch

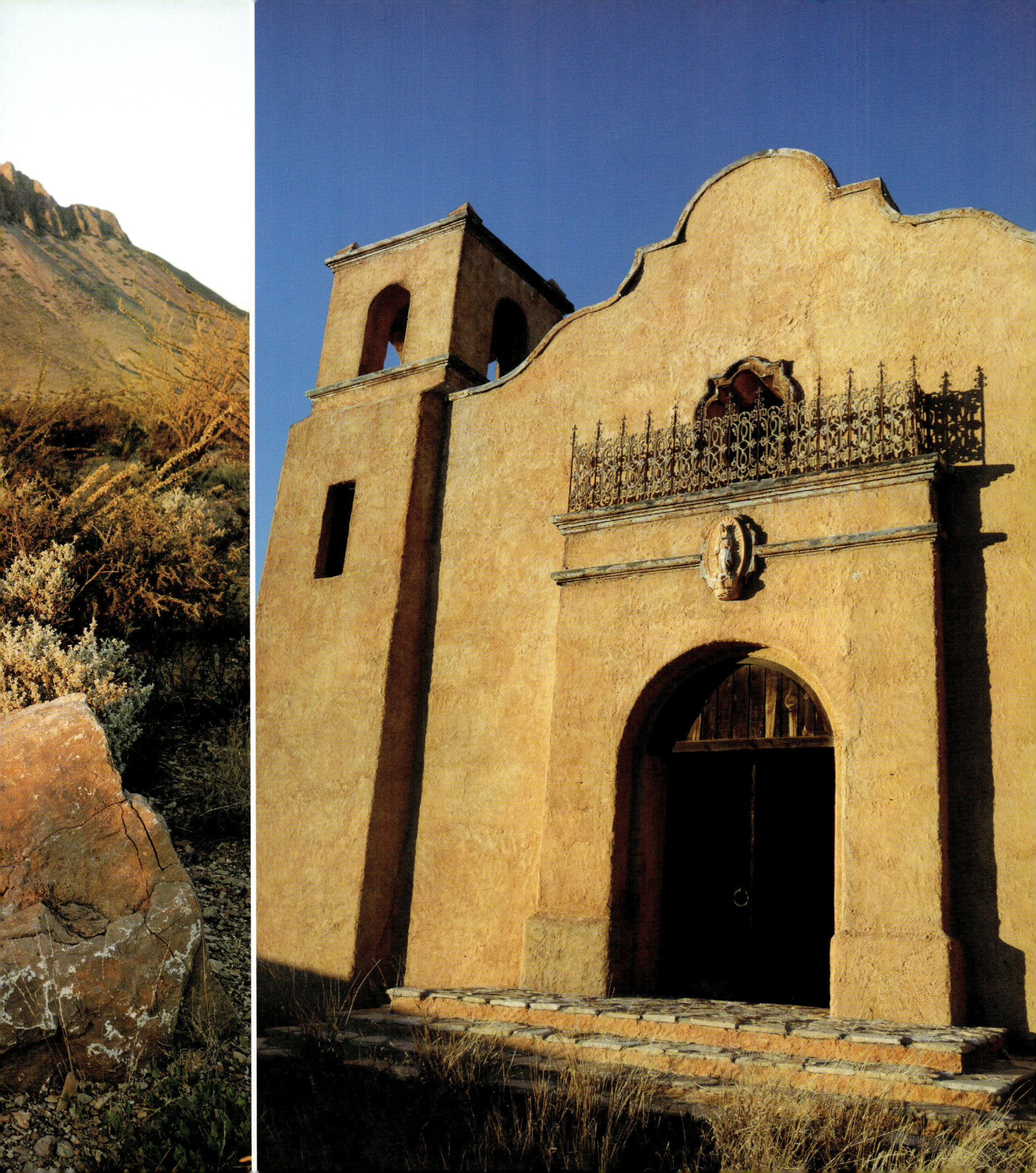

VENISON-STUFFED PEPPERS

The tenderloins are the most delicate meat found on a deer. They are located alongside the spine on the inside of the body cavity, just above the rear leg joints.

2 tenderloins from whitetail, mule deer, or antelope
Salt and pepper to taste
Garlic powder to taste
20 fresh jalapeño peppers, seeds and veins removed
20 slices bacon

Cut each tenderloin across the grain into 10 medallions. Season with salt, pepper, and garlic powder. Stuff each jalapeño with a piece of venison. Wrap the stuffed jalapeño with a slice of bacon, securing with a toothpick. Grill over hot coals until bacon is crisp.

—*Paula Cotton, ranch staff*

BUTTERMILK PIE

3 tablespoons flour
3 cups sugar
6 eggs
1 cup (2 sticks) butter, softened
1 cup buttermilk
2 teaspoons vanilla
9-inch deep-dish unbaked pie shell

Preheat oven to 400 degrees. Mix flour and sugar together. Add eggs, mixing well. Add butter, buttermilk, and vanilla, whisking well after each addition. Whisk mixture by hand; do not use an electric mixer. Pour into unbaked pie shell. Bake in preheated oven for 15 minutes, then reduce heat to 350 degrees and cook an additional 30 to 40 minutes, or until filling is set. Cool completely before slicing.

—*Sandra Lewis, ranch cook*

DENVER BISCUITS

Yield: about 60 two-inch biscuits

These biscuits can be frozen for future use. After rolling out and cutting the dough into biscuits, freeze them on cookie sheets, then transfer the biscuits to plastic bags and return them to the freezer. When you're ready to cook the biscuits, thaw them for two to three hours and proceed according to the directions.

1 quart (4 cups) milk
1 cup shortening
1 cup sugar
2 packages yeast
¼ cup warm water
8 to 9 cups flour (approximately)
2 teaspoons baking powder
1 teaspoon baking soda
2 teaspoons salt

Scald milk and add shortening and sugar. Stir until shortening is melted; remove from heat and set aside to cool until mixture is lukewarm. Dissolve yeast in warm water and let stand for 5 minutes to activate. Add yeast to cooled milk mixture and add about 4 cups of the flour, or enough flour to make a thin batter. Cover and let rise in a warm place for 2 hours, or until doubled.

Stir batter down and add baking powder, soda, salt, and the remaining 4 to 5 cups flour, or enough to make a stiff dough. (At this point, dough can be covered and refrigerated for up to one week.) Roll out to a thickness of ½ inch and cut out biscuits with a 2-inch biscuit cutter. Let rise 30 minutes, or until doubled. Preheat oven to 350 degrees and bake biscuits 12 to 15 minutes, or until golden brown.

—*Sandra Lewis, ranch cook*

Opposite, clockwise from top left: Vince Lorie with a West Texas aoudad sheep. Aoudads have keen eyes, sensitive noses, and an affinity for the roughest terrain they can find (photo courtesy of CF Ranch). Hoofing it uphill for a better view. Rifle rests are where you find them in wide-open country.

REATA RESTAURANT

⊞ **Alpine**

"It was never my intention to get into the restaurant business when we first bought the CF Ranch," said owner Al Micallef. "But when friends and business associates came out to the ranch, there weren't many places we could take them for a nice meal. This area was basically a gastronomical wasteland."

After many late-night dinner trips to the Gage Hotel in Marathon, Al decided to open a restaurant in Alpine, closer to home. His goal was to build a facility serving "cowboy cuisine" that would celebrate the rich heritage and unique culture of West Texas.

In 1995 Al and his current business partner, Mike Evans, bought a historic adobe house on North Fifth Street and converted it into the Reata Restaurant. "I've always loved the movie *Giant*," explained Al. "We named the restaurant after the ranch in the movie, which was filmed over near Marfa back in the 1950s."

Al's first hire was cowhand-turned-chef Grady Spears, who had recently left the kitchen at the Gage Hotel. From chuck-wagon suppers and Dutch ovens to stainless stoves and fine china, Grady had a wide range of talents, and it didn't take long for word to spread of his culinary expertise.

After enjoying a packed dining room in Alpine and opening another Reata in Fort Worth, Al, Mike, and Grady partnered with Ten Speed Press in 1998 for their cookbook *A Cowboy in the Kitchen*. "That book really put us on the map," said Al. "At one point it was one of the top-selling cookbooks at Amazon.com."

Reata Alpine is still running from its original location, but the Fort Worth restaurant was forced to

The Reata in Alpine: celebrating cowboy cuisine and the West Texas cattle culture

Opposite: Blind, or spineless, prickly pear on a rocky slope in Brewster County

relocate by a tornado that blasted through the middle of town in the spring of 2000. Today the Reata at Sundance Square occupies a former landmark jazz club in downtown Fort Worth. Al and his son, Mike, have also started a successful catering business, aptly named Reata on the Road.

Grady Spears is no longer with the Reatas, but Mike Micallef now oversees a talented team of chefs and managers who are committed to maintaining the tradition of legendary western cuisine and sophistication without pretension.

With no defined genetic link to antelope, deer, or goats, pronghorns are an evolutionary eccentric in the American West.

A century plant in the Chisos Mountains

138 • GRAZING ACROSS TEXAS

REATA GRILL BLEND

Yield: 1 cup

This is a great seasoning for wild game, beef, and pork.

- 4 tablespoons kosher salt
- 3 tablespoons chili powder
- 2 tablespoons granulated garlic
- 2 tablespoons sugar
- 2 tablespoons cumin
- 2 tablespoons coarsely ground black pepper
- 1 tablespoon ground thyme

Combine all ingredients and mix thoroughly. Store in an airtight container. Shake or stir before each use.

—Reata Restaurant

GRILLED VENISON BACKSTRAP WITH APRICOT GLAZE

Serves 4–6

Venison backstrap is best served medium rare to medium.

- 1 venison backstrap, white muscle sheath removed
- 2 tablespoons olive oil
- 3 tablespoons Reata Grill Blend (page 140)
- ¼ cup dry white wine
- 2 cups apricot preserves

Preheat grill to high heat. Coat backstrap with olive oil, season with Reata Grill Blend, and set aside.

In a saucepan, heat the wine until boiling and cook until reduced by half. Whisk in the apricot preserves and cook over medium heat until melted and thoroughly incorporated. Set aside.

Cook backstrap 4 minutes per side, or until an instant-read thermometer registers an internal temperature of 135 to 140 degrees (for medium rare to medium). Brush with glaze a minute or two before removing from grill. (The glaze will burn if brushed on too early.)

—Reata Restaurant

CHEESE AND BACON GRITS

Serves 6

These grits make a great Sunday brunch dish; try them with a poached egg on top. Or serve for dinner as an accompaniment to game, beef, or poultry.

- 4 cups chicken broth
- 3 tablespoons unsalted butter
- 1½ cups uncooked grits (not instant)
- 1 pound bacon, cooked and crumbled (1 cup)
- 1¾ cups grated Monterey Jack cheese
- 4 green onions, thinly sliced
- 1 tablespoon Tabasco Green Pepper Sauce
- Kosher salt to taste
- Freshly ground black pepper to taste

Preheat oven to 350 degrees. Butter an 8 × 8-inch baking dish; set aside. In a large heavy saucepan, bring the chicken broth to a boil. Lower heat to simmer, add 1 tablespoon of the butter, and stir until melted. Whisking constantly, slowly add grits. Using a long-handled wooden spoon, stir mixture until grits are thickened and all of the liquid has been absorbed, about 7 to 10 minutes. Remove from heat and stir in the remaining 2 tablespoons butter, bacon, cheese, green onions, and Tabasco. Stir until thoroughly combined and add salt and pepper. Pour into prepared baking dish and spread evenly. Bake 30 minutes, or until heated through. Serve hot.

—Reata Restaurant

CAJETA POUND CAKE

Serves 12

Cajeta is a goat's-milk caramel from Mexico. You can easily make your own, using either goat's milk or whipping cream. It can also be purchased at any Mexican grocery store or at most major supermarkets. This cake will sometimes overflow the pan, so put a piece of foil in the bottom of the oven to catch any overflow. Use at least a 12- to 15-cup Bundt pan.

1½ cups (3 sticks) unsalted butter, softened
3 cups sugar
8 eggs
4 cups sifted flour
2 teaspoons baking powder
1 teaspoon kosher salt
2 cups Cajeta Sauce

Cajeta Sauce

Yield: 4 cups

4 cups sugar
1 cup water
¼ cup unsalted butter
1 to 2 cups fresh goat's milk or heavy cream

Make the Cajeta Sauce. Combine sugar and water in a large saucepan and bring to a boil. Stir as needed to dissolve sugar, but do not stir once the mixture begins to simmer. Continue cooking at a steady boil until the mixture is reduced and the color is a light brown, about 20 to 30 minutes. When the syrup becomes light brown, watch carefully as it cooks to golden brown; it should be fairly thick. As soon as it reaches golden brown, remove from heat and slowly stir the butter into the syrup. Blend in milk until the consistency is fairly thick but the mixture is still golden brown in color. (Be careful when adding the butter and milk; the mixture will bubble up and splatter.) Cool to room temperature. Store remainder in refrigerator.

Preheat oven to 350 degrees. Grease and flour a Bundt pan and set aside. Using a mixer fitted with a paddle attachment, cream butter and sugar until the mixture is light in color and texture. Add the eggs one at a time, blending well after each addition. Stop and scrape the bowl with a spatula as needed. After all eggs have been added, beat for 3 minutes, or until light in color. In a separate bowl, sift the flour, baking powder, and salt together; add to the creamed mixture, blending at low speed. Increase the speed and beat for 2 minutes. Reduce the speed to low and fold in 2 cups of the cooled Cajeta Sauce (store the remainder in the refrigerator for another use). Pour batter into the prepared pan. Bake 1 hour and 15 minutes, or until a toothpick inserted into the center comes out clean. (Start testing after the cake has baked 1 hour.) Let cake cool in the pan 15 minutes before turning out onto a cake rack.

—*Reata Restaurant*

Opposite: The bar at the Reata
Stone ruins south of Alpine

HILL COUNTRY

ON OPENING DAY OF DEER SEASON IN 1973, my father dropped me off before daylight at a fence corner on a small ranch that we were hunting near Menard. I wouldn't be allowed to carry a gun until the following hunting season, so I climbed out of his Suburban with my Kodak Instamatic and my coat pockets jammed full of candy and jerky. He told me to sit quietly until he returned.

A couple of hours later, Dad drove up and asked if I had seen anything. "Yep, three does and a big buck crossed through the fence right down there," I pointed.

Now, unfortunately, honest-to-goodness antlered animals weren't terribly abundant on that particular swatch of Hill Country land back in those days, so you can imagine the razzing that I took from my father and brother for the remainder of our hunt. I guess you could say that I had the last laugh, though, when the film came back from the drugstore, days later, with a single, grainy, faraway image of the biggest buck we had seen all season. Yes, it was just a narrow, spindly eight-pointer—but his rack was plainly evident in the photo.

Twelve months later, I returned to that same fence corner with my dad's lever-action, open-sight .30-.30. Imagine, for a moment, a ten-year-old version of Chuck Conners as *The Rifleman.* The Kodak buck didn't show that morning, but a tribe of skinny does wandered past and I dropped one of them in her tracks at a respectable distance of about forty yards. I didn't exactly hit her where I was aiming, although at that time I considered the jaw shot a suitable alternative to the classic shoulder shot.

The Texas Hill Country, in the last thirty years, has changed more than any other region in the state. Ranch gates are much closer together and considerably more elaborate than they used to be, as numerous large landholdings have been parceled into ranchettes and estate lots. Granted, there's quite a bit of development along the Texas Coast as well, but those condos, marinas, and canal developments aren't impacting access to the resource nearly as much as the westward march of development through the Hill Country.

In the 1970s and 1980s inexpensive deer leases were easy to find near the traditional deer-

hunting towns like Llano, Johnson City, Blanco, and Fredericksburg. As the baby boomers have matured, however, many of those available leases have been bought up and fenced off as second homes and retirement retreats. It's still possible to find a relatively inexpensive deer lease on the fringes of the Hill Country, but a decent hunting property closer to Kerrville, Austin, and San Antonio has become a rare find. It was bound to happen, I suppose; the multitudes born between 1946 and 1964 have fared quite well during these past few decades of relative peace and prosperity in our country.

The Texas Hill Country may be woven a bit tighter than it used to be, but thankfully the nerve center of our state's hunting heritage remains largely intact. "Welcome Hunters" banners are still draped each fall in town squares throughout the heart of Texas, and it's hard to find a grocery or hardware store that doesn't sell sack corn, feeders, and blinds. Even though the ranches are considerably smaller than they used to be, there's still plenty of hunting going on inside their boundaries.

Within this section, you'll find a collection of cooking and hunting that represents the old and the new face of the Texas Hill Country. The German culinary influence is still apparent, and a couple of the game recipes that follow reflect that heritage. With the exception of the bobwhite quail, most indigenous species of the Texas Hill Country are doing quite well. Turkey hunting is probably as good now as it's ever been, and the same goes for doves—especially if you're standing alongside one of the colossal whitewing flyways that are spreading northward across the state. And even though the open-range bucks in the Hill Country may not grow as big as they do in South Texas, I still have fond memories of my first deer hunts with crisp mornings, acorns dropping, candy wrappers rustling, and whitetail shapes ghosting through the live oaks before sunrise.

The YO Ranch was one of the first in Texas to host hunters on a pay basis.

The main lodge and trophy room at the YO

YO RANCH

◈ **Mountain Home**

Had the early settlers in the Texas Hill Country known that they would one day have to look past their cattle herds to cover expenses, then they might have shopped elsewhere for their initial homesteads. With shallow rocky soil, very little mineral potential, and a scarcity of reliable surface water, it's no wonder that most Hill Country ranchers have tapped into recreation as a means of keeping their landholdings intact.

Charles Schreiner immigrated with his family from Alsace-Lorraine to Texas in 1852. Schreiner was intrigued by the rugged hills and canyons west of San Antonio, but he had to bide his time before he could stake a claim. After patrols with the Texas Rangers and the Confederate Army, Captain Schreiner eventually settled in Comfort, where he turned to mercantile and banking as a means of amassing capital, cattle, and land.

In 1880 Schreiner purchased 69,000 acres of land near the headwaters of the Guadalupe River. The name YO Ranch originated from a herd of cattle that Schreiner had purchased and transferred to the Hill Country from Youngs O. Coleman and the Fulton ranching empire.

The YO longhorn herd carried the ranch well until the Great Depression, when the Schreiner family realized that diversification was necessary to keep the ranch together. In 1943 ranch manager Myrtle Schreiner leased out the deer-hunting rights to Petty Geophysical Engineering. That first corporate hunting lease served as an early model for a perennial standard of recreational land access in the state of Texas.

Today the YO Ranch stands at 40,000 acres and is still run hands-on by the Schreiner family. Longhorns are still bred and sold on the YO, as are more than fifty species of African and exotic game. After 125 years the YO continues along its innovative path of diversification, and the original brand stands as an icon of ranching heritage in Texas. In addition to guided hunting, the ranch offers wildlife tours, facilities for social gatherings, and the YO Adventure Camp for young and aspiring hunters and outdoor enthusiasts.

A YO Ranch blackbuck

BACON-WRAPPED AXIS BACKSTRAP

···
Serves 4

To prepare the backstrap for this recipe, submerge it in a pan of water, cover with plastic wrap, and refrigerate for two days. Change the water at least once each day. This tenderizes the venison and helps to eliminate any gamey taste. Antelope, whitetail or mule deer, or any exotic venison can be substituted for the axis deer.

> 1 axis backstrap, white muscle sheath removed
> 8 slices thick-cut bacon
> ¼ teaspoon thyme
> ½ cup canned dark Bing cherries, undrained
> 2 cups veal demi-glace
> ½ cup light brown sugar
> ½ cup molasses

Cut each backstrap across the grain into medallions the width of a slice of the bacon. Wrap each medallion with bacon, secure with a toothpick, and sprinkle with thyme.

To prepare the sauce, combine the remaining ingredients in a saucepan and bring to a simmer; continue to simmer while medallions are cooking.

Heat a large sauté pan over medium-high heat. When pan is hot, add medallions, placing them on their edges (bacon against the skillet). Continue to cook, rolling them along on their edges until the bacon is crisp all the way around. When bacon is cooked, lay the medallions flat in the pan and cook 1 minute per side. Add the sauce to the skillet and bring to a boil; cook an additional 2 to 4 minutes for medium-rare medallions.

—*Thomas Andrysiak, chef*

Banging the horns in a live-oak mott

HUDSON'S ON THE BEND

Austin

When Jeffrey Blank's family moved to the resort town of Lakeway in the 1960s, the main travel arteries between Austin and Lake Travis carried a single lane of meandering traffic in each direction, and the fifty-odd families that lived in Lakeway considered the whitetail deer a relatively scarce and reclusive neighbor.

These days, Bee Cave Road and Ranch Road 620 carry 50,000 cars per day through miles of sprawling retail and office development, and the city of Lakeway lists 10,000 plus residents on the tax roll. Spotting a deer is no longer difficult in the rolling hills west of Austin, but shooing the prolific herds away from speeding cars, golf courses, and pricey landscaping has become a countywide predicament.

In the summer of 1966, at age sixteen, Jeff Blank began his restaurant career when the Lakeway Inn hired him to run the Beef & Bun Snack Bar at the resort's marina on Lake Travis. That turned out to be a prime gig for an avid water-skier, and between shifts Jeff would often slip away for a couple of quick runs across the lake. After attending the Hotel and Restaurant School at Oklahoma State University, Jeff was introduced to the fine dining business in 1969 when the Fairmont Hotel in Dallas hired him to work in the Venetian Room.

Seeking a new challenge in the early 1970s, Jeff left Dallas and began a seasonal circuit between Colorado and Texas. During the winter he would work and ski in Aspen; when the snows melted each spring, he'd head back to Lake Travis for hot-weather skiing and an evening maître d' shift in Lakeway. By 1984, Jeff had owned restaurants in Aspen and San Antonio, but he didn't hit the long ball until he found a little stone house for sale on Ranch Road 620 in his old neighborhood between Austin and Lake Travis.

More than twenty years have passed since Chef

The old stone house on Ranch Road 620
Opposite: November color on Texas Highway 71 near the Pedernales River

Jeff opened Hudson's on the Bend, and he'll admit that it's been a whirlwind ride. Hudson's was one of the first restaurants in Texas to serve wild game with a gourmet flair, and *Condé Nast Traveller* has listed it among its top fifty restaurants in America. The menu has evolved over the years, but Jeff's basic philosophy of big flavors and cooking fearlessly has never varied. "There are no mistakes in cooking—especially fish and game," Jeff explained as he prepped his grill during our meeting. "We may not actually serve everything we cook, but there *are* no mistakes."

Jeff is the author of two successful cookbooks, *Fired Up* and *Cooking Fearlessly*. He also offers an annual schedule of sold-out cooking schools as well as a popular line of bottled sauces and marinades that are available through the restaurant's Web site (www.hudsonsonthebend.com). With a persistently packed dining room and a reputation for innovative culinary design, Jeff Blank is at the top of a short list of chefs whenever governors, presidents, and dignitaries set out to plan a big-time feed with a Texas twist.

Hill Country commerce
Jimmy Wyndham and son, Jack, on his first dove hunt near Austin

ESPRESSO-RUBBED VENISON BACKSTRAP WITH SHINER BOCK BEER BLANC

Serves 4

This recipe can be used with either venison backstrap or unboned loin chops (pictured).

1 venison backstrap, white muscle sheath removed, or 8 venison loin chops, unboned

Espresso Rub

½ cup finely ground espresso coffee

2 tablespoons salt

1 teaspoon ancho chili powder

1 teaspoon freshly ground black pepper

Shiner Bock Beer Blanc

1 bottle (12-ounce) Shiner bock beer or any dark bock

2 shallots, diced into ¼-inch pieces

2 cloves garlic, diced into ¼-inch pieces

2 chipotle peppers in adobo sauce

¼ cup fresh lime juice

¼ cup heavy cream

2 sticks butter, cut into 1-inch cubes and softened

Salt and pepper to taste

Make the Espresso Rub by combining all ingredients, mixing well. Rub the espresso mixture into the meat and let sit for 1 hour before grilling.

Meanwhile, make the Shiner Bock Beer Blanc. In a 4-quart saucepan over medium-high heat, reduce beer to ¼ cup. Add shallots, garlic, chipotle peppers, and heavy cream. Simmer until mixture is reduced by half. Add lime juice and return to a simmer. Pour mixture into blender and purée while still very hot. With blender running, add butter cubes, one at a time. Season with salt and pepper. Keep warm over simmering water or in a thermal carafe until ready to serve.

Grill backstrap over high heat or very hot mesquite coals until medium rare (135 degrees internal temperature). Slice the backstrap into 1-inch-thick medallions and pour the warm Shiner Bock Beer Blanc over the meat. Serve immediately.

—*Jeffrey Blank, chef*

GRILLED PEACHES WITH SPICY LEMON HONEY

Serves 4

To serve this as a dessert instead of a side dish, use mascarpone cheese instead of goat cheese. The Spicy Lemon Honey can be made a day in advance.

4 firm peaches, halved and pitted

Sea salt to taste

2 tablespoons olive oil

8 tablespoons goat cheese

Spicy Lemon Honey

1 cup honey

¼ cup rice wine vinegar

Juice and zest of 3 lemons

3 serrano peppers, minced (remove seeds for a milder taste)

1 teaspoon sea salt

Make the Spicy Lemon Honey. Combine all ingredients in a medium saucepan and bring to a gentle simmer. Simmer for 5 minutes. Set aside and cool to room temperature.

Cut off a flat spot on the skin side of each peach half so that it will sit on a plate. Salt the flesh side of the peaches and rub with olive oil. Place the peach halves, flesh side down, on the grill and cook for 2 minutes. Turn the peaches over and cook an additional 2 minutes. While the skin side is grilling, put 1 tablespoon of goat cheese in each half. Place a grilled peach on each plate and drizzle liberally with the Spicy Lemon Honey. Season to taste.

—*Jeffrey Blank, chef*

QUAIL AND SPINACH SALAD WITH HONEY MUSTARD AND BACON DRESSING

The dressing and glaze can be made a day ahead and reheated just before serving. The quail can be smoked or grilled earlier in the day. Duck, pheasant, dove, or goose can all be substituted for the quail.

1 smoked or grilled quail per person
1 handful spinach per person
Sliced mushrooms
Julienned green apples
Sliced red onions

Honey Mustard and Bacon Dressing

¾ pound bacon, finely diced (1 cup)
½ cup champagne vinegar
½ cup honey
1 cup Creole mustard or coarse-grained tarragon mustard

Honey-Cilantro Ginger Glaze

1½ cups honey
¼ cup soy sauce
¼ cup Worcestershire sauce
⅓ cup minced fresh ginger
¼ cup minced garlic
¼ cup minced shallots
2 bunches cilantro, leaves only
Salt and pepper to taste
½ cup butter

To make the dressing, cook the bacon pieces in a single layer until crisp; drain and crumble. In a saucepan, mix bacon, vinegar, honey, and mustard together; bring to a gentle simmer. Set aside and keep warm.

Combine all glaze ingredients in a saucepan and bring to a simmer over medium heat; simmer for 4 minutes. Keep warm on very low heat.

Preheat oven to 250 degrees. Dip quail in warm glaze and reheat in preheated oven for 5 minutes.

To assemble the salad, toss hot dressing with cold spinach, using ¼ cup dressing per serving. Garnish with the sliced mushrooms, apples, and onions. Dip quail in warm glaze one more time and place on top of wilted spinach.

—Jeffrey Blank, chef

Preceding page: Chef Jeffrey Blank applying his maxim of "cooking fearlessly" (above). Grilled Peaches with Spicy Lemon Honey and Espresso-Rubbed Venison Chops with Shiner Bock Beer Blanc (below).

WILD BOAR SCHNITZEL

Serves 6

Allow two days for this recipe and smoke the boar one day in advance. Smoked pork tenderloin can also be used.

2 pounds boneless loin of boar
2 tablespoons Smoke Rub
Salt and pepper to taste
2 cups sourdough or French bread crumbs
2 eggs, beaten
1 cup milk
1 cup flour
½ cup clarified butter
1 Granny Smith apple, julienned
1½ cups Apple Cider Brandy Sauce

Smoke Rub

1 cup paprika
⅓ cup onion powder
⅛ teaspoon cayenne
½ teaspoon white pepper
2 teaspoons chili powder
3 tablespoons brown sugar
½ cup granulated garlic
1 teaspoon curry powder
½ teaspoon black pepper
¼ cup kosher salt

Apple Cider Brandy Sauce

¾ cup frozen apple juice concentrate, thawed
½ cup water
2 tablespoons chopped garlic
4 tablespoons diced red onion
½ cup brown sugar, packed
½ cup brandy
½ teaspoon salt
¼ teaspoon white pepper

To make the Smoke Rub, mix all ingredients together and store in an airtight container until ready to use.

Season the loin with the Smoke Rub and smoke 1 to 1½ hours, or until medium rare to medium (140 degrees internal temperature). Remove from smoker and refrigerate whole for at least 24 hours.

To make the Apple Cider Brandy Sauce, combine all ingredients in a saucepan, bring to a boil, reduce heat to a simmer, and cook for 10 minutes. Remove from heat, adjust seasonings, and keep warm.

Slice loin into medallions ½ inch to ¾ inch thick. Place medallions between two sheets of plastic wrap and pound to a thickness of ¼ inch. Sprinkle with salt and pepper. Grind bread crumbs in a food processor and set aside. In a separate bowl, whisk eggs and milk together until thoroughly combined. Dredge medallions in flour, shaking off excess; dip in the egg mixture and then in the bread crumbs. Heat the clarified butter in a large sauté pan until butter is shimmering. Carefully add medallions, cooking in batches to avoid crowding the pan. Cook 1½ to 2 minutes per side, or until the crust is set and golden brown. Remove from heat and keep warm.

Combine apple and Apple Cider Brandy Sauce in a saucepan and heat through. Spoon onto plates and top with the schnitzel.

—*Jeffrey Blank, chef*

BROKEN ARROW RANCH

◈ Ingram

As exotic game hunting grew in popularity during the early 1980s, Ingram resident Mike Hughes spotted a potential business opportunity after a vacation trip to Europe with his wife, Elizabeth. Venison and other wild game has always been popular in European restaurants, so Mike set about the task of creating American demand for a ready supply.

Since whitetail deer are native game animals (state property), they cannot be legally bought or served in restaurants. But that rule doesn't apply to our state's burgeoning population of introduced species, nor does it count for the conniving and destructive feral hog that has infiltrated every county in Texas over the past two decades.

Mike originally called his company the Texas Wild Game Cooperative when he built his first mobile harvest trailer and began contacting ranchers and restaurants in 1983. Eventually he changed the company name to Broken Arrow Ranch after family property in the Hill Country. After locating ranches around the state that were overstocked with exotic game, Mike and his crew would meet with the ranchers at night—perfectly legal, since they weren't hunting whitetails—and help them remove unwanted animals from their pastures. Axis, fallow, and sika deer were prime targets, as well as blackbuck antelope and feral hogs.

As Mike's son, Chris Hughes, explained their stringent harvest and inspection requirements, I realized that their handling of commercial wild game differs considerably from the average hunter's technique for stocking his own freezer. Chris explained that each harvest team (shooter, skinner, and state meat inspector) has a minimum goal of fifteen animals per hunt. On a good night they'll take up to forty animals, which is the maximum capacity of their refrigerated processing trailer.

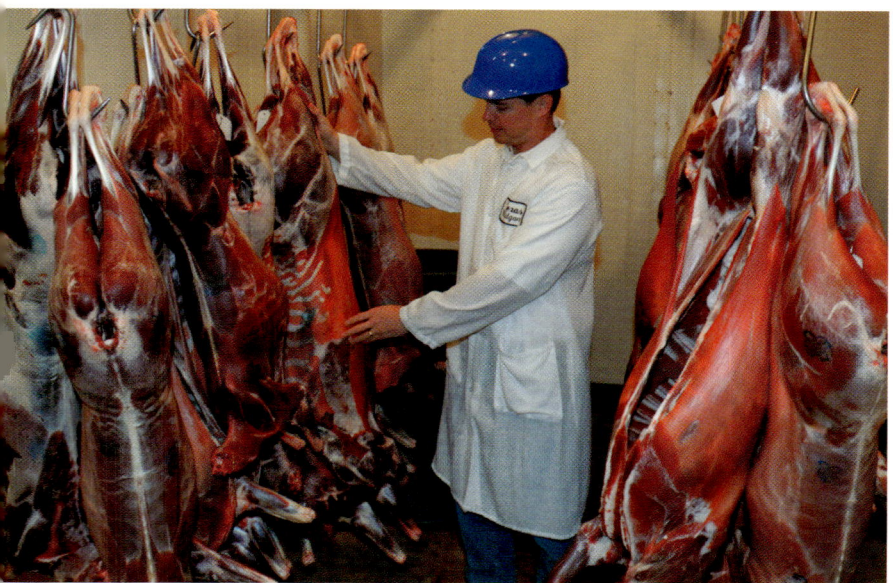

Chris Hughes inspecting the latest harvest at Broken Arrow Ranch
Opposite: A big, symmetrical eight-pointer on a low-fenced Hill Country ranch.

Each harvested animal is cleaned and skinned inside the trailer and meticulously inspected before it leaves the ranch. Back in Ingram, at Broken Arrow's processing plant, the carcasses are first hung for three to five days at 37 degrees for dry aging. From there, the animals are reduced to primary cuts (saddles and legs) and vacuum-packed for an additional sixteen- to twenty-day wet-aging period. Inventory that is not sold during this stage is then trimmed down to final cuts and flash-frozen in individual serving packs.

In 2005 Broken Arrow Ranch FedExed over 160,000 pounds of quality, aged wild game cuts to clients from New York to Hawaii. Restaurants make up the bulk of the business, but the company also sells direct, via its Web site, to private consumers around the country. "Wild game is low in fat and cholesterol, and if it's handled and prepared properly, it's as moist and tender as prime beef," Chris explained. "Our ongoing mission is to convince people that this is not your grandfather's venison that was strapped to the roof of a car and driven across Texas on an 80-degree fall day."

Opposite: Feed for deer and feed for hunters: one-stop shopping in Llano (above). A deer's-eye view of a box blind (below).

❖ A Hunter's Guide to Handling and Preparing Wild Game

Since most hunters don't have access to walk-in coolers and on-site processing facilities, I asked Chris Hughes for tips on handling wild game in the field and improving the quality of the meat.

1. Chris emphasized the importance of a "clean kill" with a minimum of stress on the animal. Now, a head shot is obviously not the correct choice when you have the buck of a lifetime framed in your crosshairs, but it's absolutely the best shot if you're harvesting does or cull bucks for the freezer. If you're hunting for horns and you don't mind giving up a little shoulder meat, try aiming for the high shoulder (just above the body's midline where the spine dips down between the animal's shoulder blades). That shot will typically drop an animal in its tracks and prevent the adrenaline buildup that occurs when the animal runs after the shot.

2. For the mildest flavor, thoroughly bleed the animal as soon as possible. The best way to do this in the field, Chris says, is to dress the animal and hang it as quickly as possible before the carcass stiffens and the blood begins to settle into the meat.

3. If you don't have access to a walk-in-cooler, this is the point where most venison quickly transitions from potentially great to marginal, at best. If you harvest a deer on a 30-degree morning and the daytime highs are in the low 60s, then the best thing you can do for the meat is to simply hang the carcass whole (shaded and screened to keep away bugs) and let it age for a couple of days. Here Chris stressed the importance of rigor mortis on the aging process. By allowing the carcass to stiffen with the meat still on the bone, the muscle fibers are held under tension and the meat will be tenderer when you reduce the animal down to serving cuts. If it's a hot day—above 70 degrees with only mild cooling at night—get the animal on ice as quickly as possible. Again, don't bone the animal all the way out before it's had time to stiffen. Simply cut the animal down to whole quarters (meat on bone) and pack the quarters into a large ice chest. As long as you keep adding ice (and draining water), you can age the meat for several days in a cooler before final processing.

4. The final steps to improve the quality of your venison are the freeze and thaw cycles. Chris suggests a rule of "freeze quickly and thaw slowly." If space allows, spread the packaged cuts around your freezer shelves so the cold air can penetrate quickly. This prevents the slow expansion of water molecules in the muscle fibers that will break down the meat and give it a grainy texture. Thawing, he says, is best accomplished by simply moving the packages of meat from your freezer to the fridge and allowing them to slowly thaw over a couple of days.

BUNKHOUSE MEATLOAF

Serves 4

2 slices fresh whole wheat bread
1 large egg
½ cup chopped onion
1 clove garlic, minced
½ cup tomato sauce
2 tablespoons chopped fresh parsley
1 teaspoon balsamic vinegar
1½ teaspoons Dijon mustard
½ teaspoon dried basil
¼ teaspoon dried thyme
¼ teaspoon dried oregano
½ teaspoon salt
½ teaspoon freshly ground black pepper
1 pound ground venison

Preheat oven to 350 degrees and lightly coat a Pyrex baking dish with cooking spray. In a food processor or blender, process bread into fine crumbs (about ¾ cup).

In a large bowl, beat egg. Add bread crumbs and all remaining ingredients except venison. Blend until well mixed. Add meat and blend again. (A spatula can be used for mixing, but it is best to use your hands.)

Place mixture in the prepared baking dish and shape to form an oval loaf. Bake 45 minutes to 1 hour, or until the internal temperature reaches 150 degrees. Let stand 10 minutes before slicing. Serve alone or with a sauce.

—*Broken Arrow Ranch*

CHRIS'S ALMOST FAMOUS CHILI

Serves 6–8

3 pounds chili meat (2 pounds venison and 1 pound wild boar)
2 tablespoons cooking oil
1 can (12-ounce) regular beer (preferably ale)
1 large onion, chopped
3 cloves garlic, finely chopped
1 jalapeño pepper, finely chopped (remove seeds and membrane for a milder chili)
2 chipotle peppers canned in adobo sauce, chopped
1 tablespoon adobo sauce (from the canned chipotle peppers)
1 tablespoon tomato paste
5 tablespoons chili powder
4 tablespoons ground cumin
1 tablespoon paprika
1 teaspoon salt
¼ teaspoon black pepper
2 teaspoons cornstarch, optional

In a heavy cast-iron or aluminum pot with a tight-fitting lid, brown meat in cooking oil. Add ½ can of beer and cook the browned meat, covered, over low heat for about 1 hour, stirring occasionally to prevent sticking.

Drain the meat juices into a skillet; sauté onion, garlic, and jalapeño in the juices until the onion is opaque. Pour this mixture into the pot and add all remaining ingredients except cornstarch. Cook covered over low heat 2½ to 3 hours, adding more beer if needed and stirring occasionally. (Make sure the chili simmers gently and never boils.) Adjust seasonings. For a thicker chili, make a slurry with the cornstarch and a little water. Stir in the slurry just before the chili has finished cooking. Serve over tamales or Fritos with cheese and sour cream.

—*Broken Arrow Ranch*

Hunting dollars flood the Hill Country each year between Labor Day and Christmas. Paint up a sign and get in on the action.

Opposite: A shrine, of sorts, to the major player in the Texas hunting scene

ROASTED WILD BOAR LEG WITH MUSTARD-CAPER SAUCE

The wild boar leg can be roasted in the oven or in an outdoor pit with indirect heat.

>1 wild boar leg
>Salt and pepper to taste
>Bacon strips, optional

Mustard-Caper Sauce

>6 tablespoons butter
>½ cup dry white wine
>2 tablespoons Dijon mustard
>½ teaspoon Worcestershire sauce
>3 tablespoons capers, well drained

Preheat oven to 400 degrees. Sprinkle meat with salt and pepper and place in a large roasting pan. Cover with bacon strips. Roast 15 to 20 minutes, or until leg is nicely browned. Reduce oven temperature to 250 degrees. After about 3 hours of cooking time, insert meat thermometer into the thickest part of the leg and check temperature every 30 minutes or so. Remove leg from oven when internal temperature reaches 160 degrees. (The cooking time for a 4- to 5-pound leg will be 4 to 5 hours.) Keep warm.

To make the sauce, melt butter in a saucepan over low heat; mix in wine, mustard, Worcestershire, and capers. Stir to blend. Slice the meat and serve warm with Mustard-Caper Sauce.

—*Broken Arrow Ranch*

SAVORY VENISON STEW

Serves 4

This recipe was created for feeding a hunting camp crowd and can easily be doubled.

>1 pound venison stew meat, cut into 1-inch chunks
>1 bay leaf
>1 tablespoon pickling spice, wrapped in cheesecloth and tied with string
>1 cup coarsely chopped onion
>⅛ teaspoon garlic powder
>¼ teaspoon ground black pepper
>2 carrots, cut into ½-inch slices
>2 celery stalks, cut into ½-inch slices
>2 large red-skinned potatoes, cut into ½-inch cubes
>2 chicken bouillon cubes
>2 cups water
>1 teaspoon red wine vinegar
>1 can (8-ounce) tomato sauce

Spray a small stock pot with cooking spray and quickly brown the venison chunks on all sides. Add remaining ingredients to pot and simmer for 1½ hours, or until venison is tender and vegetables are cooked. Remove bay leaf and spice bag before serving.

—*Broken Arrow Ranch*

VENISON KABOBS

Serves 4

½ cup freshly squeezed orange juice
2 tablespoons rice vinegar
3 tablespoons soy sauce
2 tablespoons peanut oil
1 tablespoon chopped fresh ginger
2 cloves garlic, sliced into ovals
3 green onions, chopped
2 tablespoons chopped fresh cilantro
1 pound venison, cut into 2-inch chunks
1 medium onion, cut into 8 wedges
1 medium red bell pepper, cored, seeded, and cut into 8 squares
8 medium mushroom caps
8 cherry tomatoes
4 servings of cooked rice

In a 1-gallon sealable plastic bag, combine orange juice, rice vinegar, soy sauce, peanut oil, ginger, garlic, green onions, and cilantro; stir to blend. Add venison chunks and seal bag, squeezing out air and turning to coat the venison. Marinate venison up to 2 hours at room temperature, or longer in the refrigerator, turning bag occasionally. Allow meat to remain at room temperature for 30 minutes before grilling. Drain marinade into a small saucepan and bring to a boil; set aside.

In a large pan, combine the onion, bell pepper, mushrooms, and cherry tomatoes. Pour boiling water over them and let them sit in the water for just 10 seconds; then drain and rinse with cold water.

Preheat broiler or grill 20 minutes. Thread vegetables and meat onto skewers, beginning and ending with onion wedges. Set skewers on rack, keeping rack about 2 to 3 inches from heat. Broil or grill about 3 minutes per side, basting with the marinade when turning.

Heat remaining marinade and bring to a boil; boil for 1 minute. Serve marinade with kabobs over cooked rice.

—Broken Arrow Ranch

The blackbuck antelope, native to India, Pakistan, and Nepal, has fared remarkably well in the Texas Hill Country.

EXECUTIVE OUTFITTERS

⊞ **Brownwood**

In the fall of 1964, Richard Lee, a principal with Life Insurance Company of the Southwest, invited a prospective client from Dallas on a dove hunt near his home in Coleman. Dallas Airomotive eventually signed on as Richard's first group health insurance client, and from that point forward he was pegged as the designated corporate entertainer for the company. For the next twenty-five years, Richard continued entertaining insurance clients with a combination of leased sunflowers fields, seasonal cooks and guides, and rental houses in Brownwood.

Upon his retirement from the insurance business in 1990, Richard formed Executive Hunts with partners Donnie Durham, Pat Caudle, and Don Huff. Their plan was to offer quality dove hunting at a fair price for companies looking to entertain their clients in a relaxed outdoor setting. Within a few years their business had grown to the point that piecemeal lodging was no longer an option. After selling off part of the company and changing its name to Executive Outfitters, Richard contracted with the Texas 4-H Conference Center on Lake Brownwood for up to 120 beds per hunt and well over 1,000 hunters per season.

In 1999, at the age of seventy-five, Richard Lee announced his second retirement and sold Executive Outfitters to longtime friend and rancher Ted Taylor of Coleman. Today the Taylor family (Ted, wife Sonya, son Ben, and daughter-in-law Meredith) are still using Richard Lee's proud and proven business plan for running a large-scale outfitting operation in our state's most prolific dove-hunting area.

Opposite: A wet spring will produce head-high sunflowers and clouds of doves in the fall

Army surplus ammo boxes, loaded up for dove season

Hill Country • 169

Each summer, the Taylors call on their local farming and ranching contacts in Coleman, Brown, and Callahan counties and lease up the best sunflower fields available. By opening day, they'll have up to fifty fields under contract, and as the season progresses, they'll use a system of relentless scouting and field rotation to make sure that the doves aren't overpressured.

Hunters are still housed at the 4-H Center, where they can also shoot clays, fish for bass, and socialize with their clients and business associates between hunts. Meals are served buffet style, and the Taylors count their generous, home-style cooking as their absolute top priority. "Doves are migratory birds," Ted explains. "At some point you might have bad weather or a marginal hunt, but we'll never serve you a bad meal."

On December 29, 2005, Richard Lee suffered a fatal heart attack while field-dressing a deer that his wife of sixty years, Bernice, had just shot on their lease east of Coleman. He was eighty-one years old, and he was still doing what he loved most at the exact moment of his passing. The Texas 4-H Conference Center recently honored him by designating the lakeside facility as the Richard Lee Recreational Area. He is remembered by friends, family, and literally thousands of dove hunters across the country for his adventurous spirit and his innovative work in the Texas outdoors.

Stalks breaking and seeds flying, a Lab crashes through the sunflowers with his prize.

FRIED DOVES

For a spicier dish, add Cavender's or Tony Chachere's Cajun seasoning to the flour.

> Vegetable oil for frying
> Flour
> Salt and pepper
> 3 or 4 dove breasts per person
> Buttermilk

Fill fryer with enough oil to cover the birds; preheat to 375 degrees. Season flour with salt and pepper and mix well. Dip each dove breast into the buttermilk and then dredge in seasoned flour. Cook the birds in hot oil until they float to the top and are golden brown.

—Sonya Taylor

BACON-WRAPPED DOVES

> 3 or 4 dove breasts per person
> Onion slivers
> Fresh jalapeño pepper slices
> Bacon
> Garlic salt to taste
> Freshly ground black pepper to taste

Using a sharp knife, make a slit along each side of the breastbone of each bird. Insert a sliver of onion and a slice of jalapeño into each slit and tightly wrap the dove breast with bacon, securing with a toothpick. Season the doves with garlic salt and pepper and grill over medium heat. Turn the dove frequently to prevent charring and flare-ups. Cook until bacon is crisp.

—Sonya Taylor

BOURBON SWEET POTATOES

Serves 8

6 sweet potatoes
½ cup (1 stick) butter, melted
½ cup brown sugar
⅓ cup orange juice
¼ cup bourbon
½ teaspoon salt
½ teaspoon pumpkin pie spice
½ cup chopped pecans

Boil unpeeled sweet potatoes 30 to 35 minutes, or until fork-tender. Drain and cool.

Preheat oven to 375 degrees. Peel potatoes and mash in a medium mixing bowl. Add melted butter, brown sugar, orange juice, bourbon, salt, and spice and mix until blended. Spoon mixture into a lightly greased 1½-quart baking dish. Sprinkle with chopped pecans. Bake 45 minutes.

—*Sonya Taylor*

Opposite: Hungry dove hunters at the Richard Lee Recreational Center on Lake Brownwood (above). Josh "Treebark" Weaver finishing up pork chops for 100 hunters (below).

Guns, hunters, stools, and shells: an efficient system for dispersing dove hunters

JOSHUA CREEK RANCH

⬧ **Boerne**

When Ann and Joe Kercheville bought 1,200 acres north of Boerne in 1986, their plan was to build a home on the property and move their registered longhorn herd from the smaller piece of land where they were living south of town.

"We never had any plans to develop a hunting business," Ann explained, "but when the real estate market and the longhorn business collapsed just after we bought the new ranch, we realized we might need to change our plans."

On a trip to Scotland in 1988, Ann and Joe participated in a traditional driven pheasant shoot and realized that their new ranch on Joshua Creek might lend itself to the same type of program. "The lay of the land was perfect," Ann said. "We had these beautiful fields on either side of the creek, and there were several high bluffs that we could use for drive sites."

After months of land clearing and converting the existing stone ranch house into a functional lodge, the Kerchevilles opened Joshua Creek Ranch in the fall of 1990. Their plan was to offer the same type of driven pheasant shoots that they had experienced in Scotland as well as guided field hunts with pointing and flushing dogs for released quail, pheasant, chukar, and Hungarian partridge. To broaden the shooting experience at Joshua Creek, Ann and Joe also built a challenging sporting clays course with a spectacular Hill Country view.

As their clientele has grown over the years, the Kerchevilles have added a wobble trap station near the main lodge, and they've developed more areas of the ranch for wing shooting. They also offer deer hunt-

The main lodge at Joshua Creek Ranch
Opposite: A beautiful English setter and a stylish point

ing from a number of blinds located on the ranch and fly-fishing for stocked rainbow trout in Joshua Creek's spring-fed pools and riffles.

Ann explained that corporate entertaining has always been a large part of their business, and their goal from the beginning was to offer a complete experience where the group host could focus on clients and not worry about the quality of the meals, lodging, birds, dogs, and guides. Joshua Creek has a kennel of finished pointing and flushing dogs and a crew of staff guides that run the majority of their hunts each year. They also have select contract guides with their own dogs that are called in, as needed, to take care of larger hunting groups.

Austin, San Antonio, and Houston are their biggest markets, but Ann says that they've entertained guests from all over the United States and a few foreign countries as well. "This has been a wonderful experience," she admits, "and the most enjoyable aspect, which we never considered in the early days, is the number of friends and lasting relationships that we've formed with our hunters and guests over the years."

Bob Woodward prepping one of his German shorthairs (above). Bob lining up on a flushing bobwhite (right).

PHEASANT ROYALE

Serves 1

1 pheasant breast, filleted (2 pieces)
Garlic salt to taste
Pepper to taste
Fresh spinach leaves
Thinly sliced pastrami
Shredded Pepper Jack cheese, enough to cover each breast
½ cup vegetable oil

Cream Sauce

4 tablespoons butter
1 to 2 pints heavy cream, depending on number of servings
¼ cup white wine, optional

Preheat oven to 350 degrees. Fillet breast meat from bone; wash well and pat dry. Place the 2 breast fillets between two sheets of plastic wrap and pound gently until flat. Sprinkle fillets with garlic salt and pepper. Cover each fillet with several spinach leaves. Place a slice of pastrami over spinach and sprinkle with cheese. Roll each breast lengthwise and secure with toothpicks.

In a skillet, brown pheasant rolls in vegetable oil; transfer rolls to a baking dish. Cover with foil and bake for 30 minutes. Do not overcook. Remove from oven and let stand covered.

To make the sauce, drain excess oil from skillet and melt butter over medium heat. When butter is very hot, add cream, whisking constantly. Cook, stirring, until cream thickens. Add wine.

To serve, remove toothpicks from pheasant rolls and slice into ½-inch-thick pieces. Arrange slices on plate and drizzle with cream sauce.

—*Joshua Creek Ranch*

PHEASANT POT PIE

This dish can also be prepared as one large pot pie by using a 13 × 9 × 2-inch baking dish and reducing the amount of pie dough by about one-third.

   2 whole pheasants
   3 cups sliced carrots
   1 cup pearl onions, peeled and halved
   3 cups cubed potatoes
   5 cups pheasant broth
   1 tablespoon chicken broth base
   1 cup half-and-half
   1 cup sour cream
   4 slices Pepper Jack cheese
   ½ cup cornstarch
   3 cups green peas
   Dough for 3 single-crust pies

Place pheasants in large stock pot and cover with water. Bring to a boil and cook for about 40 minutes, or until meat is tender. Let cool in broth. Remove the meat from the bones and cut into bite-size pieces. Reserve 5 cups of broth.

In a saucepan, boil carrots, onions, and potatoes until crisp-tender; drain.

Preheat oven to 350 degrees. In a separate saucepan, combine 4 cups of the reserved pheasant broth with chicken broth base, half-and-half, sour cream, and cheese. Bring to a boil, stirring constantly, and add cornstarch that has been dissolved in the remaining 1 cup of pheasant broth. Cook sauce until thickened; add chopped meat and cooked vegetables. Spoon mixture into six 12- to 16-ounce ovenproof bowls and top each with pie dough. Cut slits in crust. Bake 30 to 45 minutes, or until crust is browned.

—*Joshua Creek Ranch*

Opposite: Pheasant cover at Joshua Creek
The ring-necked pheasant: how can such an ornate bird hide so effectively?

GRILLED ORANGE DUCK

Serves 6–8

This recipe works best with milder-tasting ducks: dabbling ducks like mallards, pintails, widgeon, and teal. The barbecue sauce can be made in advance and stored in the refrigerator for as long as a month. Or you can substitute any prepared barbecue sauce.

> 6 duck breasts, filleted (12 pieces)
> ¾ cup grated orange peel
> ¼ cup lemon pepper
> 2 cups orange marmalade
> ½ cup orange juice
> ½ cup soy sauce
> 4 cups barbecue sauce

Barbecue Sauce

> 1 bottle (20-ounce) Woody's Original Barbecue Sauce
> 1 bottle (20-ounce) ketchup
> ½ cup butter
> 1 teaspoon liquid smoke
> Juice of 3 lemons or limes
> 1 onion, minced
> ¼ cup brown sugar

To make the barbecue sauce, mix all ingredients together in a saucepan and cook over medium heat for 15 minutes. Set aside.

Place duck breasts on a chopping board and lightly pound from the underside of the breast until flat. Arrange breasts in a 1-inch-deep baking pan. Sprinkle orange peel and lemon pepper on each breast.

Mix marmalade, orange juice, soy sauce, and 2 cups of the barbecue sauce; spread over the duck breasts. Marinate breasts at room temperature for 45 minutes.

Heat grill to 400 degrees, then reduce heat to 225 degrees. Lay breasts on grill, skin side down. Brush with barbecue sauce and grill 3 to 4 minutes per side. Reduce heat to low and brush again with barbecue sauce. Don't overcook (remember, the breasts are thin and duck breasts are best served medium rare). Cut each breast diagonally into 6 to 8 slices and serve immediately. Serve with warm or cold barbecue sauce on the side.

—*Joshua Creek Ranch*

Sensory overload

GRILLED VENISON WITH GREEN PEPPERCORN SAUCE

Serves 3–4

Green peppercorns are the dark green immature berry of the peppercorn vine and have a milder flavor than the mature black berry. They can be found at major supermarkets and gourmet shops.

> 1 venison backstrap, white muscle sheath removed
> Salt and pepper to taste
> Minced garlic to taste

Green Peppercorn Sauce

Yield: 3 cups

> ½ cup butter
> ½ cup chopped red onion
> ½ cup chopped fresh parsley
> 2 teaspoons minced garlic
> 2 teaspoons green peppercorns
> 1½ packages Knorr Peppercorn Sauce Mix
> ⅔ cup red wine
> 1½ cups water
> 1 cup half-and-half

Season the backstrap with salt, pepper, and minced garlic; refrigerate, covered, for several hours.

About 30 minutes before grilling the meat, make the Green Peppercorn Sauce. Melt butter in large saucepan. Add onion and cook until almost translucent. Add parsley, garlic, peppercorns, and peppercorn seasoning mix and stir until smooth. Add wine and water and bring to a boil. Reduce heat to low and stir in half-and-half. Cook over low until smooth and thick, about 10 to 12 minutes. Remove from heat and keep warm.

Heat grill until hot and cook the backstrap until an instant-read thermometer registers an internal temperature of 135 degrees (medium rare). Remove from grill and thinly slice the backstrap across the grain three-fourths of the way through. Serve with Green Peppercorn Sauce spooned over the top.

—*Joshua Creek Ranch*

KAHLUA PECAN PIE

> 9-inch uncooked piecrust
> ½ cup toffee bits
> 4 eggs, slightly beaten
> 1 cup light corn syrup
> ½ cup brown sugar, packed
> 4 tablespoons butter, melted
> 1 tablespoon vanilla
> ⅓ cup Kahlua liqueur
> 1 cup pecans, coarsely chopped

Preheat oven to 350 degrees. Cover the bottom of the piecrust with toffee bits. In a mixing bowl, combine eggs, corn syrup, brown sugar, butter, vanilla, and liqueur. Mix well and add pecans. Pour mixture into piecrust. Bake for 50 to 55 minutes, or until set.

—*Joshua Creek Ranch*

Opposite: Moving in for the flush (above). An English cocker spaniel retrieving a chukar (below).

A downed bird in deep grass

ROUGH CREEK LODGE & RESORT

⊞ **Glen Rose**

Like many avid bird hunters in Texas, Dallas physicians Rodney Moore and Harwin Jamison have experienced quail hunting in our state from a number of angles. They've booked guided hunts in various places, and at one time they had a quail lease near Childress and a trailer full of bird dogs.

"The lease was great as long as we had birds to hunt," Harwin remembered, "but then we had a couple of dry years back to back and the last time we went up there we only killed two birds." Rodney described the long drives up from Dallas and back, the task of buying groceries and cooking their own meals, the marginal accommodations, and the constant care that their dogs required. "We finally realized that we were putting forth too much effort for the amount of enjoyment that our lease was providing," he explained.

In the fall of 2006 I spent a morning photographing Rodney and Harwin on a quail, pheasant, and chukar hunt at Rough Creek Lodge near Glen Rose. They had driven in from Dallas (only ninety minutes) the night before, and after a restful night's sleep and a breakfast that they didn't have to cook, they saddled up with their guide at 8:30 a.m. and departed for a pasture that they knew would be full of birds. Three hours later, they were back at the lodge and enjoying a wonderful lunch next to the lodge's massive stone fireplace while the staff cleaned and packaged their birds for the drive home.

Rough Creek Lodge opened in 1998 on an 11,000-acre ranch that straddles the boundaries of Erath, Bosque, and Somervell counties. The goal was to attract a mixed hunting and recreational clientele and provide a turnkey outdoor experience for executives and families that value their recreational time. "When

Harwin Jamison drawing down on a departing rooster
Rough Creek Lodge & Resort near Glen Rose

we first opened, we were mainly a hunting preserve, and corporate bookings made up the majority of our business," explained manager Paul Boccafogli. As the clientele became more diverse, they realized that there was significant potential for expansion.

In recent years, Rough Creek has added a sporting clays course, rifle and archery ranges, a fishing dock, biking and horseback trails, and a family swimming pool with a climbing wall and zip lines just outside the gated pool deck.

Wing shooting is still a large part of Rough Creek's business, and there are currently eight guides on staff with fully rigged trucks and a kennel with over fifty pointers and labs. In an average year Rough Creek releases from 60,000 to 65,000 birds between October and the end of March. In one of our parched and sweltering drought years you won't find that many native birds in an entire Texas county, much less on one Texas ranch.

Rodney Moore dusting a cockbird

DUCK AND BLACK BEAN CHILI

Serves 6

This is a wonderful alternative to traditional chili. Dried ancho peppers can be found in most major supermarkets or Hispanic grocery stores.

1 tablespoon cumin seeds
¼ cup vegetable oil
3 duck breasts, filleted (6 pieces, about 2 pounds), skinned, and cut into ¼-inch pieces
1 onion, diced
3 cloves garlic, chopped (1 tablespoon)
½ cup diced red bell pepper
½ cup diced yellow bell pepper
½ cup diced poblano pepper
1 cup Ancho Purée
1 to 2 cups cooked, drained black beans
3 cups duck or chicken stock
Kosher salt to taste
Masa or corn meal for thickening, optional

Ancho Purée

3 or 4 ancho peppers, seeded
Hot water

Make the Ancho Purée. Place peppers in hot water to cover and soak for at least 10 minutes; drain. Transfer to a blender, add 1 cup hot water, and purée until smooth. Set aside.

Heat a small skillet over medium-high heat, add cumin seeds, and stir until seeds begin to brown and become aromatic. Set aside to cool.

Heat oil in a large pot. Add duck and sear until meat is browned and most of the moisture has evaporated, about 10 minutes. Add onion, garlic, and peppers and sauté 3 minutes. Add Ancho Purée, toasted cumin seeds, black beans, stock, and salt. Bring to a boil, reduce heat, and simmer 15 minutes. If chili is too thin, mix a small amount of masa with an equal amount of broth and stir into chili; stir until thickened to the desired consistency. Adjust seasonings and serve.

—*Gerard Thompson, chef*

PHEASANT SALAD

Serves 4

2 pheasant breasts, filleted (4 pieces)
1 pound mixed baby lettuces
¼ cup chopped walnuts
¼ cup Maytag (or any good-quality) blue cheese, crumbled
¼ cup dried berries (such as cranberries, cherries, blueberries)

Marinade

½ cup vegetable oil
¼ cup balsamic vinegar
1 teaspoon honey
1 teaspoon fresh thyme
1 shallot, finely chopped
1 teaspoon freshly ground pepper

Vinaigrette

1 cup olive oil
⅓ cup balsamic vinegar
2 teaspoons finely chopped shallots
1 teaspoon orange zest
Kosher salt and freshly ground pepper to taste

To make the marinade, combine ingredients and mix well. Pour marinade into a sealable plastic bag, add pheasant breasts, and marinate in refrigerator at least 4 hours.

When ready to assemble salad, grill pheasant until done and let rest 10 minutes. Cut into thin strips.

To make the vinaigrette, combine ingredients and whisk together thoroughly.

In a large salad bowl, mix lettuce, walnuts, blue cheese, berries, and pheasant strips. Toss with vinaigrette and serve immediately.

—*Gerard Thompson, chef*

ROAST PHEASANT

Serves 6

6 pheasant breasts (6 to 8 ounces each)
1 tablespoon balsamic vinegar
1 clove garlic, minced
1 tablespoon chopped fresh rosemary
1 teaspoon honey
1 shallot, minced
1 tablespoon orange juice
1 cup vegetable oil

Rinse pheasant breasts and pat dry. Mix remaining ingredients together and pour over pheasant breasts. Marinate in the refrigerator for at least 4 hours. Grill over hot coals or sear in a hot skillet and finish in the oven at 350 degrees for 12 to 15 minutes.

—*Gerard Thompson, chef*

WILD MUSHROOM AND SWEET GARLIC BREAD PUDDING

Serves 6

This is an unusual side dish that complements grilled meats, game, or poultry. The pudding can be assembled about an hour before baking, set aside, and then baked while the rest of the meal is being prepared. Use a combination of wild fresh mushrooms, such as morel, porcini, shiitake, or chanterelle. Experiment with the herbs or use what is available; any combination of the herbs listed, or all of them, can be used.

> 1 head garlic
>
> Olive oil
>
> 3 tablespoons butter
>
> 1 shallot, finely diced
>
> 2 cups chopped assorted fresh wild mushrooms
>
> 1 tablespoon chopped assorted herbs (such as thyme, rosemary, oregano, and Italian parsley)
>
> 1 cup heavy cream
>
> 2 large eggs
>
> 1 loaf (10-ounce) sourdough bread, cut into cubes (about 4 cups)
>
> Kosher salt and freshly cracked black pepper to taste

Preheat oven to 350 degrees. Cut the top off the head of garlic and place in a lightly greased baking dish. Drizzle with olive oil. Bake 45 minutes, or until cloves are soft and lightly browned. Remove from oven and set aside to cool. When cool, squeeze garlic from cloves and chop. Measure ½ cup and set aside; reserve the remainder for another use.

Increase oven temperature to 375 degrees. Grease a large six-hole muffin tin. Melt butter over medium heat and add shallot and mushrooms. Sauté 3 to 5 minutes, or until mushrooms are tender. Add herbs and set aside to cool. In a stainless steel bowl, whisk together cream and eggs. Add diced bread, mushroom mixture, and roasted garlic, mixing well until bread has absorbed most of the liquid. Season with salt and pepper. Divide mixture evenly among the muffin cups and bake 15 to 20 minutes, or until golden brown. Remove from muffin tin and serve immediately.

—Gerard Thompson, chef

Opposite: An English pointer at full stride (above). Honoring a point with a mouthful of quail (below).

Hand delivery from a fine pointer

VENISON AND SWEET POTATO HASH

Serves 4–6

This is a wonderful and unusual dish for dinner or brunch. Try serving with red pepper sauce and poached or fried eggs on top of the hash.

> 1 Idaho potato, peeled and cut into medium cubes
> 1 sweet potato, peeled and cut into medium cubes
> ¼ cup vegetable oil
> 2 cups diced venison (½-inch cubes)
> Salt and pepper to taste
> 1 small red bell pepper, diced
> 1 small yellow bell pepper, diced
> 1 cup corn
> 1 bunch green onions, chopped

Simmer the potato cubes in salted water just until tender; do not cook until soft. Drain and immerse the potatoes in ice water to stop the cooking; drain. Heat a large skillet over high heat and add vegetable oil. When oil is hot, add drained potatoes and sauté until golden brown. Add venison and cook until browned. Season with salt and pepper. Add bell peppers and corn and cook, stirring constantly, until peppers are tender. Add green onions and cook an additional 2 minutes. Adjust seasonings.

—*Gerard Thompson, chef*

CHEDDAR-BACON BISCUITS

Yield: about 16 biscuits

These biscuits are delicious with any game meal. They also make a great on-the-go breakfast. The recipe can easily be doubled, and the biscuits can be cut out and frozen for up to two weeks. Thaw the number of biscuits needed and bake as directed.

> 2 cups all-purpose flour
> 1 tablespoon baking powder
> ½ tablespoon sugar
> 1½ teaspoons salt
> ¼ cup grated Cheddar cheese
> ¼ cup cooked, crumbled bacon (about 5 thin slices)
> Chopped chives
> 1½ cups heavy cream

Preheat oven to 425 degrees. In a large mixing bowl, combine all dry ingredients. Add cheese, bacon, and chives and mix well. Stir in cream and mix just until all ingredients are incorporated. On a floured surface, knead dough about 5 times, or just until well mixed. Roll dough to a thickness of ½ inch and cut with a 2-inch biscuit cutter. Bake just until biscuits begin to brown on top. Serve hot with lots of butter.

—*Gerard Thompson, chef*

WARM APPLE TART

Serves 8–10

Pastry

- 1¼ cups flour
- ¼ cup sugar
- ¼ teaspoon salt
- ½ cup (1 stick) chilled butter, cut into pieces
- 1 large egg yolk
- 1½ tablespoons ice water

Filling

- 1 large egg
- 1¼ cups sour cream
- ¼ cup granulated sugar
- ¼ cup light brown sugar
- Pinch of salt
- 1 teaspoon vanilla
- ¼ cup flour
- 4 Granny Smith apples, peeled and sliced

Streusel Topping

- ¾ cup granulated sugar
- ¾ cup brown sugar
- ¾ cup flour
- 1 teaspoon cinnamon
- 6 tablespoons butter
- 1 cup coarsely chopped walnuts

Preheat oven to 350 degrees. To make the pastry, combine flour, sugar, and salt in a food processor; add butter and process until mixture resembles coarse meal. Add egg yolk and water and mix until dough begins to form a ball. Turn out onto a floured surface and roll out crust for a 9- or 10-inch pie pan. Transfer crust to pie pan. Line crust with aluminum foil and fill with pie weights or dried beans. Bake 18 to 20 minutes, or until edges of crust begin to brown. Remove from oven and cool.

To make the filling, combine egg, sour cream, granulated sugar, brown sugar, salt, vanilla, and flour in a large bowl; mix well. Stir in apple slices. Fill baked pie shell with mixture and bake in preheated oven for 35 minutes.

Meanwhile, make the Streusel Topping. In a food processor, pulse together granulated sugar, brown sugar, flour, and cinnamon until combined. Add butter and pulse 3 or 4 times, or until coarsely chopped. Add walnuts and pulse another 3 or 4 times, or until mixture is crumbly. Do not overmix.

Remove pie from oven and spread Streusel Topping over the filling (the pie will be very full). Bake an additional 20 to 30 minutes, or until topping is golden brown. Serve warm.

—*Gerard Thompson, chef*

Opposite: Boathouse on the lodge's managed bass lake
Great room and fireplace at Rough Creek Lodge

BRUSH COUNTRY

HAVING SPENT NEARLY THREE-FOURTHS OF MY HUNTING SEASONS watching the sun rise and set over the brushy plains near the Rio Grande, I get a kick out those who speak of South Texas weather in terms of averages. As of today, August 30, 2006 (the day that I'm writing this chapter), the town of Spofford in Kinney County has received less than three inches of rain since the first of the year. If it rains nineteen inches in the next three months (or the next three days, which is not impossible), then the town of Spofford will officially have met its average annual rainfall. Those who keep the official weather records in South Texas should probably become more familiar with the term "weighted average."

According to descriptions by Spanish explorers in the 1600s, the region we now know as the Brush Country was at one time considerably less brushy. They described trees and thickets along the creek and river drainages, but most of South Texas, when the Spanish arrived, was a vast prairie where herds of antelope, bison, and deer could be seen from great distances. It is generally assumed that the overstocking of cattle, sheep, and goats by the first settlers decimated the grasslands, thereby removing fuel for

naturally occurring wildfires that kept the spread of noxious brush in check. In those days, unstocking animals from the range was considerably more difficult than stocking.

So why is it that the Brush Country is so often victimized by erratic weather cycles? To the east is the Gulf of Mexico. For most of the year, it pushes humid air inland on a southeast breeze. In some years those breezes bring hurricanes and rainfall measured in feet, but in most years they bring scattered showers, at best.

To the west, across the Rio Grande, lies the Chihuahan Desert. Those persistent, torching winds from the southwest tend to stifle the development of thunderstorms; yet occasionally they'll usher in a wobbling and sodden air mass from the Pacific that will stall over South Texas with flooding rains—rainfall measured in feet.

So if South Texas is arguably one of our state's more inhospitable patches of scrubland, then how is it

possible that good hunting leases in the Brush Country typically start at around ten dollars per acre? It's a simple formula of supply and demand.

In a green year, even the low-fenced ranches in South Texas are capable of producing whitetail bucks scoring 200-plus on the Boone & Crockett scale. And while a Brush Country quail hunter might bemoan a ten-covey day in a poor hatch year, a dyed-in-the-wool bird hunter from Georgia or the Carolinas might consider that the hunt of a lifetime. And even though deer and quail generate most of the lease dollars, if you're lucky enough to find a pasture with a sunflower field, a few live oak trees, and reliable surface water, then you can probably extend your season with doves, ducks, spring gobblers, feral hogs, and year-round bass fishing.

Within this section you'll find a broad and intriguing compilation of hunting and cooking and a glimpse

of ranching heritage that predates the lawless years when no one really gave a damn who claimed title to the land between the Nueces and the Rio Grande.

While some might presume that all South Texas cooking involves mesquite wood, beans, and whatever one might carve off the meat pole and wrap in a flour tortilla (not that there's anything wrong with that), I am pleased to report that a few chefs and camp cooks south of San Antonio are working hard to dispel that myth. As ranches have changed hands and elegant lodges have risen from the brush behind elaborate gated entries, haute cuisine has slowly worked its way into the fabric of Brush Country cooking.

It's a logical succession if you think about it. As package hunts have nosed into the five-figure category in recent years, firepit dinners that are spooned from a can have become less than companionable.

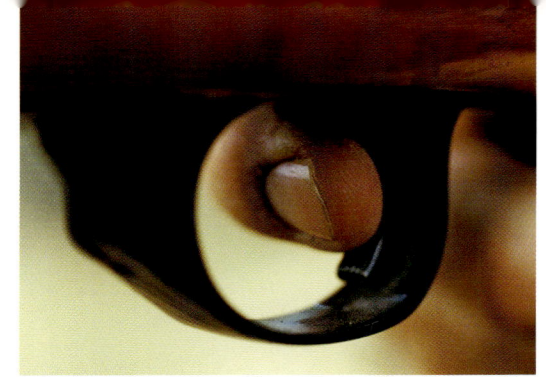

HINDES RANCH

⊞ Charlotte

On some Texas road maps there is still a little spot marked "Hindes" on Texas Highway 97, south of Charlotte in Atascosa County. The town was named for George Hindes, a rancher who settled there in the early 1900s. At one point the town of Hindes had a schoolhouse with 200 pupils, a bank, a store, and a post office. The town was lively and prosperous until the 1930s, when the train stopped running and the schoolhouse burned to the ground.

There is still a small green Highway Department sign marking the original location of the town. It sits just a few yards north of a ranch gating leading to the home of George's great-great-grandson, Roy Hindes III ("Little Roy") and his wife, Pam. If you converse with anyone long enough about cattle ranching or deer management in South Texas, you'll eventually turn up the Hindes name. The lineage goes like this: Little Roy Hindes is the son of Roy Hindes II ("Big Roy"), who is the son of Leroy Hindes, who is the son of David Hindes, who is the son of George Hindes. Little Roy now has a grown son, Roy Hindes IV, who goes by Cuatro. Cuatro also has a son, Roy Hindes V.

When I asked Little Roy if George was the original Hindes settler in the area, he replied, "Not exactly. George's father was Moses Hindes. He founded the town of Tilden and was killed by Comanches in 1865."

In the early 1970s Big Roy was running the Hindes Ranch and looking at his deer herd as a source of annual income to supplement his cattle and farming operation. Unfortunately, most of South Texas during that time had become terribly overpopulated with

Ranch trophies in Pam and Roy Hindes's living room
Opposite: A mature buck in heavy cover

198 • GRAZING ACROSS TEXAS

A playground fight between two adolescents

deer after years of indiscriminate buck harvest and no pressure on the does. Ten-point bucks were hard to come by, and a mature deer (if you could find one) would dress out at only 100 pounds or so.

In 1972 Little Roy was going to college in Uvalde when he heard about the deer management successes of Al Brothers and Murphy Ray on the H. B. Zachry ranches in Webb, Zapata, and Jim Hogg counties. He asked them if they would come out to meet with his dad and explain their theories. The rest, as they say, is history.

That year, the Hindes Ranch became one of the first in South Texas to erect a deer-proof fence. As Brothers and Ray explained it, you're not building this fence to keep your deer in; you're trying to keep everyone else's deer out. Once the fence was built, the Hindeses set about managing the basic components of nutrition, age, and genetics in their deer herd. Rotational grazing practices were applied to keep the range in good shape. Selective culling was used to improve the standing gene pool. And young quality bucks were allowed to grow into old trophy bucks. By the early 1980s, word of big deer at the Hindes had reached the hunting community and the ranch began offering a limited number of guided trophy hunts.

Big Roy passed away in 1999, and today Little Roy and Cuatro are still guiding some of the same hunters that they started out with. Their bucks have appeared in magazines and books around the country, and dozens of ranches in Texas are now using the basic management model that Al Brothers and Murphy Ray applied to the Hindes Ranch over thirty years ago.

"We're not trying to do anything real fancy here," Little Roy explained. "We've got a comfortable lodge and a good group of hunters. We love the land, and we try to do our best with what we have."

Roy with his tracking dogs Gus and Fidel, known statewide for their ability to trail wounded deer

SWISS VENISON

Serves 4

To add extra heat to this dish, add a chopped, fresh jalapeño. Serve over rice.

Flour
Salt
Pepper
1 venison backstrap, white muscle sheath removed, sliced thin
Vegetable oil for frying
1 can (14-ounce) diced tomatoes
1¼ cups water
1 large onion, diced
1 large bell pepper, diced
4 ribs celery, chopped

Mix flour, salt, and pepper and dredge venison slices in flour mixture. Heat oil in a large skillet and fry meat until browned. (The meat may have to be cooked in several batches.) Drain on paper towels. Transfer venison to a 4-quart pot. Add remaining ingredients and stir to combine. Bring to a boil, cover, and reduce heat. Simmer 45 minutes, or until meat is tender. Serve warm.

—*Pam Hindes*

VENISON CARNE GUISADA

Serves 6–8

3 tablespoons vegetable oil
6 cups lean cubed venison
2 fresh tomatoes, coarsely chopped
1 large bell pepper, coarsely chopped
2 generous tablespoons minced garlic
1 teaspoon salt or to taste
Pepper to taste
1 can (15-ounce) tomato sauce

Heat vegetable oil and brown venison cubes in batches until golden. Transfer browned venison to a large Dutch oven. In a blender or food processor, purée tomatoes, pepper, garlic, salt, and pepper. Combine tomato sauce with the pureed vegetables and pour over the browned venison. Bring to a boil, reduce heat, and simmer 2 hours. Serve with warm flour tortillas.

—*Pam Hindes*

DOVES AND DUMPLINGS

Serves 4

A wonderful dish, just like old-fashioned chicken and dumplings. Quail can be substituted for the doves.

12 doves
1½ quarts water
Salt and pepper to taste
2½ cups milk
1 cup flour
2 teaspoons baking powder
½ teaspoon salt
2 tablespoons vegetable oil

Place doves in a large Dutch oven. Add water and season with salt and pepper. Bring to a boil, reduce heat, and simmer 45 minutes, or until tender. Cool doves in broth. When doves are cool enough to handle, remove meat from bones, discarding bones; return meat to broth Add 2 cups of the milk to the dove broth and bring to a gentle boil.

In a mixing bowl, combine flour, baking powder, and salt. Whisk together the remaining ½ cup milk and vegetable oil. Pour over the dry ingredients and stir just until moistened.

Drop the dumpling dough, by tablespoons, into the bubbling broth. Cover with a tight-fitting lid and return mixture to a gentle boil. Reduce heat and simmer 12 to 15 minutes; do not lift the lid during this time.

—*Pam Hindes*

BUTTERSCOTCH CUSTARD PIE

Little Roy claims that this pie (along with the .270 that Pam's father gave him) closed the deal on their courtship.

> 4 egg yolks, whites reserved
> 1 cup light brown sugar
> 5 tablespoons flour
> 3 cups whole milk
> 1 teaspoon vanilla
> Dash of salt
> 1 tablespoon butter
> 9-inch piecrust, baked

Meringue

> 4 egg whites at room temperature
> ½ teaspoon vanilla
> ¼ teaspoon cream of tartar
> 8 tablespoons sugar

Beat egg yolks until well combined. Stir brown sugar and flour together and add to beaten egg yolks. Whisk in milk, vanilla, salt, and butter. Stirring constantly, cook over medium heat until thickened, about 7 to 10 minutes. Pour custard into baked piecrust and set aside.

Preheat oven to 375 degrees. To make the meringue, beat reserved egg whites with vanilla and cream of tartar until soft peaks form. Gradually add sugar, beating meringue until stiff and glossy and all sugar is dissolved. Spread meringue over cooled pie filling, covering to the edges of the pastry all around. Bake 12 to 15 minutes, or until meringue is golden brown. Cool thoroughly before serving.

—Pam Hindes

PRALINE BARS

Yield: 50 bars

These bars freeze well—if they last that long!

> 2 cups brown sugar
> 1 cup (2 sticks) butter, softened
> 1 egg, beaten
> 1½ cups flour
> ¼ teaspoon salt
> ½ teaspoon baking powder
> 1 cup chopped pecans
> 1 teaspoon vanilla

Praline Icing

> 1 cup brown sugar
> ½ cup heavy cream
> 1 cup sifted powdered sugar

Preheat oven to 350 degrees. Grease a 9 × 13-inch baking pan. Cream together brown sugar and butter. Add beaten egg and mix well. Stir in flour, salt, and baking powder and mix until blended. Add pecans and vanilla and spread mixture into prepared pan. Bake for 20 to 25 minutes.

To make the icing, combine brown sugar and cream in a small saucepan. Heat to a boil, stirring constantly. Cook, stirring constantly, for 2 minutes. Remove from heat and whisk in powdered sugar. Spread icing over the baked mixture while it is still warm. Cool completely and cut into 2-inch bars.

—Pam Hindes

Roy with a massive pair of sheds; he's been managing age, nutrition, and genetics on the Hindes Ranch since 1972.

PERLITZ RANCH

◈ **Crystal City**

Peer out the windows of any blind on the Perlitz Ranch in Zavala County, and you'll notice a consistent theme: lots of big bucks and no feeders. Instead of propping up a corn slinger out in the brush to attract deer, Jimmy Perlitz runs his program a bit differently.

"We had automatic feeders for a while, but I got tired of the hassles and the constant maintenance," Jimmy explained. He and his guides still use corn to sweeten the setup when they're hunting, but they spread it up and down the senderos using truck-mounted feeders when they arrive at each blind. "This way we're not wasting a lot of corn on coons, hogs, and javelina at blinds where we're not sitting." Jimmy starts his road corning program every year in October, feeding selected blinds morning and evening. Just like an automatic feeder, the deer learn quickly to respond to the sound of spinning corn—and they respond at a time that's convenient for the hunter instead of a preprogrammed time. "If it's 90 degrees in the afternoon, we'll hang around the house a little longer and feed the roads when we get to the blind. That way we're not baking in the heat and waiting for a feeder to go off when the deer aren't moving in the first place." This type of feeding regimen may appear too labor-intensive to the casual whitetail hunter, but the Perlitz family typically hosts forty to forty-five guided deer hunters in a season, and their consistent hunting results are a fair endorsement of their technique.

The Perlitz Ranch has been in Jimmy's family since 1924 when his great-grandfather, Jesse Stuart, bought the 9,000-acre spread with money that he made

Leaving the lodge for the afternoon hunt
Opposite: Primed for the rigors of the coming rut

using mule teams to dig pipelines for the oil industry. The motivation for their guided hunting program came in 1985 with the construction of a high fence and the adoption of an intensive management plan. After several years of culling and feeding, they hosted their first group of hunters in 1992.

Jimmy explained that they were fortunate, early on, to cultivate a relationship with Realtree Outdoors. A number of television shows and magazine articles were produced on the ranch with celebrity hunters like Jeff Foxworthy, Jay Novacek, Chipper Jones, Sammy Kershaw, and Davey Alison.

In a typical year the Perlitz Ranch divides its harvest between a prescribed number of trophy and management buck hunters. Even though Jimmy's phone rings constantly during the weeks leading up to deer season, he emphatically states that he is not looking for the one-time trophy hunter. "We've got plenty of good bucks on the ranch, but our first priority is hospitality and enjoyment," Jimmy explained. "We're looking for long-term relationships, and a lot of our hunters have been coming here for years."

Jordan Case with a 170-class Perlitz Ranch trophy. A six-year-old with 200-plus inches of antler: would you take him now or let him go another year?

Opposite: Game room in the old ranch house (left). Culls and casualties in the Perlitz barn (right).

VENISON PICCATA

Serves 4

1 venison backstrap, white muscle sheath removed
2 tablespoons vegetable oil
6 to 8 tablespoons butter
¾ cup flour
Salt and freshly ground pepper to taste
4 tablespoons fresh lemon juice
2 tablespoons finely chopped parsley
½ lemon, thinly sliced

Slice the backstrap across the grain into ½-inch-thick medallions. Pound each medallion to a thickness of ⅛ inch with a tenderizing mallet. In a skillet over medium-high heat, heat the oil and 2 tablespoons of the butter until very hot (the meat must cook quickly, or it will be tough). Dip both sides of the venison in flour and shake off the excess. Add the venison to the skillet; do not crowd. Cook about 1 minute per side, or until lightly browned. Transfer to a warm platter and season with salt and pepper. Add more butter as needed and repeat until all meat is cooked. Set meat aside. Remove skillet from heat.

To make the sauce, pour lemon juice into the skillet, scraping up any loose browned bits. Add the remaining butter, stirring until melted. Stir in the parsley. Return the venison medallions to the skillet, turning them in the sauce. Heat the sauce and venison together, garnish with the lemon slices, and serve immediately.

—*Perlitz Ranch*

BARBECUED WILD TURKEY

This dish tastes just like chopped brisket. Serve with bowls of relish, chopped onions, and extra barbecue sauce for sandwiches.

1 wild turkey
4 stalks celery, chopped
1 onion, chopped
Garlic salt to taste
¼ cup liquid smoke
1 bottle (10-ounce) Worcestershire sauce
1 bottle (18-ounce) hickory-smoked barbecue sauce

Bone the turkey, cut into large pieces, and put into a roasting pan. In a separate bowl, combine celery, onion, garlic salt, liquid smoke, and Worcestershire sauce and pour over the turkey pieces. Refrigerate for at least 24 hours.

Preheat oven to 300 degrees. Cover pan tightly with two layers of aluminum foil. Bake 5 hours. Strain marinade and set aside. Shred turkey meat and return to pan. Pour barbecue sauce over meat and add strained marinade to taste. Mix well and cover. Bake for an additional 1 hour. Serve on buns.

—*Perlitz Ranch*

SOUTHWEST BAKED BEANS

Serves 6–8

2 tablespoons bacon drippings or vegetable oil
1 medium onion, chopped
3 cans (14-ounce) pinto beans, drained and rinsed
3 tablespoons brown sugar
1 can (8-ounce) tomato sauce
½ cup prepared chili sauce
1 can (4-ounce) chopped green chilies
½ teaspoon cumin
½ teaspoon chili powder
1 teaspoon salt
½ teaspoon freshly ground pepper
5 slices bacon

Preheat oven to 325 degrees. In a heavy skillet, heat bacon drippings and add onion; sauté until onion is translucent, about 2 minutes. Transfer onion to a medium bowl and add all remaining ingredients except bacon slices. Mix lightly and pour into a 2-quart casserole. Arrange bacon slices on top. Cover and bake 1½ hours. Remove cover and bake an additional 30 minutes, or until sauce has thickened and top has browned.

—Perlitz Ranch

*Opposite: An ill-advised posture for a two-year-old buck
Checking out the day's video footage*

SALADO SECO RANCH

⊞ **Spofford**

In the fall of my eighth grade school year, my father bought a small piece of Kinney County ranchland between Bracketville and Eagle Pass. The property had plenty of surface water (seasonal, of course) and a small house sitting next to a sequence of live oaks that followed Las Moras Creek from its wellspring in Bracketville, past the ranch house, to its final merger with the Rio Grande near Quemado.

The house was nothing special: a wood frame structure over pier and beam, with a screened porch, lots of curling linoleum, aluminum shower stalls, sulphuric well water, and a framed nude-on-velvet flea market masterwork hanging over the mantel. The painting made it through my mom's second visit, but it was one of the first things thrown into the burn barrel when the serious housekeeping started.

On my first trip to the ranch in October of 1977, my brother, father, and I spent two days driving around and dodging quail coveys, herding turkeys single file down the roads, and counting more deer than we thought any single piece of land could carry (I'll revisit that topic in a moment). My father's original plan with this property was to slightly improve it, hold it, and sell it.

Over thirty hunting seasons have now passed since that first visit. Within that time our family has grown from its nucleus of five to a multilevel gaggle of fourteen, and the Salado Seco Ranch has been significantly improved but never sold. During that time, the original house has been expanded, then remodeled, then flooded (twice), then finally demolished in favor of new construction at a slightly higher elevation above the creek.

A place to gather at the Salado Seco Ranch
Opposite: By-products of an extended wet spell

210 • GRAZING ACROSS TEXAS

Like most land in South Texas, we are subject to the cruel and erratic cycles of drought and monsoon. During green years our tanks are loaded with ducks, quail limits are possible before lunchtime, and the marauding turkey flocks start gathering at the deer feeders a half hour before they spin. When the rains stop and the tanks dry up and the quail switch to survival mode, we tend to spend less time with shotguns and more time nurturing the deer herd and trying to make sure we never see them as skinny and abundant as they were back in 1977.

Rain or shine, though—year after year—what my family does persistently and remarkably well at the Salado Seco is gather. We gather for the dove opener, and we eat. We gather a few weeks later to guide our annual group of deer hunters, and then we eat some more. At Thanksgiving we eat enough to last us until Christmas, and then we typically gather one more time to nibble and graze through the first days of the New Year.

In the following pages you'll find a selection of my family's favorite game recipes. Now, obviously, I can't promote these dishes with total impartiality, but I can tell you that they have consistently served a big family of big eaters for three decades of gathering, hunting, watching football, and wondering when it will start raining next—or stop.

Chris McKeown lining up on a blazing bobwhite

SCALLOPS OF VENISON

Serves 6

18 slices venison backstrap, pounded to a thickness of ¼ inch

Salt and pepper to taste

4 tablespoons flour

¼ cup clarified butter

4 shallots, finely chopped

¼ cup red wine vinegar

1 cup heavy cream

1 tablespoon Dijon mustard

2 tablespoons unsalted butter, cut into small pieces

Season venison with salt and pepper and lightly dust with flour. Heat a large skillet over medium-high heat and add clarified butter. When butter is hot, add venison, a few slices at a time; do not crowd the pan. Cook 1 to 2 minutes per side. Transfer to a platter and keep warm.

Pour off grease. Add shallots and vinegar, scraping up the browned bits. Cook over medium heat until vinegar is reduced by half. Add cream and cook, stirring, until sauce is slightly thickened. Remove from heat and stir in mustard. Whisk in the butter pieces, one piece at a time. Spoon sauce over warm venison and serve immediately.

—David Brown

BARBECUED DOVES

Serves 4

The sauce for this dish is unusual and very good with dove and quail. The recipe makes a generous amount of sauce, but any leftovers can be refrigerated for about a week. The sauce also goes well with grilled chicken. To reheat, pour into a saucepan and heat over low heat; do not let it boil, or it will separate.

12 doves
4 cups beef broth or consommé

Barbecue Sauce

2 cups (4 sticks) butter
1 bottle (5-ounce) A-1 sauce
2 tablespoons mustard
Juice of 3 lemons
2 dashes of Tabasco sauce
1 tablespoon sugar
1 tablespoon salt
Garlic salt to taste, optional

Place doves in a large saucepan and pour broth over to cover by 1 inch; add water if needed. Bring to boil, reduce heat, and simmer 30 to 45 minutes, or until doves are tender but not falling apart. Set aside and preheat grill.

To prepare the sauce, combine all ingredients and heat slowly over low heat. Be careful not to let the sauce boil, or it will separate.

Place doves on a hot grill and baste with sauce, turning frequently. Cook 8 to 10 minutes. Serve immediately with extra barbecue sauce.

—*Carolyn Brown*

Opposite: Barbecued Doves
Blake Brown on a September dove hunt

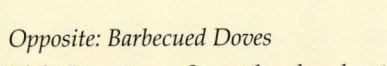

Brush Country • 215

DOVE EMPANADAS

Yield: about 90 empanadas

These empanadas take a little time to make but are well worth the effort. The pastry and dove mixture can be made a day ahead, refrigerated, and then assembled the following day. After the empanadas have been frozen on cookie sheets, they can be transferred to sealable containers, returned to the freezer, and baked at a later time.

15 doves
Seasoned salt
½ cup (1 stick) butter
½ onion, minced
2 cloves garlic, minced
1 red bell pepper, minced
1 fresh jalapeño pepper, seeded and minced
5 ounces slivered almonds, toasted and finely chopped
1 cup chopped cilantro
1¼ teaspoons ground cumin
1 teaspoon kosher salt
¾ teaspoon allspice
½ teaspoon cayenne
½ teaspoon cinnamon
2 tablespoons red wine vinegar

Cream Cheese Pastry
1 cup (2 sticks) butter, softened
8 ounces cream cheese, softened
2 cups flour
Dash of salt

Preheat oven to 300 degrees. Generously sprinkle doves with seasoned salt. Wrap tightly in foil and bake for 3 hours, or until tender; cool. Remove meat from bone and finely chop in a food processor.

In a large skillet, melt butter over medium-high heat. Sauté onion, garlic, bell pepper, and jalapeño pepper until soft. Add almonds, cilantro, and dove meat; cook for 1 minute. Add spices and vinegar, mixing well. Set aside to cool.

Make the Cream Cheese Pastry. In an electric mixer or food processor, blend butter and cream cheese. Add flour and salt; mix well. Form dough into a ball, wrap in waxed paper, and refrigerate at least 30 minutes or overnight.

On a floured surface, roll pastry to a thickness of ⅛ inch. With a 2-inch biscuit cutter, cut circles from pastry. Place 1 teaspoon of dove mixture on each pastry circle, fold over, and pinch edges to seal. Prick tops with fork. Place empanadas 1 inch apart on cookie sheets and freeze for several hours. When ready to bake, preheat oven to 425 degrees. Bake frozen empanadas 10 to 12 minutes, or until golden brown. Serve immediately.

—Ellen McKeown

Nellie fetching a drake pintail
Opposite: David Brown (left) and foreman Ambrose Watson scoring a whitetail

DOVE POT PIE

Serves 4–6

The doves can be cooked and boned a day in advance, refrigerated, then returned to room temperature before proceeding with the recipe. To save even more time, a refrigerated piecrust can be used instead of making pastry.

> 12 to 15 doves
> Salt and pepper to taste
> Garlic powder to taste

Filling

> 6 tablespoons butter
> 1 cup chopped onion
> 1 cup chopped celery
> ½ cup chopped green bell pepper
> ¼ cup chopped fresh parsley
> ¼ cup chopped fresh cilantro
> 2 heaping tablespoons flour
> 8 ounces fresh mushrooms, sliced
> 1 cup frozen petite green peas, optional
> Dash of Tabasco sauce
> ¼ cup dry white wine
> ⅓ cup chicken broth
> Salt and pepper to taste

Pastry

> 1½ cups all-purpose flour
> 1 teaspoon kosher salt
> ½ teaspoon baking powder
> ¼ cup vegetable shortening, chilled
> ¼ cup cold unsalted butter, diced
> 5 to 6 tablespoons ice water

Preheat oven to 300 degrees. Generously sprinkle doves with salt, pepper, and garlic powder. Wrap tightly in foil and cook 3 hours, or until tender. Cool and remove meat from bones. Set meat aside.

To make the pastry, mix flour, salt, and baking powder in a food processor. Add the shortening and butter and, using the metal blade, pulse 8 to 10 times. With the motor running, add the ice water; process just until the dough is moistened and a ball is starting to form. On a piece of waxed paper, shape dough into a flat disk and refrigerate 30 minutes.

To make the filling, melt butter and sauté onion, celery, bell pepper, parsley, and cilantro. Stir in flour and mix well. Add mushrooms, peas, Tabasco, wine, and chicken broth. Add dove meat, season with salt and pepper, and pour mixture into a 2-quart baking dish. (The mixture will be thick.)

Preheat oven to 400 degrees. On a lightly floured surface, roll out pastry in the shape of the baking dish. Place on top of dove mixture and crimp the edges. Bake 30 minutes, or until crust is browned.

—Carolyn Brown

ROAST DUCK WITH CURRANT SAUCE

Serves 2

This recipe works best with dabbling ducks like pintails, mallards, widgeons, teal, and gadwalls.

> 2 whole ducks, plucked and cleaned with skin and fat remaining
> Salt and pepper to taste
> 2 apples
> 2 onions
> 1 cup chicken broth

Currant Sauce

> 1 jar (12-ounce) currant jelly
> 2 tablespoons Dijon mustard
> 1 teaspoon cumin

Rinse ducks and pat dry. Salt and pepper each duck, inside and out. Slice apples and onions into large chunks and place in breast cavity of each duck. In a Crock-Pot or slow-cooker, stand each duck on end, breast side down. Pour chicken broth around ducks. Cook on high for 3 hours.

To make the sauce, combine ingredients in a small saucepan. Cook slowly over low heat until jelly melts. Stir well and serve with warm duck meat.

— *David Brown*

RANCH BEANS

Serves 10–12

Serve these beans with corn bread or warm tortillas. The heat of the beans can be increased by adding more jalapeños.

> 2 pounds dry pinto beans, cleaned
> 1 tablespoon kosher salt
> ½ medium onion, thickly sliced
> Cloves of 1 head garlic, peeled
> 2 smoked ham hocks
> 1 pound bacon, diced
> ¼ medium onion, chopped
> 2 or 3 fresh jalapeño peppers, stemmed and sliced
> 3 cloves garlic, minced
> 1 can (14-ounce) chopped tomatoes
> ½ cup chopped fresh cilantro

Rinse beans and put in large pot with water to cover by about 3 inches. Add salt, sliced onion, garlic, and ham hocks. Bring to a boil, reduce heat to medium low, and boil gently for 1 hour, or until beans are tender.

While beans are cooking, fry bacon until it is almost crisp; add chopped onion and cook for 4 minutes. Add jalapeños and minced garlic and sauté an additional 2 minutes. Pour in the tomatoes and their juice and simmer 4 minutes, or until most of the liquid is gone.

When beans are tender, add tomato mixture and stir in chopped cilantro. Return beans to a boil, reduce heat to a simmer, and cook an additional 5 to 8 minutes. Adjust seasonings.

— *Martha Novel, ranch staff*

Russell McKeown sighting in his .243

SALSA ROJA

Yield: 2 cups

3 medium ripe tomatoes
3 small fresh jalapeño peppers
¼ small onion, coarsely chopped
2 cloves garlic
1 teaspoon salt
¼ teaspoon cumin

Quarter the tomatoes and cut the peppers in half. Put tomatoes, peppers, and onions in a microwave-safe dish and cover lightly with plastic wrap. Cook in microwave on high for 3½ minutes, or until peppers begin to soften. Transfer to a blender and add remaining ingredients. Pulse 5 to 6 times. Refrigerate.

—*Martha Novel, ranch staff*

TOMATILLO SAUCE

Yield: 2 cups

12 small tomatillos (about 1 pound), husks removed
2 fresh jalapeño peppers, stems removed
3 cloves garlic, peeled
¼ medium onion
1 cup coarsely chopped cilantro
1 teaspoon salt
¼ teaspoon freshly ground pepper
1 tablespoon olive oil

In a medium saucepan, bring 3 cups salted water to a boil. Add whole tomatillos and jalapeños and cook for about 5 minutes, or just until tender. Drain and cool to room temperature. Transfer to a blender and add all remaining ingredients except olive oil. Blend, using quick pulses, until well combined but not smooth. Adjust seasonings to taste.

In a medium skillet, heat olive oil. Add tomatillo mixture and cook over medium-high heat until mixture boils, stirring frequently. Cook an additional 2 minutes. Cool and refrigerate for up to 3 or 4 days.

—*Martha Novel, ranch staff*

SANDY OAKS RANCH

◆ Devine

Like most Texas quail-hunting guides, Foard Houston didn't wake up one morning with three dozen bird dogs and several charge accounts with his local feed mill and veterinary clinic. Ask any guide with enough dogs on payroll to last a full quail season, and he'll affirm that total immersion in passionate lunacy tends to develop gradually over time.

Foard grew up hunting quail on his family's ranch south of San Antonio, but he didn't get into dog ownership until he graduated from college. His first pair of bird dogs was originally designated for personal enjoyment, but that plan changed in the fall of 1990 when a friend offered Foard a payday to hunt over his dogs. For the next ten years, Foard's kennel grew proportionately alongside his reputation as a top quail guide and dog handler.

In those days he was mainly freelancing on other people's ranches. For a daily fee he would show up with a tricked-out quail rig and a string of pointers. Have dogs, will travel. The advantage of that program was the lack of pressure (and overhead) on the quail side of the equation. Foard didn't have to produce birds; that part was up to the landowner. All he had to do was produce dogs that could find birds.

After years of chasing rainfall and wild quail around South Texas, Foard eventually decided to hedge his bets and cut down on travel time during hunting season. After obtaining the necessary game preserve permits for the family ranch near Devine, Foard set about building a lodge and improving the habitat for a released-quail operation.

Poolside at Sandy Oaks Ranch
Opposite: Rooting a single bobwhite from a tasajillo clump

Brush Country • 221

Sandy Oaks Ranch opened for business in the fall of 2000 with a spacious main lodge, a swimming pool, a patio bar and outdoor fireplace, and guest rooms for up to eight hunters. A clay range and pigeon rings are available for tune-up shooting, and a covered kennel facility out back houses Foard's dogs.

These days Foard still does quite a bit of freelance guiding—especially in the wet years when the hatches are big. When wild bird numbers are down, however, he can fall back on released birds to extend his season and keep his dogs busy. Quail hunting remains his primary pursuit, but Foard also offers dove hunting in September and October and year-round fly-fishing for bass on a number of private lakes in the area.

Pass-shooting whitewings over a croton field
A Lab on the move with a mouthful of dove

Springer spaniels are great to have on the truck for flushing and fetching (above). A mid-day dog wallow (below).

Opposite: Foard and his quail rig at first light (above). Damp and green on opening weekend (below).

DOVE CARNE GUISADA

Serves 4

½ tablespoon shortening
1½ pounds cubed dove breasts (about 30 doves)
1 onion, chopped
1 can (14.5-ounce) stewed tomatoes
1 can (10-ounce) diced tomatoes and green chilies
2 fresh jalapeño peppers, seeded and diced
1 tablespoon chili powder
1 tablespoon ground cumin
3 cloves garlic, minced
Salt and pepper to taste
Flour tortillas

Melt the shortening in a large saucepan over medium-high heat. Add dove meat and cook until browned. Add onion and sauté until tender. Stir in stewed tomatoes, tomatoes and green chilies, chili powder, cumin, garlic, salt, and pepper. Bring to a boil, reduce heat to low, cover, and simmer 1 hour, or until dove meat is tender. Thin with water if mixture is too thick. Serve hot with flour tortillas.

—*Sandy Oaks Ranch*

TAILGATE QUAIL

This is a quick and easy way to prepare birds for lunch or dinner in the field.

2 or 3 quail per person, skinned and cleaned
Half-and-half, enough to cover birds
Flour
Salt and pepper to taste
Shortening for frying

Build a small fire in a safe area (out of the wind and away from tall grass). Wash quail thoroughly in cold water. Place quail in a large bowl, cover with half-and-half, and set aside. In a small bowl, combine flour with salt and pepper. When the fire has burned down, place a fire grate over the hot coals. In an iron skillet over the hot coals, heat shortening until shimmering. Dredge quail in the seasoned flour and fry until golden brown.

—*Sandy Oaks Ranch*

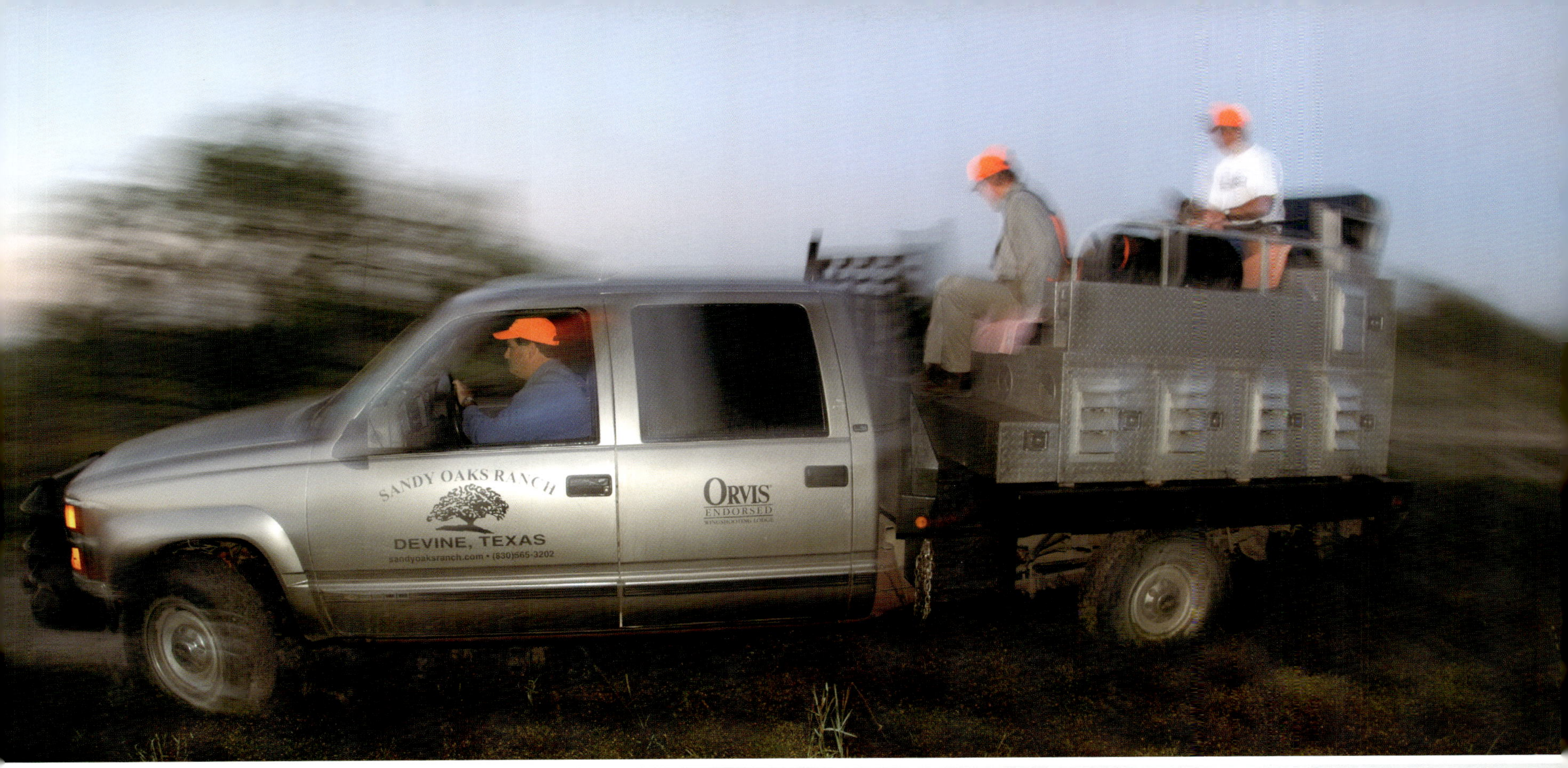
SANDY OAKS RANCH
DEVINE, TEXAS
sandyoaksranch.com • (830)665-3202
ORVIS
ENDORSED

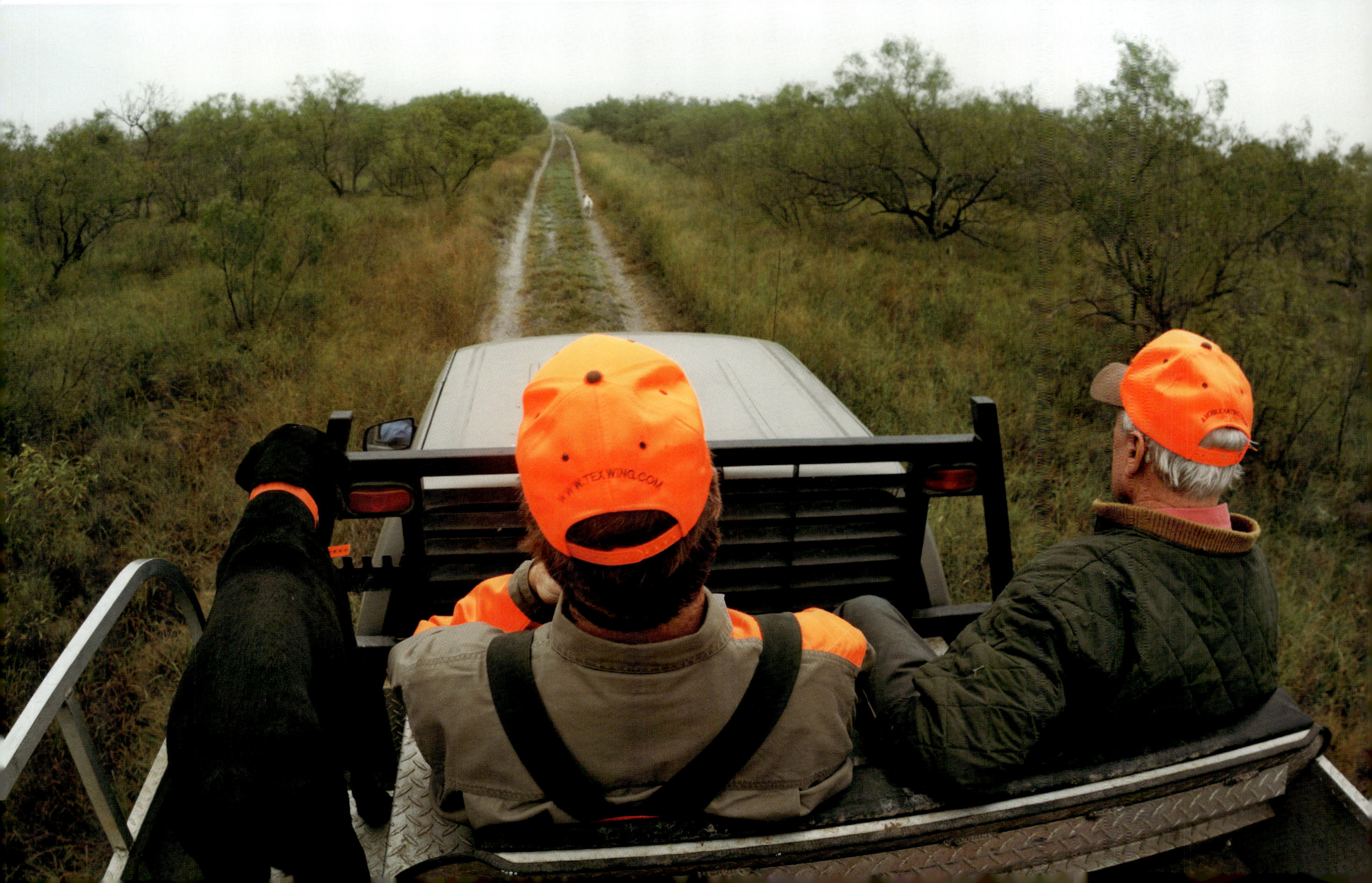
WWW.TEXWING.COM

FRIED GREEN BEANS

Serves 6–8

2 pounds fresh green beans, trimmed and cut into 3-inch lengths
½ cup (1 stick) butter
6 slices bacon, chopped
1 medium onion, sliced
1 tablespoon minced garlic

Cook the green beans in boiling salted water 8 to 10 minutes, or until crisp-tender. Drain and immerse in a bowl of ice water to stop the cooking process. Drain and set aside.

In a large skillet, melt butter and fry bacon until it begins to brown. Add onion and garlic and fry until tender and bacon is cooked. Add drained green beans to skillet and stir-fry until tender.

—Sandy Oaks Ranch

Jumping bass on a ranch pond near Yancey (left). Releasing a chunky largemouth (above).

LA BANDERA RANCH

◈ **Carrizo Springs**

Grab a Texas map and a pencil. Now draw a line from Laredo north to Cotulla, then west to Eagle Pass, and then back south to Laredo. What you've cordoned off, according to most serious whitetail deer hunters, is a sportsman's dreamland of thornbrush, red dirt, sparse rainfall, and giant antlers. Whitetails in the "Golden Triangle" grow to magnificent proportions without really trying. The ranches are big, the protein content in the native browse is outstanding, and the naturally occurring genetics are arguably the best in the world.

If you take a spin through the Boone & Crockett Club record book, you'll notice an inordinate number of entries from Dimmit, Webb, and Maverick counties. Granted, there are countless managed ranches across Texas—and the United States—that are turning out gargantuan whitetails these days, but most of them are doing it with intensive feeding, culling, habitat enhancement, and, in some cases, genetic intervention. Ranches in this storied corner of South Texas were producing huge bucks decades before anyone knew what those terms meant—and they're still doing it today with comparatively little effort.

In 2001 Austin restaurant owner Jack Carmody had just put the finishing touches on a showplace of a ranch when he was killed in a speedboat racing accident near Corpus Christi. His La Bandera Ranch consisted of 31,000 acres and a magnificent lodge located southwest of Carrizo Springs in the heart of the Golden Triangle. When La Bandera was offered for sale after Carmody's tragic death, avid big game hunter Bob Hixson of Arkansas recognized the area's

Opposite: A substantial buck shadowing a doe during the rut (left)
One of La Bandera's truck-mounted hydraulic hunting blinds (right)
Hunting trophies from around the world at La Bandera Ranch

potential for record-book whitetails, so he purchased the ranch with the hope of perpetuating Carmody's vision.

Today Hixson and his staff offer superlative accommodations, gourmet meals, and guided hunting for whitetails, quail, and doves. Hunters can choose from three lodges: the rustic La Sombrilla Lodge, Ponderosa Lodge, or the five-star 17,000-square-foot Southwest Lodge. Ranch amenities include a 5,000-foot lighted runway, heated swimming pool and sauna, sporting clays course, rifle and pistol ranges, and stocked bass lakes.

And what about the deer on La Bandera? They've already harvested a significant number of trophies, and it'll be interesting to see what a low-fenced ranch in prime country will consistently turn out if those accidental giants are given a persistent pass to grow old and reproduce. In the meantime, though, La Bandera has already made waves with its unmatched service and accommodations. In case you were wondering, that resounding clink emanating from southern Dimmit County is the sound of the bar being raised.

Birds, in there (above). Quail hunter pushing a pear flat at sunrise (right).

VENISON CHILI

Serves 8

This chili is prepared in a slow-cooker or Crock-Pot, which allows the cook to assemble the recipe early in the day and forget about it until dinnertime. The long simmer creates a very flavorful chili.

> 5 pounds ground venison
> 5 cloves garlic, minced
> 1 yellow onion, chopped
> 1 can (28-ounce) chopped tomatoes with juice
> 1 can (4-ounce) chopped green chilies
> 6 to 8 tablespoons chili powder
> 2 teaspoons dried oregano
> 1 teaspoon ground cumin
> Salt and freshly ground pepper to taste
> ⅓ cup yellow cornmeal
> 2 cups beef broth
> 1 can (15-ounce) small red beans, drained, optional
> Sour cream, chopped red onion, grated cheese, and cilantro for garnish

In a large sauté pan over medium-high heat, brown half the venison. Using a slotted spoon, transfer the venison to a large slow-cooker. Repeat with the remaining venison. Add garlic, onion, tomatoes, green chilies, chili powder, oregano, cumin, salt, pepper, cornmeal, and beef broth to the slow-cooker and stir to blend. Cover and cook on high setting for 6 hours. During the last hour of cooking, add drained beans.

—*La Bandera Ranch*

Brush Country • 231

QUAIL IN WINE SAUCE

Serves 4

A wonderful recipe for wild quail that keeps them moist and tender. Serve over white rice.

> 1 medium onion, coarsely chopped
> 8 quail
> 1 cup flour
> 1 teaspoon salt
> 1 teaspoon freshly ground pepper
> ½ cup (1 stick) butter
> 8 ounces fresh mushrooms, sliced
> ¼ cup chicken broth
> ½ cup dry white wine
> ½ cup whipping cream
> ½ cup chopped fresh parsley

Spread chopped onion in the bottom of a Crock-Pot or slow-cooker. Rinse quail and pat dry. In a shallow bowl, mix flour, salt, and pepper. Melt butter in a large skillet over medium-high heat. Lightly dredge quail in seasoned flour and brown in melted butter, about 4 minutes per side. Remove from skillet and place on top of onions in pot. Using the same skillet, sauté mushrooms lightly and transfer to pot. Add chicken broth to skillet and bring to a boil, scraping up browned bits; cook about 2 minutes, or until reduced by one-third. Pour over quail. Pour wine over quail and cook on high setting for 3 hours. Check for tenderness and cook longer if needed. Remove quail when they are fork-tender and transfer to a serving dish. Just before serving, add cream to the wine sauce and pour over quail. Sprinkle with fresh parsley.

—*La Bandera Ranch*

VENISON SAUSAGE AND BISCUIT CASSEROLE

Serves 8–10

This is a quick and easy breakfast dish to serve after the morning hunt. A mixture of Pepper Jack and Cheddar cheeses can be substituted for the Cheddar for an even spicier dish. If a milder dish is preferred, omit the green chilies and cayenne pepper.

> 2 pounds venison pan sausage
> 1 cup chopped onion
> 2 cans (4-ounce) chopped green chilies, drained
> 2 cups biscuit mix
> 4 ounces grated Cheddar cheese (1 cup)
> 1 cup buttermilk
> 1 teaspoon poultry seasoning
> ¼ teaspoon cayenne pepper
> ¼ teaspoon ground cumin

Preheat oven to 425 degrees. Grease a 9 × 13-inch baking dish and set aside. Brown the sausage lightly in a medium skillet, stirring until crumbly. Add onion and sauté until translucent, about 4 minutes. Stir in green chilies. Pour into prepared dish.

In a medium bowl, combine biscuit mix, cheese, buttermilk, and spices; mix until a sticky dough forms. Drop by tablespoonfuls onto the sausage mixture. Bake 20 minutes, or until biscuits are lightly browned.

—*La Bandera Ranch*

Opposite: Poolside at the 17,000-square-foot Southwest Lodge (above). The main dining room with African and whitetail trophies (below).

MCALLEN RANCH

⊞ Edinburg

In a time when ranches are flipping faster than the courthouses can record the deeds, it's inspiring to note a six-generation family landholding that can be traced back to the absolute birthright of South Texas ranching.

Irish immigrant John McAllen first worked as a store clerk when he arrived in the Rio Grande Valley in the early 1850s. By 1860 McAllen was earning a living in commodities with purchases of cotton, sugar, and salt, which were transported by steamship from Hidalgo to the Port of Brownsville. In 1862 McAllen married Salomé Ballí Dominguez Young; her family owned the Santa Anita Ranch, which was part of the original 200,000-acre Spanish land grant signed to Jose Manuel Gomez in 1791. In 1893 the Santa Anita was divided, with the McAllen family retaining ownership of the San Juanito division—subsequently named the McAllen Ranch.

Today the ranch is owned and operated by John McAllen's great-grandson Jim McAllen and his sons and daughters. They are best known for their registered Beefmaster cattle herd, but the McAllen Ranch was also one of the first in Texas to capture and study whitetail deer in a managed environment. After purchasing the Guajolota division in the late 1960s, Jim erected a high fenced enclosure on the property and began experimenting with deer densities, culling, and age-class structure. This was long before high-protein feed was available, and Jim produced some significant bucks on the ranch's native browse alone.

David Coleman and his twenty-three-point McAllen Ranch giant. The buck scored 227⅞ and won the Low Fence division of the 2006 Los Cazadores contest.

Opposite: High-racking on a damp January day on McAllen's Guajolota division (above). Banging horns and glassing senderos (below).

A promising young buck with his fashionable pre-rut headwear

Opposite: Dinnertime at the Guajolota Lodge

Each year the McAllen family hosts a limited number of guided deer hunters on the Guajolota and the headquarters pastures as well. Hunters are housed in a comfortable, full-service lodge, with meals prepared on site by the ranch chef. The terrain varies from thick brush that is cut with numerous senderos to wide-open fields and savannahs. Ground blinds are their preferred hunting method, but horn rattling and safari-style hunting from high-rack trucks is also available.

Even though the McAllens see their research on captive deer as one of their signature achievements, the ranch may eventually become better known for a buck harvested in one of the low-fence pastures. In December of 2006, hunter David Coleman of Columbus, Mississippi, harvested a monster buck on the McAllen Ranch with twenty-three points and a net B&C score of 227⅞. Oddly enough, the buck grew the massive rack in a year when Hidalgo County had no measurable rain until mid-summer. While most whitetail hunters hold firmly to the adage that big rains produce big horns, this buck symbolizes what South Texas deer hunting is really all about. On any given ranch, on any given day, you just never know what might step out of the brush.

Jim's daughter, Melissa McAllen Guerra, is the celebrated chef of their family. Melissa has authored two successful cookbooks, *Dishes from the Wild Horse Desert: Norteño Cooking of South Texas* and *The Texas Provincial Kitchen*, a companion volume to her PBS television show by the same name. Melissa also sells a selection of authentic Mexican ingredients, cookware, and other products through her online store (www.melissaguerra.com).

VENISON TAMPIQUEÑA

Serves 4–6

The traditional tampiqueña is made with a beef fillet that is butterflied or sliced thin and quickly seared. Venison backstrap (butterflied) or a thin steak cut from a ham will also work well. Serve with the traditional accompaniments of guacamole, refried beans, and tostada triangles. Bottled sour orange juice can be found at most Hispanic food stores.

- 2 pounds of venison backstrap or ham, sliced thin into 4 to 6 individual steaks
- 2 cups sour orange juice or apple cider vinegar
- Salt and freshly cracked black peppercorns
- 3 poblano peppers, thoroughly washed
- 2 tablespoons olive oil
- 1 medium red onion, sliced into rounds
- 1 white onion, sliced into rounds
- 2 carrots, sliced into rounds

Place the venison slices in a nonreactive dish. Pour the sour orange juice over the venison and season with salt and cracked peppercorns. Cover and refrigerate at least 20 minutes.

While the meat is marinating, roast the poblano peppers. Place 1 or 2 peppers at a time onto the burner over a medium flame. Using tongs, turn them so that they roast and blacken evenly, about 5 minutes. Be careful that they don't burn and develop an ashy layer on the skin. (Or roast in the oven directly beneath the broiler element until the skins blister, about 10 minutes.)

Place the roasted peppers in a plastic bag, seal tightly to keep the steam from escaping, and allow to sweat for 15 minutes. Remove the peppers and peel away the layers of charred skin and the stem. Cut a slit in each and remove the clusters of seeds. Rinse under cold water to remove any remaining skin or seeds; pat dry.

Coat a large cast-iron skillet with olive oil and heat over medium-high heat until the oil is almost smoking. Add the venison and sear it for 5 to 7 minutes on each side, depending on thickness and the preferred degree of doneness. (For medium rare, remove the meat when it reaches an internal temperature of 135 degrees.) Add the onions, carrots, and roasted peppers to the pan. Over medium heat, cook the vegetables until the onions are caramelized. Pour the mixture over the venison and serve.

—Melissa Guerra

VENISON CORTADILLO

Serves 6

Cortadillo, which means "that which is cut," comes from the northern Mexican state of Coahuila. The traditional cortadillo is made with beef, but it also works well with venison.

> 2 tablespoons corn oil
> 1 small onion, chopped
> 2 pounds venison, cut into ¼ × 2-inch slices
> 1 pound ripe tomatoes (about 4), peeled and seeded
> 2 whole serrano peppers
> 2 cloves garlic, minced
> Salt and pepper to taste

Heat oil in a 10-inch lidded skillet over medium heat. Add onion and sauté until transparent, about 5 minutes. Add venison and cook until the meat is well browned, about 5 minutes.

Purée tomatoes in a food processor or blender. Add tomato purée, peppers, garlic, salt, and pepper to the meat. Stir to combine well. Cover and reduce heat; stirring occasionally, simmer 45 to 60 minutes, or until tender. Uncover for the last 10 minutes to reduce and thicken the stewing liquid.

—Melissa Guerra

VENISON HENRY

Serves 4

> 3 tablespoons butter
> ¾ cup flour
> ½ cup grated Parmesan cheese
> 1½ pounds venison, thinly sliced

Sauce

> 3 tablespoons butter
> 1 cup sliced fresh mushrooms
> 3 green onions, sliced
> 2 tablespoons chopped fresh parsley
> 1 tablespoon cornstarch
> ½ cup beef broth
> ½ cup red or white wine
> Salt and pepper to taste

In a large skillet, melt butter over medium-high heat. Meanwhile, combine flour and cheese in a shallow dish. Dredge venison in flour mixture and fry in the butter, about 1 minute per side. Drain cooked venison on paper towels.

To make the sauce, melt butter in the same skillet and sauté mushrooms, onions, and parsley until tender. Add cornstarch and mix well. Slowly add broth and wine and continue to stir until mixture thickens. Add salt and pepper. Return venison to skillet to heat. Serve immediately.

—Melissa Guerra

Weathered sheds on an old log corral

FLAN

Serves 8

This one of Melissa's most requested recipes. Her flan is very rich and serves well with coffee and fresh fruit. Flan must be baked in a water bath, which requires a metal baking pan large enough to hold the casserole dish.

- 1 cup sugar
- ½ cup water
- 5 drops lemon juice
- 4 eggs
- 4 egg yolks
- 3 cups whole milk
- 1 cup heavy cream
- 1 teaspoon vanilla extract

Preheat oven to 350 degrees. In a 1-quart saucepan, stir together sugar, water, and lemon juice. Cook over medium heat until the mixture boils. Cook the mixture until it turns amber in color (it should register 320 to 356 degrees on a candy thermometer), about 10 minutes. Remove from heat and pour into a 2½-quart round casserole or soufflé dish. Set aside to cool.

Whisk together eggs and egg yolks in a large bowl until thick. In a 2-quart saucepan, heat milk and cream until tiny bubbles form around the edges and the mixture is on the verge of boiling. Remove from heat. Using a whisk, whip the eggs continuously while drizzling in a small amount of the hot milk mixture. Continue until you have added about 1 cup of the milk mixture. Pour the milk and egg mixture into the saucepan and whisk until well combined. Add vanilla and whisk until combined.

Pour the custard mixture into the prepared casserole dish (strain the mixture if it contains filaments of cooked egg).

To prepare the water bath, fill a teakettle with water and bring to a boil. Lay a small dishtowel in a metal baking pan, place the pan on the oven rack, and place the casserole dish into the pan. Pour boiling water into the metal pan—not into the flan! (For best results, the water bath should be at least 1 inch deep around the casserole dish.) Carefully push the oven rack into the oven, being careful not to slosh any water into the flan. Bake 50 to 60 minutes, or until a knife inserted in the center comes out clear.

Remove the casserole carefully from the water bath and allow the flan to cool completely. Before serving, carefully loosen the edges of the flan from the dish and invert onto a serving platter. If any liquid caramel remains in the dish, pour it over the flan.

—*Melissa Guerra*

GULF COAST

SEVERAL YEARS AGO I WAS SITTING ON THE FERRYBOAT *J.C. DINGWALL* in Port Aransas when a family of summer migrants in a minivan squeezed into the lane next to me. It was mid-morning in early July and there was no wind. The sky was heavy with cumulus buildups, and the humidity was draped over the scene like a damp beach towel. With my windows rolled down and engine turned off, I was anxiously awaiting any small amount of breeze that the *Dingwall* might create by actually moving us from one side of the channel to the other.

Two feet away from my truck, a young girl in the backseat of the minivan rolled down her window and poked her head out for a gasp of fresh air. About halfway through her inhale, she clamped her mouth closed, crinkled up her nose in disgust, and ducked back into their car.

"Eeewww, Mama," she squealed, "what is that awful smell?"

Naturally, everyone within earshot—her mother, father, two siblings, the ferry attendant, two other carloads of beachgoers, and myself—all took a big simultaneous whiff. I was thinking of a potential answer to her question at the exact moment that her father spoke up.

"That's the coast, sweetheart," he announced in his best tour-guide voice. "It's the salty air, and the sand, and the seaweed, and all the neat things that make this such a great place."

Way to go, Dad. I couldn't have explained it better myself. The ferry attendant couldn't hear the father's reply over the drone of the engine, and he was still looking around, perplexed, and sampling the air like maybe someone's shrimp cooler needed another bag of ice.

With both hands clasped over her nose and mouth, the little girl cautiously leaned toward the car window again and cracked her palms just enough to let in another small sample of the offending atmosphere. "Well, it doesn't smell like home," she announced, "but I guess I can get used to it."

Most Texans will readily admit that our 375 miles of coastline are somewhat lacking in certain sparkling and idyllic brochure amenities. We don't have sugar-white sand, persistently perfect weather, and Caribbean water clarity—but we do have great hunting and fishing, and we're still proudly trailing South Florida in the statistical hierarchy of crowds, crime, and corruption.

If you took away the paint-peeling winds, our brownish beaches, and a climate that can rust out a galvanized boat trailer in less than a year, then the Texas coast would be absolutely perfect. Perfection tends to spawn congestion, and it's also a tough title to defend on an annual basis.

Within this chapter you'll find a diverse selection of coastal sporting and dining opportunity from the inland marshes, the shallow bay systems, and the blue-water depths. Just as the terrain and climates differ between the Sabine and South Padre Island, you will also find a diversity of cultural influence on the cooking between the upper and lower coasts. Heading east out of Galveston it's hard to find a chef who doesn't preach the religion of cayenne pepper, fluffy rice, and roux. From Corpus Christi south to the Rio Grande you'll find the spices and traditions of Mexico's Tamaulipas, Veracruz, and Bay of Campeche.

While private landholdings limit recreational access in most areas of our state, the Texas coast is a wide-

open gateway of hunting and fishing opportunities. Of course, you'll have to charter a boat to catch anything of any size offshore, but our inland waterways offer a variety of easy and inexpensive access for jetty jockeys, surf casters, kayakers, and waders.

Inevitably, though, if you spend enough time on the Texas coast, you'll eventually experience that pang of exasperation when you roll out of bed at 6:30 a.m. and find the flags snapping, the halyards humming, and the palm fronds whipping violently. While Plan B might not completely make up for smooth water and a solid tug on your line, there's certainly no shame in switching to shellfish when all else fails. If it takes a trip to the fish house or a couple of hours on the dock with a crab net to fill the pot, then we've also got you covered with some great shellfish recipes—perfect fare for those blustery non-brochure occasions.

GAIDO'S RESTAURANT

◈ **Galveston**

On September 4, 1900, a cyclonic mass of rain and wind traversed the island nation of Cuba and then slipped into the Gulf of Mexico near Key West, Florida. After twenty-four hours of torrential rain and flooding, the Cuban forecasters predicted that the storm would continue moving northwestward with significant strengthening. In Washington, D.C., however, the U.S. Weather Bureau forecasted a dying storm with an erratic northeasterly track across mainland Florida and the eastern seaboard.

On the morning of September 8, Galveston residents gathered at the beachfront to marvel at the luminous pink skies and the massive swells that were gathering offshore and crashing onto the sand. Sadly, the only people who could have predicted what really lay in store for Galveston that day were the freighter captains south of the Mississippi Delta who had perished overnight among sixty-foot waves and winds estimated at 120 miles per hour.

At dawn, on September 9, the affluent island city of Galveston had been obliterated by an overwhelming storm surge and cataclysmic winds that mariners of that era described as "the Devil's voice." The eventual death toll was estimated at 8,000 souls, with over two-thirds of Galveston's homes and buildings destroyed. Undaunted by their extraordinary losses and determined to rebuild the most prosperous port city west of New Orleans, the people of Galveston spent the next ten years dredging, filling, and constructing a concrete seawall that would eventually raise the city over fifteen feet above mean tide level.

Galveston was booming again when San Jacinto (S. J.) Gaido opened a small sandwich shop atop Mur-

Nearly a century of fine dining in Galveston
Opposite: A subsurface view of a big bull dolphin (mahi-mahi)

doch's Bathhouse on Seawall Boulevard in 1911. The Interurban Railway was completed across Galveston Bay in 1912, and easy access to the mainland allowed an unprecedented boom in tourism and industry. After adapting a full seafood menu and elegant table service, Gaido's soon gained a reputation as one of the finest restaurants on the Gulf Coast.

Today Gaido's Restaurant is still family-owned, with S. J.'s great-grandsons Rick and Michael Gaido managing the daily current of fresh seafood and loyal patrons through the doors. The restaurant has moved a few yards inland—it's no longer perched atop a rickety wooden pier—but it remains an iconic fixture along Seawall Boulevard, and it's still preparing and serving seafood much the same as it did nearly one hundred years ago. Shrimp and oysters are still peeled and shucked by hand; breads and sauces are prepared from scratch daily; and the Gaido family remains committed to serving the freshest and finest ingredients available.

Name recognition goes a long way in the restaurant business. Ask anyone who's ever spent much time in Galveston about a good place to eat, and they'll probably mention Gaido's. It's a name that goes with the city, a city known for an unnamed hurricane that nearly scraped it off the map over a century ago.

LUMP CRAB AU GRATIN

Serve as an appetizer with thin, lightly toasted slices of French bread. You can also fill small prebaked pastry shells with the crab mixture and bake until browned on top. As an entrée, serve with a green salad and a chilled white wine.

>2 tablespoons Worcestershire sauce
>2 cups half-and-half
>1 teaspoon seasoned salt
>2 tablespoons butter
>1 tablespoon minced garlic
>2½ tablespoons flour
>2 tablespoons sherry
>Chopped fresh parsley to taste
>1 pound lump crabmeat (2 cups)

Preheat oven to 375 degrees. In a small saucepan, combine Worcestershire sauce, half-and-half, and seasoned salt; heat until the mixture is just at the boiling point. Remove from heat.

In a separate saucepan, heat butter and garlic together until butter is melted. Whisk in flour and stir constantly to make a roux; make sure the flour does not brown or stick to the pan. Cook 1 minute. While whisking, slowly add the half-and-half mixture to the roux. Continue to cook, stirring constantly, until mixture is thick, about 6 to 8 minutes. Stir in sherry and mix well. Remove from heat and add parsley and crabmeat. Pour into a casserole dish and bake until bubbly and browned on top, about 15 to 20 minutes.

—*Gaido's Restaurant*

Opposite: The main dining room at Gaido's
Shrimp Pegues with Brown Sugar Glaze

SHRIMP PEGUES WITH BROWN SUGAR GLAZE

>1 cup brown sugar
>¼ cup fresh lemon juice
>2 tablespoons molasses
>1 tablespoon honey
>8 jumbo shrimp, peeled and deveined
>1 cup dried bread crumbs or commercial breading mix
>2 ounces Cheddar Jack cheese, grated
>4 slices bacon, cut in half
>Olive oil

In a 2-quart mixing bowl, combine brown sugar, lemon juice, molasses, and honey; stir until thoroughly mixed.

Butterfly each shrimp. Mix together bread crumbs and grated cheese. Stuff each shrimp with approximately ¼ cup of the bread crumb mixture. Wrap each stuffed shrimp with a piece of bacon and secure with a toothpick. Heat olive oil over medium heat and add shrimp. Cook until bacon is browned. Dip each shrimp into brown sugar glaze and serve immediately.

—*Gaido's Restaurant*

MAHI SAPORITO

Serves 4

Mahi-mahi is the Hawaiian name for dolphin fish (not Flipper). In Mexico the fish is called *dorado* for its golden color.

> 2 cups cracker crumbs
> 1 head garlic, roasted and peeled
> 1 tablespoon oregano
> ¾ teaspoon dried thyme
> ½ tablespoon kosher salt
> ¾ teaspoon ground black pepper
> 1 tablespoon granulated garlic
> 2 eggs
> 4 tablespoons unsalted butter
> 4 mahi-mahi fillets

Place cracker crumbs and roasted garlic in a food processor and pulse until thoroughly combined. Transfer to a bowl and add oregano, thyme, salt, pepper, and granulated garlic; mix well. Whisk eggs in a small bowl to make an egg bath. In a large skillet, melt butter over medium heat. Dip each fillet in the egg bath, shaking off excess, then roll in the cracker crumb mixture, coating thoroughly. Sauté until golden brown on all sides and fish is thoroughly cooked, about 6 minutes per side.

—*Gaido's Restaurant*

Forty miles out and flat calm (left). Sport fishers at sunset (below).

BUCKSNAG HUNTING CLUB

◆ Garwood

In 1968 legendary waterfowl guide Jimmy Reel purchased the old Chapman Hotel in Garwood with a notion that his clientele might benefit from an exclusive private hunting club. Originally constructed in 1910, the historic facility required an extensive renovation before he could open it up for membership. He named the fledgling club after Bucksnag Creek, which meanders through the Garwood Prairie, and the club stands today as an icon of waterfowling tradition in the rice fields of Southeast Texas.

Jimmy Reel was the originator of the "Texas rag" decoy spread, and he also pioneered the practice of pumping water and flooding grain fields to attract migratory ducks and geese. Hunting pressure has since forced the evolution of the rag spread along the Texas coast, and today's waterfowl hunters are behind the curve if they're not using some combination of windsocks, wobblers, kites, and shells in their decoy spreads. Even so, as decoys, clothing, calling methods, and bag limits have changed over the years, the Bucksnag experience remains largely intact. The old wooden bar still stands as the traditional gathering spot after the hunt. The guest rooms are furnished with hand-sewn quilting, iron bed frames, and antique dressers. And you can still sit on the front porch in a wooden rocker and watch the town of Garwood inch along at a snail's pace.

Jimmy Reel passed away in 1976, but the Bucksnag Hunting Club is still operated by a limited membership—many of them have been with the club since its inception. Time may further change the way ducks and geese are hunted on the Garwood Prairie, but it's doubtful that the Bucksnag tradition will evolve much more than it has in the past forty years.

The Bucksnag Hunting Club in Garwood

Opposite: Snows and blues leaving a winter wheat field. Swinging on a pair of snow geese

BUCKSNAG GOOSE

This recipe can also be used for duck by reducing the total cooking time by one hour. The method of preparation produces meat that is moist and tender. Soaking the geese in the vinegar mixture and then the baking soda mixture reduces the gamey taste and tenderizes the meat. Allow one-fourth to one-half goose per person. Serve with wild rice.

2 to 4 whole geese, plucked
Distilled vinegar
Baking soda

3 cups dry white wine
3 cups water
10 to 12 heaping tablespoons flour
1 pound mushrooms, sliced
1½ onions, thickly sliced
Soy sauce
Worcestershire sauce
Celery salt
Coarsely ground black pepper
2 to 4 white onions, halved
2 to 4 small turnips, halved

Place geese in an extra-large Ziploc bag. Cover geese with a mixture of one part distilled vinegar and two parts water. Refrigerate at least 1 hour but preferably overnight. Remove geese and rinse, discarding vinegar mixture. Return geese to plastic bag and add more water to cover. Pour baking soda into water until it becomes cloudy. Return to refrigerator and soak an additional 1 hour.

Preheat oven to 425 degrees. In a large roasting pan with a tight-fitting lid, mix white wine and water. Add flour and whisk until smooth. Add mushrooms and sliced onions. Season liberally with soy sauce, Worcestershire sauce, celery salt, and black pepper; mix well. (This mixture, along with the goose drippings, is used to make the gravy.)

Place geese on a rack in the roasting pan. Stuff each goose with half an onion and half a turnip. Season liberally with soy sauce, Worcestershire sauce, celery salt, and pepper. Cover and roast 30 minutes. Baste geese with gravy and reduce heat to 285 degrees. Cook an additional 4½ hours, basting every 30 minutes.

Remove from oven and carve. The breast meat should almost fall away from the bone. Stir gravy. If it is too thin, thicken it with a small amount of sifted flour. Whisk well to prevent lumps.

—David Wolff, club member

A quiet spot facing a street with no traffic

A feeding flock of snows and blues

Some call the blue phase of the snow goose an "eagle-head." Waterfowl roost on the Garwood prairie

BAYFLATS LODGE

⊞ **Seadrift**

While growing up in Victoria, Chris Martin spent considerable time exploring the vast network of bays and marshes around Seadrift on the middle coast. Later, as a commissioned sales rep for Bridgestone Firestone Corporation, he returned to those waters to entertain prospective clients with waterfowl hunts and bay fishing trips for speckled trout and redfish.

After eighteen years in commercial sales, Chris decided in 1998 to pursue his captain's license and a career change. Armed with an extensive list of business contacts, he and his wife, Deb, opened Bayflats Lodge with a goal of attracting corporate hunting and fishing business to a relatively untapped resource on the Texas coast.

"Rockport and Port O'Connor get a lot of traffic," Chris explained, "but we're set up right between them on a bay system with very little fishing and hunting pressure."

With a vast network of shorelines, back lakes, shell reefs, and marshes within a few miles of the lodge, Chris and his stable of full-time guides can spread out their clientele and avoid the pitfall of harassing the same populations of fish and birds on a daily basis.

In addition to their remote location, Chris and Deb take pride in their attention to detail. The lodge and boats are meticulously maintained, and their loaner tackle is in better shape than most people's personal gear. For corporate groups or family gatherings, the Martins can host accomplished anglers or first-timers with equal attention and proficiency. If you want to anchor and fish with live bait, that's not a problem. If you prefer casting lures and don't mind wading and

Chris and Deb Martin's new lodge near Seadrift.
Opposite: A substantial speckled trout. Blake Brown launching lures on San Antonio Bay.

grinding, there's a guide at Bayflats (especially Chris) who's ready to accommodate you.

During the waterfowl seasons, Chris and his guides use mobility and persistent scouting to track the ducks and geese as they move back and forth between the bays and inland marshes. By deploying a rotation of airboats, ATVs, sunken pits, and shore blinds, they can put you within easy range of decoying birds.

After eight years of building a persistent repeat clientele, the Martins finally outgrew their original converted bay house. In the spring of 2007 they opened a new 10,000-square-foot waterfront facility with a spacious main lodge, private guest suites, and an outdoor kitchen pavilion. Guests can expect the same level of comfort and service to which they've grown accustomed with additional space to stretch out and socialize.

Guides T. J. Christensen (front) and Harold Dworaczyk calling ducks
Adjusting the decoy spread

GRILLED SPECKLED TROUT

Speckled trout are delicate fish that require proper handling. To keep fillets fresh and firm, try to ice and clean the trout as soon as possible after they have been caught. Specks are best when cooked and served fresh. They degrade quickly in the freezer.

1 to 3 trout fillets per person
Freshly ground black pepper to taste
4 tablespoons butter
¼ teaspoon minced garlic
Lemon wedges

Preheat grill to medium-high setting. If cooking with mesquite or charcoal, make sure to spread the coals evenly.

Season fillets with pepper. In a small saucepan, melt butter and add minced garlic. Baste both sides of fillets with butter mixture and place in a greased grilling basket (a piece of wire screen can also be used). This keeps the fillets from falling through the grill grate. Cover the grill and cook until fillets begin to brown slightly along the edges. Baste again with butter just before removing from grill. Serve with lemon wedges.

—*Bayflats Lodge*

Trout fillets on the grill (left). Hand delivery (right).

GRILLED DUCK BREAST

The type of duck used for grilling must be chosen carefully. Pintails, widgeons, teal, and gadwalls are typically fine-tasting birds as they feed mainly on aquatic plants. Of the diving ducks (bottom-dredgers), redheads are normally the best for grilling. Bluebills, buffleheads, ruddies, ringnecks, and shovelers are typically very gamey when harvested in the bays. Save those species for soups and gumbos.

For a less gamey flavor, the fillets in this recipe can be place in a dish filled with half of the vinegar and oil mixture, covered with plastic wrap, and marinated in the refrigerator for one or two hours before grilling. Grilled duck is best served rare to medium rare; otherwise, it becomes dry and tough.

2 to 4 duck breast fillets per person
⅛ cup balsamic vinegar
⅛ cup red wine vinegar
¼ cup olive oil
¼ cup vegetable oil
Salt and pepper to taste
Garlic powder to taste

For larger fillets (not teal), use a tenderizing mallet to slightly flatten the fillets. (This will keep the fillet from curling on the grill and ensure uniform cooking.) Thoroughly mix the vinegars and oils; shake or whisk until completely combined.

Preheat grill to highest heat setting. If cooking with mesquite or charcoal, make sure to spread the coals evenly. Baste fillets with vinegar and oil mixture, then season with salt, pepper, and garlic powder. Grill 3 to 4 minutes for teal or 5 to 6 minutes for larger birds.

—*Bayflats Lodge*

DUCK CAKES

This is an excellent appetizer served with spicy mustard. The duck cakes can also be served as a salad over a bed of baby lettuce with a vinegarette dressing. The ducks can be roasted one day ahead.

1 onion, thickly sliced
3 medium ducks
5 tablespoons extra-virgin olive oil plus additional for frying
½ medium red bell pepper, diced
½ medium yellow bell pepper, diced
1 shallot, finely chopped
⅓ cup hazelnuts, toasted and chopped
2 eggs, lightly beaten
2½ tablespoons mayonnaise
½ teaspoon salt
¼ teaspoon freshly ground black pepper
1½ tablespoons fresh thyme leaves, or 1½ teaspoons dried
1 cup plain bread crumbs

Preheat oven to 450 degrees. Line the bottom of a roasting pan with onion slices. Place ducks, breast down, on the onions and cover with lid or heavy-duty aluminum foil. Roast 15 minutes; reduce oven to the lowest setting and roast an additional 6 to 8 hours. Cool ducks, remove meat from bones, and chop.

Heat olive oil in a medium skillet. Sauté peppers and shallot for 5 minutes. Transfer to a bowl and add duck meat, hazelnuts, eggs, mayonnaise, salt, pepper, thyme, and ⅓ cup of the bread crumbs. Mix well and form into 2-inch cakes. Dredge cakes in the remaining ⅔ cup bread crumbs.

Pour olive oil into a frying pan to a depth of 1 inch and heat over medium-high heat. When oil is hot, fry cakes until golden brown on both sides. Drain on paper towels and serve immediately.

—*Bayflats Lodge*

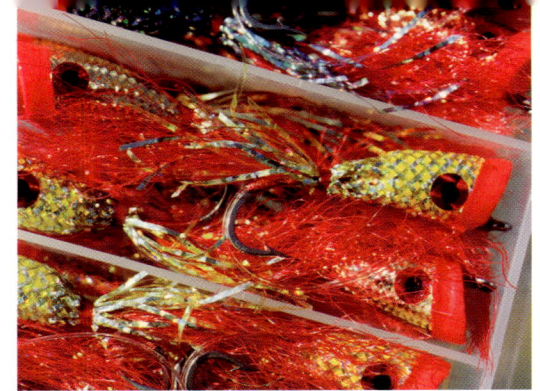

REDFISH LODGE

◈ **Rockport**

When Jim Conklin, Canada's largest carnival operator, bought a sandy spit of land called Rattlesnake Point back in 1983, he had no idea that he would one day own one of the finest fishing lodges on the Texas coast. Jim's original plan was to subdivide the property and develop luxury bay-front homes on the narrow peninsula dividing Copano and Port Bay.

The Conklin family had been vacationing and fishing for years around Rockport, but an untimely crash in the real estate market forced a change of plan. Lot sales stalled not long after building the first spec home on the property, and Jim reasoned that a commercial operation might fare well when the Texas economy eventually regained its footing.

In 1992 he sent his daughter, Melissa, and her husband, Phil Rogers, to Rockport with instructions to open their home and transform it into a fishing and hunting lodge. Many of the locals gave them little chance of success, as they presumed that the stately private sporting clubs on the Texas coast had already captured the well-heeled hunting and fishing crowd that Jim was hoping to attract.

Recognizing that the local experts could get them quickly up to speed, Phil and Melissa chose to concentrate on the room and board side of the equation while farming the guiding out to the most qualified local anglers. Rockport guide James Fox was the first to bring his clients aboard at Redfish Lodge, and over the next few years a number of other guides joined the mix. In 1994 the lodge hired Port Isabel fly-fishing guide Chuck Scates and his wife, Lynn, and set them up as on-site managers. Brian Holden, who is now the club manager, joined the team as a full-time guide, and from there Chuck went to work hiring out the remainder of his in-house team.

Redfish Lodge on Copano Bay
Opposite: Could an avid bay caster ever tire of this scene?

The original Conklin home still stands as the primary facility on Rattlesnake Point. Redfish Lodge has built an indelibly loyal clientele and is known as a top facility for corporate entertaining on the Texas coast. The Conklins learned early on that the weather and the fish might not always cooperate, but the sporting world will beat a path to your door if you're consistent with great service, fine accommodations, and memorable meals.

MirrOlure's popular Top Dog, an effective trout and redfish plug. Redfish on the fly.

Gulf Coast • 267

BACARDI RUM BLACKENED TROUT

Serves 6–8

¾ cup vegetable oil

½ cup Bacardi rum

¼ cup dried parsley flakes

1 tablespoon garlic powder

6 to 8 fresh speckled trout fillets

¼ cup olive oil

1 orange

Blackened Spice Mix

1½ tablespoons seasoned salt

½ tablespoon salt

1½ tablespoons ground white pepper

2 tablespoons paprika

1½ tablespoons garlic powder

1 tablespoon chili powder

1 tablespoon ground mustard seed

In a shallow dish, mix together the vegetable oil, rum, parsley, and garlic powder. Dip fillets in mixture, transfer to a separate dish, and marinate at room temperature for about 1 hour.

Prepare the Blackened Spice Mix by combining all ingredients and mixing well. Coat one side of each fillet with spice mix, covering completely.

Heat olive oil in a large skillet over medium heat. Add fillets, seasoned side down, and cook 2 minutes. Turn and cook an additional 2 minutes, or until fish is opaque. Remove from heat and squeeze fresh orange juice over fish. Serve immediately.

—Chris Lee, chef

Opposite: Chef Chris Lee

PINEAPPLE-RUM SHRIMP

Serves 2

The amount of cayenne used in this recipe can be adjusted according to the amount of heat preferred. Serve over fluffy white rice.

> 3 tablespoons olive oil
> 1 dozen jumbo shrimp, peeled and butterflied with tail on
> 1 tablespoon minced garlic
> ¼ to ½ teaspoon cayenne
> ½ teaspoon paprika
> 4 small green onions, chopped (about ½ cup)
> 1 cup fresh pineapple cubes (1-inch)
> ¼ cup Bacardi rum

In a large, deep skillet or wok, heat olive oil over medium-high heat. Add shrimp and garlic and cook 1 minute. Add remaining ingredients and cook an additional 2 to 3 minutes. Serve immediately.

—Chris Lee, chef

CHAMPAGNE CRAB DIP

Serves 12–15

> ½ cup mayonnaise
> 8 ounces cream cheese, softened
> ¼ cup minced shallots or green onions
> ¼ cup minced red bell pepper
> ¼ cup minced purple onion
> 2 cloves garlic, minced
> ½ teaspoon paprika
> ¼ teaspoon cayenne
> ½ teaspoon Old Bay seasoning
> ½ cup champagne
> 8 ounces fresh lump crabmeat

In a food processor, combine mayonnaise and cream cheese; add shallots, bell pepper, purple onion, and garlic. Process mixture until almost smooth. Add paprika, cayenne, Old Bay seasoning, and champagne; pulse 2 or 3 times, or until combined. Transfer mixture to a bowl and gently stir in crabmeat. Chill 1 hour. Serve with tortilla chips.

—Chris Lee, chef

COFFEE RUB DUCK BREASTS

Serves 4–6

This recipe works best with the dabbling species, such pintails, widgeons, teal, and gadwalls. Of the diving species, redheads tend to have the mildest flavor.

> 3 duck breasts with skin on, filleted (6 pieces)
> ¼ cup olive oil

Coffee Rub

> ½ cup ground coffee
> ¼ cup seasoned salt
> 1 tablespoon garlic powder
> 1½ tablespoons ground black pepper
> 1½ tablespoons paprika
> 1 tablespoon sugar

Make the Coffee Rub by mixing all ingredients together.

Preheat oven to 425 degrees. Thoroughly rub both sides of each duck breast with the Coffee Rub. Line a baking sheet with foil. In a large skillet, heat olive oil over medium heat. Cooking only a few at a time, brown the breasts for 1 minute on each side and transfer to the baking sheet. Repeat with remaining duck breasts. Bake 8 to 10 minutes, or until the internal temperature reaches 135 to 140 degrees (for medium rare). Serve immediately.

—Chris Lee, chef

TROUT-MANGO CEVICHE

Serves 8–10

The acid in the lime juice "cooks" the fish as it marinates. Serve with fried corn tortilla chips. The amount of cayenne used in the recipe can be adjusted according to the amount of heat preferred.

4 fresh trout fillets, sliced thin
1 cup diced fresh tomatoes
½ cup diced purple onion
1½ tablespoons minced fresh garlic
1¼ cups fresh lime juice
½ to 1 teaspoon cayenne
1½ teaspoons paprika
1 cup diced fresh mango
½ cup finely chopped fresh cilantro
Salt to taste

In a large, nonreactive bowl, mix trout fillets, tomatoes, onion, garlic, lime juice, cayenne, and paprika, making sure all ingredients are evenly coated with lime juice. Refrigerate at least 10 minutes or up to 1 hour. Just before serving, add mango and cilantro and mix well. Season with salt. Serve immediately.

—*Chris Lee, chef*

Opposite: Good food and good company

PORT "A" SEAFOOD COMPANY

◈ **Port Aransas**

Some may proclaim knowledge of a certain industry, but Linda Gilley has lived her profession from every imaginable angle. Over the past twenty years, there aren't too many jobs involving shrimp, fish, and crabs that she hasn't experienced firsthand.

When Linda and her late husband, Buddy, moved from Beaumont to Port Aransas in 1990, they decided that Buddy's commercial fishing background might allow them to make a successful start in the restaurant business.

In 1992 the Gilleys purchased Yankee and Betty's Seafood Galley restaurant and later renamed it in honor of Buddy's primary passion: flounder fishing. Gilley's Flounder Run enjoyed a six-year stay on Alister Street, but the couple eventually decided that a smaller, family-operated business would better suit their tastes.

In 1999 the Gilleys opened Port "A" Seafood Company and rapidly developed a loyal, statewide clientele. Early on, Linda and their son Colby would tend the store while Buddy gigged flounder and managed the catch from their own pair of shrimp boats and a number of contract vessels between Port Aransas and Louisiana. Since Buddy's death in November of 2006, Linda's brother, Kenny Greene, has joined the team as general manager, and Colby has assumed his dad's commercial fishing role.

Port "A" Seafood is proud of its "always fresh" catch, but according to Linda, there is also an exacting degree of service and presentation to which the restaurant adheres. "Customers appreciate the gifts, marinades, and home-cooked extras that we sell," Linda explained, "and they also appreciate a clean store that doesn't smell like a fish house."

Linda Gilley and crew
Opposite: Clearing the jetties at sunrise

Fourth of July in Port Aransas

FRESH TUNA PÂTÉ

Serves 12–16 as an appetizer

18 ounces ahi-grade tuna
¼ cup freshly squeezed lemon juice
⅔ cup finely chopped red onion
1 cup mayonnaise
½ cup sun-dried tomatoes
¼ cup fresh basil leaves
Salt and pepper to taste

Lightly steam fresh tuna until opaque but not dry. Drain any excess moisture. Transfer to a food processor and add lemon juice, red onion, mayonnaise, tomatoes, and basil. Pulse until consistency is smooth and spreadable. Add salt and pepper to taste. Pack into a serving crock and refrigerate at least 2 hours before serving. Serve with crackers.

—Port "A" Seafood Company

YAKITORI SAUCE

Yakitori is a Japanese method of grilling chicken on skewers with a spicy sauce. This adaptation of the sauce is great for basting and marinating tuna steaks, grilled fish, and shrimp.

½ cup soy sauce
2 tablespoons canola oil
2 tablespoons fresh lemon juice
1 tablespoon white sesame seeds
2 green onions, thinly sliced
1 clove garlic, finely minced

Place all ingredients in a medium bowl and blend until oil is thoroughly incorporated.

—Port "A" Seafood Company

C. J.'S SHRIMP CEVICHE

Serves 3–4

1½ pounds fresh shrimp, peeled and cleaned
2 Roma tomatoes
1 large red onion
1 fresh jalapeño pepper
4 fresh serrano peppers
1½ tablespoons fresh cilantro
¼ cup extra-virgin olive oil
1½ tablespoons salt
1 tablespoon freshly ground black pepper
4 fresh lemons
4 fresh limes

Lightly steam shrimp; drain and chop into small bite-size pieces. Be careful not to overcook the shrimp, or it will become tough after marinating in the citrus juices. Finely chop tomatoes, onion, peppers, and cilantro; mix with shrimp. Add olive oil, salt, and pepper; squeeze the lemons and limes over the mixture. Stir gently but thoroughly. Refrigerate 3 hours, stirring every hour. Serve with corn tortilla chips or crackers.

—Colby Gilley, Port "A" Seafood Company

A sampling of fine seafood from the Coastal Bend

REMOULADE SAUCE

Yield: 2 cups

This is a wonderful sauce for crab cakes and shrimp.

2 tablespoons freshly squeezed lemon juice
1 tablespoon distilled white vinegar
4 tablespoons Cajun or Creole mustard
2 tablespoons prepared horseradish
½ teaspoon salt
1 teaspoon black pepper
2 teaspoons paprika
Cayenne pepper to taste
2 tablespoons ketchup
½ tablespoon sugar
1 cup canola oil
½ cup finely chopped celery
½ cup minced green onions

In a food processor fitted with metal blade, add all ingredients in order except oil, celery, and green onions. Pulse 5 or 6 times to blend. With the machine running, slowly add oil and mix for several minutes, or until mixture has thickened to the consistency of a thin mayonnaise and oil is completely incorporated. Add celery and green onions and continue mixing for an additional 1 minute, or until well blended. Refrigerate at least 1 hour before serving (the mixture will thicken as it chills).

—Port "A" Seafood Company

Yellowfin tuna: strong on the hook and mild on the grill (below)
Opposite: Kingfish aren't necessarily the greatest-tasting fish in the Gulf, but they're a ton of fun to catch.

SHELLS PASTA & SEAFOOD

◈ **Port Aransas**

Heber Stone IV and family had a long history in the restaurant business before moving to Port Aransas in 1988. With past interests in several Austin and Hill Country restaurants, the Stones recognized a promising opportunity when they first arrived on Mustang Island. In a town dominated for decades by fried fish, shrimp, and oysters, Heber felt that a quaint eatery offering fresh grilled and sautéed seafood might prosper in a sleepy fishing town that appeared on the verge of a significant population and tourism boom.

In January of 1996, Heber and his son, Heber V, opened Shells Pasta & Seafood on the corner of Eleventh Street and Avenue G. Word spread quickly around town that the Stone family was serving fresh gourmet seafood at a fair price. With fewer than a dozen tables in the small dining room, it wasn't long before lines started forming well before dinnertime.

The Stones have recently added shaded patio seating, but Shells hasn't expanded nearly as fast as the tax base of Port Aransas. "We prefer an intimate and unpretentious atmosphere," explains Heber V. "On any given night you might find couples dressed up for a date, sitting right next to a group of anglers wearing shorts and flip-flops."

Beyond its fresh seafood, Shells is known for its extensive list of wines from Italy, California, and Texas. All breads and desserts are made from scratch, and the seafood and pasta menu reflects a broad range of influence from Asia and Latin America. It's doubtful that you'll find a fried seafood sampler on their menu, but that means you'll have plenty of room for a great appetizer, entrée, and dessert.

The Heber Stone family
Opposite: Sport fishers in the harbor at Port Aransas

Gulf Coast • 279

GRILLED AMBERJACK WITH TOMATILLO SAUCE

Serves 4

4 (8-ounce) amberjack fillets

Tomatillo Sauce

4 or 5 medium tomatillos (about ½ pound)
¼ cup fresh lime juice
¼ cup chicken stock or broth
1 fresh jalapeño pepper
4 cilantro sprigs
1 tablespoon minced garlic
½ cup chopped onion
Salt and pepper to taste

To make the sauce, remove husks from tomatillos and boil until soft, about 10 minutes. Cool slightly. Transfer to food processor or blender and add remaining ingredients. Blend until smooth and set aside.

Grill amberjack fillets until opaque and serve with Tomatillo Sauce.

—*Shells Pasta & Seafood*

Lars Koster with an amberjack, a belligerent battler around the rigs and rock piles in the Gulf

CRAB FINGER DRESSING

Yield: 5 cups

This recipe makes more than enough dressing to marinate a pound of crab fingers; however, it will keep for a week in the refrigerator and is excellent as a marinade for fresh, boiled shrimp and even as a salad dressing. Be sure to use fresh garlic; the prepared minced garlic sold in jars at supermarkets can give this dressing a bitter taste.

> 24 cloves or 2 heads fresh garlic, coarsely chopped (½ cup)
> 2⅔ tablespoons Dijon mustard
> 1¼ tablespoons salt
> 1 teaspoon pepper
> ⅔ cup balsamic vinegar
> 1 cup red wine vinegar
> ⅓ cup walnut oil
> 2⅔ cups olive oil
> 1 pound fresh crab fingers

In a food processor, combine garlic, mustard, salt, pepper, and vinegars and pulse 3 or 4 times, or until well blended. With machine running, slowly add oils and process until well blended. Pour 2 cups of the dressing over the crab fingers and chill at least 30 minutes before serving. Refrigerate the remaining dressing for another use.

—Shells Pasta & Seafood

TUNA STEAK WITH JAPANESE MAYONNAISE

Serves 6

The wasabi powder and Sriracha sauce can be found with the Asian foods in most major supermarkets.

> 6 (4-ounce) yellowfin tuna fillets
> Freshly ground pepper to taste

Japanese Mayonnaise

> ¾ cup good-quality mayonnaise
> ¼ teaspoon wasabi powder
> 1 tablespoon Sriracha sauce
> 1 tablespoon sour cream
> 1 tablespoon whipping cream
> 2 or 3 drops sesame oil

To make the mayonnaise, whisk all ingredients together and set aside.

Season tuna fillets on both sides with pepper. Heat skillet or grill to high heat. Sear tuna on both sides, being careful not to overcook. Serve with Japanese Mayonnaise.

—Shells Pasta & Seafood

Below: Shells, a quaint establishment serving great seafood in Port Aransas. John Wagster launching a plug near Wilson's Cut.

Clockwise from top: A meticulously organized selection of leaders, jigs, and feathers. Little boat, big water. Allyson Smith (left) and Emily Brown: two keepers and one throwback on a fine summer evening.

LISABELLA'S BISTRO

⊞ Port Aransas

After fourteen years in the hotel catering and food service business in San Antonio, Kris Amundsen decided that a sandwich shop in the downtown tourist and business district might offer a new challenge and a break from the established routine. His business plan was nearly complete in the summer of 2004 when friends invited Kris, his wife, Lisa, and their three children to Port Aransas for a weekend on the beach.

"Lisa's grandmother had a beach house in Port Aransas that she built back in 1964," Kris recalled. "We've always loved the island, and we spent a lot of time there before she finally sold the house in 2000."

By the time they returned to San Antonio, their business plan had unofficially changed and the Amundsens were making plans to revisit Port Aransas for a research trip. A few weeks later Kris and Lisa drove back down and spent a couple of days dining around town and visiting with realtors about the business climate on Mustang Island.

"The sandwich shop idea didn't seem right for Port Aransas," Kris explained, "so we started thinking about an upscale seafood bistro with a home-style atmosphere." When their realtor called and announced that the two-story yellow house on Cotter Street was for sale, the Amundsens jumped at the opportunity and moved to Port Aransas.

Fine seafood on Cotter Street

Opposite: Moment of truth for Mike Siegman on Redfish Bay

In May of 2005 Lisabella's opened next door to the old Tarpon Inn. The restaurant's menu is constantly evolving, but its specialty will always be fresh seafood. "We get our fish from Hawaii, the Atlantic, and right here in the Gulf," Kris explained. "Our intent is to serve absolutely the best ingredients available."

Since most fresh seafood is seasonal, Kris and Lisa are constantly changing their menu with an offering of seven to nine fresh entrées per night. "I guess you could best describe our menu as fusion cooking," said Kris. "We like to combine different regional influences into one great dish."

Recreation and industry at the tip of the North Jetty

Coy Radley waiting for the grab

GRILLED WAHOO
WITH COCONUT CURRY SAUCE

Serves 6

This sauce also makes an excellent marinade for grilled shrimp.

    6 (8-ounce) wahoo fillets

Coconut Curry Sauce

    1 tablespoon olive oil
    ¼ cup finely diced red onion
    1½ tablespoons curry powder
    ½ teaspoon cayenne pepper
    ½ teaspoon paprika
    ¼ cup honey
    2 cups heavy cream
    1 can (14-ounce) coconut milk
    Pinch of salt
    Pepper to taste

Make the Coconut Curry Sauce. In a medium saucepan, heat olive oil over medium heat. Sauté onion, curry powder, cayenne, and paprika about 30 seconds. Add honey, cream, coconut milk, salt, and pepper. Reduce heat to a simmer and cook until sauce thickens, about 8 to 10 minutes. Remove from heat and keep warm.

    Preheat oven to 375 degrees. Grill wahoo fillets 2 minutes per side, then finish in the oven for 6 to 8 minutes. Serve with warm Coconut Curry Sauce.

    —*Luke Amundsen, Lisabella's Bistro*

BLUE CRAB ENCHILADAS WITH MANGO-JALAPEÑO CREAM SAUCE

Allow two enchiladas per person as a main course or one per person as an appetizer. Mango purée can be purchased frozen at specialty grocery stores, or you can make your own.

Vegetable oil
12 fresh corn tortillas
1 pound fresh lump crabmeat
3 large red bell peppers, roasted, peeled, and diced
6 large poblano peppers, roasted, peeled, and diced
12 ounces Pepper Jack cheese, grated

Mango-Jalapeño Cream Sauce

¾ cup butter
½ cup diced Roma tomatoes
½ cup diced red onion
½ cup diced fresh mango
1½ fresh jalapeño peppers, diced (remove seeds for a milder sauce)
2 cups heavy cream
½ cup mango purée (see note)
Salt and ground white pepper to taste

Make the Mango-Jalapeño Cream Sauce. In a medium saucepan, slowly melt butter. Add tomatoes, onion, mango, and jalapeños; cook 1 minute. Add cream and bring to a boil. Reduce heat to a simmer and stir in mango purée. Season with salt and white pepper, set aside, and keep warm.

Preheat oven to 375 degrees. Lightly grease a baking sheet and set aside. In a small skillet, heat oil over medium heat. To soften tortillas, dip each into hot oil for 10 seconds and place on paper towels to drain. Pat tortillas dry to remove excess oil.

Fill each tortilla with 3 tablespoons of the crabmeat and 1 tablespoon each of the diced peppers and grated cheese. Roll gently (not too tightly) and place on the prepared baking sheet. Pour 1 tablespoon of the Mango-Jalapeño Cream Sauce over each enchilada and sprinkle with the remaining cheese. Bake about 7 minutes, or until cheese is lightly browned on the edges. Remove from oven and place on warmed plates. Cover with warm cream sauce and serve immediately.

NOTE: To make your own mango purée, combine the flesh of 1 medium mango with 2 tablespoons sugar in a food processor and process until smooth. Yield: about 1 cup.

—*Lisabella's Bistro*

GRILLED RED SNAPPER WITH CILANTRO-LIME BUTTER

··
Serves 4

4 (6- to 8-ounce) snapper fillets
½ cup olive oil
4 tablespoons lime juice
Salt and pepper to taste
4 lime wedges
4 cilantro sprigs

Cilantro-Lime Butter

1 tablespoon olive oil
½ shallot, finely chopped
2 cloves garlic, finely minced
1 cup heavy cream
2 tablespoons fresh lime juice
½ cup (1 stick) chilled butter, cut into small pieces
¾ cup chopped cilantro
Salt and black pepper to taste
Cayenne pepper to taste

Make the Cilantro-Lime Butter. In a small saucepan, heat olive oil over medium heat. Add shallot and garlic and sauté until tender. Whisk in cream and lime juice and bring to a boil, stirring occasionally. Cook until reduced by half. Whisk in butter, a few pieces at a time, allowing butter to melt and combine with sauce before adding more. Stir in cilantro and adjust seasonings. Remove from heat and keep warm.

Preheat oven to 375 degrees. Place snapper fillets in a shallow nonreactive dish. Combine olive oil, lime juice, and seasonings and pour over fillets. Marinate at room temperature.

While fillets are marinating, preheat grill to high. Remove fillets from marinade and grill over hot coals for 2 to 3 minutes. Transfer to a baking sheet and finish cooking in preheated oven until flesh is opaque and flakes easily with a fork, about 5 to 8 minutes. Garnish each fillet with a lime wedge and cilantro sprig; serve immediately with Cilantro-Lime Butter.

—Lisabella's Bistro

Will Myers demonstrating his inimitable kinship with redfish (above). Daniel Dain with a red snapper dinner for three (below).

PORT BAY HUNTING & FISHING CLUB

◈ **Rockport**

In 1912 Danish immigrant Andrew Sorenson purchased 240 acres of land on the eastern shore of Port Bay, near Rockport. With an established reputation as a hunting and fishing guide, Sorenson built the Port Bay Hunting & Fishing Club on his new property and set about recruiting an exclusive membership of waterfowl and bay-fishing enthusiasts. Private shares in the club were sold at $150 per person, and the offering was closed when the club roster reached one hundred members. Many of the original charter members were from Texas, but the Port Bay Club also attracted sportsmen from New York, Chicago, St. Louis, Cincinnati, and Atlanta.

My grandfather joined the club around 1930, and at that time the highway infrastructure to the Texas coast was relatively spotty. From his home in Corsicana, he would load his gear onto the train and connect with the old San Antonio and Aransas Pass Railroad to reach the club. As a child, my father recalls the excitement of waiting at the train station in Corsicana for my grandfather's return from the hunt. This was long before Igloo, Coleman, and injection-molded plastic, so the ducks, drawn and plucked, rode home on the train from Port Bay in wooden barrels packed with ice.

In 1971 I was able to tag along on my first Port Bay duck hunt with my father and grandfather. Rail travel to the coast was no longer necessary, but the club still utilized its established traditions of wooden

Policy and practice of a century-old sporting club on the Texas coast

Opposite: Wooden skiffs in formation

skiffs, wooden decoys, a limited membership, and fabulous hunting and fishing. From the age of five through my high school years, we spent the week between Christmas and New Year's Day at Port Bay, and those memories of decoying ducks, blasting north winds, and the clang of the 5:00 a.m. wake-up bell are forever etched in my mind.

Today the Port Bay Club is still ginning along in its original clubhouse facility, which will soon celebrate its one-hundredth birthday. The old wooden decoys have been retired—except for very special occasions—but the wooden skiffs, the boat blinds, the wake-up bell, and a century of hunting and fishing tradition are still in place.

Banking pintails over Lower Bay
Opposite, left to right: A drake widgeon, one of the more vocal and communal ducks on the Texas coast. Lab on a mission.

LEIGH ANN'S SEAFOOD SEASONING

Yield: 3½ cups

This is a bold and spicy mixture. Sprinkle on fish and seafood before baking, broiling, or grilling.

> 1 bag whole-spice crab boil
> 2 tablespoons red pepper flakes
> 3 tablespoons Old Bay seasoning
> ¼ cup Tony Chachere's or Zatarain's Creole seasoning
> ¼ cup lemon pepper seasoning
> 1 tablespoon dried oregano
> 1 tablespoon dried basil
> 1 tablespoon dried rosemary
> 1 tablespoon dried thyme
> 1 tablespoon dried tarragon
> Pinch of dried sage, optional
> 4 tablespoons garlic powder
> 2 tablespoons onion powder
> ¾ cup paprika
> 1½ tablespoons whole black peppercorns
> 2 tablespoons kosher salt

Mix all ingredients together. Working in batches, grind mixture in a spice grinder until finely ground. Store in a glass jar in a cool dark place.

—Leigh Ann Brister, chef

REDFISH CAKES

Yield: about 20 cakes

Black drum, speckled trout, or flounder can be used in this recipe instead of redfish. The cakes can be pan-fried instead of baked. The bread crumbs can be made from any bread, including biscuits and corn bread.

> 1½ pounds fresh redfish, diced
> 2 tablespoons finely diced red bell pepper
> 2 tablespoons finely diced yellow bell pepper
> 2 tablespoons finely chopped green onion tops
> 2 tablespoons finely diced red onion
> 1 tablespoon dried parsley flakes
> 1 tablespoon Leigh Ann's Seafood Seasoning or to taste (page 293)
> 1 cup cold cooked rice
> 1 cup fresh bread crumbs plus additional as needed
> 1 egg, beaten, or ¼ cup mayonnaise

Preheat oven to 450 degrees. Line a baking sheet with parchment. Gently mix together fish, peppers, onions, seasonings, rice, and bread crumbs. Add egg and just enough additional crumbs to bind mixture. Using a 2-ounce ice cream scoop or a ¼-cup measuring cup, scoop up portions and drop on the prepared baking sheet. Flatten cakes slightly and spray with cooking spray. Bake about 20 minutes.

—Leigh Ann Brister, chef

STUFFED WHOLE FLOUNDER

Serves 4–6

The Seafood and Cheese Stuffing can also be used to make seafood cakes or to stuff fish fillets. The mixture freezes well.

    4 (1½-pound) whole flounder, cleaned and scaled with heads removed
    4 cups Seafood and Cheese Stuffing

Seafood and Cheese Stuffing

Yield: about 6 cups

    ½ pound cooked crabmeat or chopped imitation crab
    ½ pound cooked tiny shrimp or crawfish
    ½ pound shredded cheese (a combination of at least two different types, such as Cheddar, mozzarella, Monterey Jack, Colby, provolone, or Swiss)
    ⅓ cup finely diced red bell pepper
    ⅓ cup finely diced yellow bell pepper
    ⅓ cup finely diced orange bell pepper
    1 cup finely diced red onion
    ¼ cup thinly sliced green onion tops
    ¼ cup finely diced celery
    1 loaf (24-ounce) bread, made into crumbs
    1 tablespoon Worcestershire sauce
    ½ tablespoon Tabasco sauce, or to taste
    2 tablespoons Cajun or Creole seasoning, or to taste
    ¼ cup Dijon mustard
    Mayonnaise as needed

To make the Seafood and Cheese Stuffing, combine all ingredients except mayonnaise, mixing well. Add just enough mayonnaise to bind the mixture together.

    Preheat oven to 400 degrees. Lightly grease a baking sheet. Working with one flounder at a time, slice the dark side of each fish down the middle. Without cutting all the way through, slice toward each side to create a pocket. Fill each pocket with about 1 cup of the stuffing, mounding it on top. Place fish on the prepared baking sheet and bake 20 minutes, or until fish is opaque. Serve immediately.

—Leigh Ann Brister, chef

Flounder on ice (abpve). Speckled trout from the shell reefs in Copano Bay (below).

HOT AND SPICY SPECK PO' BOY

Yield: 1 sandwich

Serve this sandwich with Yogurt-Fried Red Onion Rings and extra Remoulade Slaw on the side. The sauce used in the slaw can be made in advance and stored in the refrigerator.

- 1 pound fresh speckled trout fillets, cut into strips
- 1 cup buttermilk
- 2 tablespoons Tony Chachere's Creole seasoning
- ¼ cup hot pepper sauce
- Oil for frying
- Flour for dredging
- 2 thick slices French bread
- Mayonnaise
- Leaf lettuce
- 1 slice ripe tomato
- 2 slices Tasso ham, warmed in a skillet
- Yogurt-Fried Red Onion Rings (page 295)

Red Remoulade Sauce

Yield: about 4 cups

- 1½ cups thick homemade mayonnaise or best-quality prepared mayonnaise
- ½ cup Creole mustard
- 1 tablespoon Worcestershire sauce
- 1 teaspoon hot sauce
- ½ cup Heinz Hot & Spicy Ketchup or chili sauce
- ¼ cup minced red bell pepper
- ¼ cup minced yellow bell pepper
- ½ cup minced celery
- 2 tablespoons minced garlic
- ¼ cup minced fresh parsley
- ½ tablespoon fresh lemon juice
- Salt and freshly ground pepper to taste

Remoulade Slaw

- 4 cups shredded iceberg lettuce
- ¾ cup shredded red cabbage
- ¾ cup Red Remoulade Sauce

Place fish strips in a nonreactive container. In a separate bowl, mix buttermilk, Creole seasoning, and pepper sauce. Pour over fish, cover, and refrigerate 1 hour.

Meanwhile, prepare the Red Remoulade Sauce by combining all ingredients and mixing well. Refrigerate until ready to use.

Heat oil to 350 degrees. Drain fish strips and dredge in flour. Fry until golden brown and drain on paper towels.

While fish strips are frying, prepare the Remoulade Slaw by combining all ingredients. Set aside.

To assemble the sandwich, spread a thin coating of mayonnaise on one side of each bread slice. Heat a griddle or skillet over medium-high heat and toast bread slices, mayonnaise side down, until golden brown. Place lettuce, tomato slice, fish strips, ham, and ¼ cup Remoulade Slaw on the untoasted side of one slice. Sprinkle with additional hot pepper sauce for a spicier sandwich. Top with the second slice of bread and serve immediately.

—Leigh Ann Brister, chef

YOGURT-FRIED RED ONION RINGS

- 1 large red onion, sliced ¼ inch thick
- 2 tablespoons vinegar
- ½ cup plain yogurt
- Seasonings to taste (such as salt, pepper, Cajun, etc.)
- Flour for dredging
- Oil for frying

Preheat oven to 200 degrees. Separate onion slices into rings and place in a large Ziploc bag; add vinegar, mix thoroughly, and then drain. Mix yogurt and seasonings in a small bowl. Fill a deep pot half full of oil and heat to 375 degrees. Dip onion rings in seasoned yogurt, dredge in flour, and fry a few at a time until golden and crispy. Drain on paper towels and keep warm in oven.

—Leigh Ann Brister, chef

LODGE ON THE ARROYO

⬖ Arroyo City

Waco native Ray Box is an avid angler and consummate do-it-yourselfer. After graduating from Southwest Texas State in 1977, Ray moved to New Braunfels and took a job teaching drafting and photography before launching a successful career as a builder and remodeler. While renovating and expanding the old Grist Mill in historic Gruene, Ray warehoused his shop and materials in a vacant storefront just down the street from the evolving restaurant and dance hall.

As the Grist Mill project neared completion, Ray recognized a potential business opportunity sitting just a few minutes away from the trout fishery on the Guadalupe River. In 1989 he leased his former warehouse and set about converting it, by hand, into a full-service fly shop. Gruene Outfitters did well during the fly-fishing boom of the 1990s, but the real test came when the Internet allowed virtual storefronts to sidestep the brick-and-mortar fly shops and saturate the market with inexpensive tackle. A number of Texas fly-fishing retailers have closed their doors in recent years, but Gruene Outfitters is still going strong, and Ray feels that his proximity to Austin, San Antonio, and the Guadalupe as well as the popularity of historic Gruene have served him well.

In the fall of 2000, Ray couldn't pass up an opportunity to diversify when he found a home for sale in Arroyo City on the banks of the Arroyo Colorado with quick access to the prolific flats fishery on the Lower Laguna Madre. After converting the home into a quaint, eight-bed facility, Ray opened Lodge on

The dining room at Lodge on the Arroyo
Opposite: Redfish rooting shrimp out of the grass beds

the Arroyo with an idea that professionals with limited time for arranging piecemeal fishing trips might seek out a small lodge located just minutes from tailing redfish and the Valley International Airport in Harlingen.

Having fished in the salt since 1979, Ray admits that the shallow flats hold a special allure. He loves to see a tarpon jump, but it's the Texas redfish that really gets him going. "Sight-casting to reds is exciting and rewarding," Ray explained. "They're not easy to catch, and it requires interaction between the angler and guide. If I could fish for only one species, it would probably have to be redfish."

Ray Box hosing down his skiff (above). An eclectic selection of redfish and trout flies (right).

GRILLED REDFISH VERACRUZ

1 or 2 redfish fillets per person
Lemon juice
Melted butter
Salt and pepper to taste

Veracruz Sauce

2 tablespoons olive oil
1 onion, chopped
2 cloves garlic, minced
5 or 6 medium tomatoes, chopped (3 cups)
½ cup prepared salsa or diced Rotel tomatoes
1 cup sliced green olives with pimientos
Salt and pepper to taste

Make the Veracruz Sauce. Heat olive oil over medium-high heat and sauté onion and garlic until tender. Add tomatoes, salsa, and olives, stirring until thoroughly combined. Season with salt and pepper. Reduce heat to low, cover, and simmer while grilling fish.

Preheat grill to high. Brush fillets with lemon juice and melted butter. Season with salt and pepper. Place fish on a wire screen and cook until the center of the fillet flakes and the edges begin to brown. Serve with Veracruz Sauce.

—Lodge on the Arroyo

BROILED REDFISH PARMESAN ON THE HALF SHELL

1 or 2 redfish fillets per person, with skin on
Garlic salt to taste
Lemon pepper to taste
2 tablespoons mayonnaise per fillet
¼ cup grated Parmesan cheese per fillet

Arrange oven rack 5 to 6 inches from heat source. Pat fillets dry and place them, skin side down, on a cookie sheet. Season fillets with garlic salt and lemon pepper. Spread mayonnaise in a thin, even layer over each fillet. Sprinkle cheese over mayonnaise. Broil until top is golden brown and fish is flaky throughout.

—Lodge on the Arroyo

MARIA'S SAUTÉED TROUT WITH CILANTRO

Serves 2

2 or 3 speckled trout fillets per person
Salt and pepper to taste
2 tablespoons olive oil
¼ cup white wine
¼ cup chopped fresh cilantro
Lime wedges

Pat fillets dry and season both sides with salt and pepper. In a large skillet, heat olive oil over medium-high heat. Add fillets to skillet and cook until the undersides begin to brown. Turn, add wine, and continue cooking until fish begins to flake. Remove from heat, sprinkle cilantro over each fillet, and serve immediately with lime wedges.

—Maria Ruiz, lodge cook

Snook are making a comeback on the lower Texas coast after decades of overharvest and a couple of killer freezes during the 1980s.

Opposite: A push pole can be a fine tool for deflecting an errant backcast (above). Speckled trout (below).

EAST TEXAS

TECHNICALLY, I AM NOT FROM EAST TEXAS. Depending on which official geographical analysis of the state you are referencing, my hometown of Corsicana is categorized as part of the Prairies and Lakes, Blackland Prairie, or Post Oak region of Texas. Technically, I guess I'm a multi-categorized Texan; I am a man without a region.

But even though I wasn't actually born in the Piney Woods proper, I did spend quite a bit of my youth east of the Trinity River where my family had a lake house on Cedar Creek Reservoir. We had red dirt, pine trees, sandburs, dewberries, and copperheads in our yard, and my father poured and molded his own plastic worms for bass fishing. If nothing else, that one should at least get me a few style points.

I haven't been back to Cedar Creek in over twenty years; and since I've spent significant time in other regions of the state during that time, I can now look back, somewhat objectively, and offer evidence to support my claim that East Texas is at least partially responsible for my upbringing.

Of the people I've met in my adult life who are not from East Texas, I've yet to find anyone who will

admit that they've ever aspired to trap coons for spending money, gigged frogs on a date, or missed a day of school because of a skunk (that was my brother, not me). And furthermore, I've yet to find anyone who has ever hunted gar at night with a crossbow, fished for carp with homemade dough balls, or used worms and a hand line to catch bream for trotline bait. Incidentally, I gave up that business in the summer of my fourth-grade year when I pulled up my set one morning and found a 5:1 ratio of snakes to catfish.

So at the risk of carrying this burden of proof any further and turning this chapter into some Foxworthy-like testament, I'll stop now and let the record speak for itself. I might've been born west of the Trinity, but when it comes to Piney Woods folk, I can hobnob with the best of them.

Distinct proliferations and collapses have occurred in the various fish and game species in East Texas since I was a kid. Leading the demise list, sadly, is the bobwhite quail. I can remember flushing a few wild coveys in the open pastures around my hometown in the mid-1970s, but that was before fire ants,

and before coastal Bermuda grass and fence-to-fence farming converted the quail country in East Texas into a hygienic bi-culture of improved pastures and cropland.

The feral hog occupation of East Texas is both a good and a bad thing, depending on your perspective. If your livelihood depends on grain, fruit, or vegetable production, then you probably don't think too highly of their proclivity for trampling and root-plowing. Outfitters, on the other hand, are typically a bit more passive in their distaste for feral hogs; they hate them only up until the point that a hog hunter writes them a check.

With respect to waterfowl, the losses and victories mainly relate to the health of their nesting grounds. Mallards and pintails nest in Canada and the northern prairies, where persistent drought and plowing have reduced their nesting cover. Wood ducks nest right here in Texas, and they love the cozy little wooden boxes that we've nailed up throughout their range.

In the category of significant wildlife triumphs in East Texas, there are two notable victors. When I was a

kid, an eight-pound bass could win you a trophy—maybe even a new trolling motor—and a hero shot in the local paper. That same fish today might still win you a token tournament prize, but now it's the fourteen-pounder that'll take home the major chips. Big bass are now worth big bucks; and wherever there's money, there's also sound management. The whitetail deer has likewise done remarkably well in recent years. In 1970 a legitimate buck sighting in the river bottoms of Anderson County would fuel a week's worth of coffee shop conversation. Today there are reported densities of one deer per ten acres on some of those farms.

The cooking culture of the Piney Woods has been largely influenced by the westward migration of Cajun and Old South plantation-style dishes (if it dies, it fries). Within these pages you'll find a time-honored selection of game and fish favorites from the lakes, pine forests, and bottomlands. The views may be tighter and the landholdings significantly smaller in East Texas, but this is one area of the state where all manner of hunting and fishing pursuits are represented: rod, gun, bow, gig, and string.

COON CREEK CLUB

In January of 1902, East Texans J. H. Miller, J. A. Pondren, and S. L. French drew up a private charter for an exclusive hunting and fishing club located eight miles south of the town square in Athens. Their plan was to construct a clubhouse and a series of dams on Coon Creek, which flowed through the sandy hills and fertile hardwood bottoms of southern Henderson County. During the warmer months they planned to fish for bass, bream, and crappie; in the fall they would stow their rods and hunt for ducks and squirrels.

For many years the Coon Creek Club was primarily a gentleman's retreat for the 145 voting members and their guests. Membership criteria were strict, and the mission statement was clear: Coon Creek was a sporting club where businessmen could escape the stress and demands of professional life. Casual dress was required; relaxation and fellowship were encouraged.

The original clubhouse lasted until 1942, when it was destroyed by fire. At that point, a new main lodge was built, and many of the members began constructing private lakefront homes on the club's grounds. The fabulous fishing at Coon Creek was interrupted in 1944 when flooding rains breached the dams and drained the lakes. Reconstruction was exhaustive, but the lakes were eventually rebuilt and the club's main attraction soon returned to form.

Today the original Coon Creek property has expanded to over 7,500 acres, but the membership remains fixed at 145 voters. Wives and children are welcomed, and family festivities are scheduled for most holiday weekends. Bass fishing still reigns supreme,

The Orval Anding Room, where daily blind and lake assignments are drawn and posted

Opposite: Bryan Pickens casting for October bass. Decades-old boathouses at Coon Creek.

and the lakes at Coon Creek are now managed by a committee of members that oversees the stocking of forage fish, weed control, brood pond management, and harvest recommendations.

As whitetails have increased in East Texas after decades of overharvest, the club has also adapted an intensive management program with habitat enhancement, supplemental feeding, and strict harvest criteria. Each season, for a member to qualify for a trophy whitetail, he must first harvest a prescribed number of does, cull bucks, and feral hogs.

Even though habitat, game, and fish management principles have changed significantly over the years, the traditional premise of the Coon Creek Club remains intact. There are no tennis courts, ATVs are not allowed, and over the years the members have voted down several motions for a community swimming pool. Coon Creek is a sporting club, not a country club. Swimming in the lakes isn't prohibited, but it's not exactly encouraged, either. Each year the club receives a limited number of alligator permits; the largest bagged, to date, taped out at twelve feet two inches.

An mid-size bass caught on a jig-n-pig (above). Working the lily pads with a topwater plug (below).

310 • GRAZING ACROSS TEXAS

CRAPPIE-STUFFED CHAYOTE SQUASH

Serves 4

6 boned crappie fillets
Butter for sautéeing
2 chayote squash, peeled and halved
2 or 3 green onions, minced
2 or 3 cloves garlic, minced
2 teaspoons fresh thyme leaves
2 tablespoons fresh lemon juice
3 crackers, crushed
Salt and pepper to taste
Grated mozzarella cheese

Preheat oven to 350 degrees. Sauté crappie fillets in butter until tender. Set aside to cool. Place squash, cut side down, in a microwave-safe dish, add water to a depth of about ¼ inch, and microwave until fork-tender, about 8 minutes. Sauté green onions, garlic, and thyme in butter until tender. Transfer to a bowl and add fillets; mix until well combined. Stir in lemon juice and crackers and season with salt and pepper. Spoon fish into squash halves and top with grated cheese. Bake until heated throughout, about 20 minutes.

—Bea McCall Watson, club member

BEER BATTER FISH

3 eggs, separated
1 clove garlic, cut in half
1 cup beer
1 cup flour
1 teaspoon salt
½ teaspoon paprika
Bass or crappie fillets

Beat egg whites until stiff and set aside. Rub a mixing bowl with garlic and add beer, flour, salt, and paprika, mixing well. Just before frying the fillets, fold egg whites into beer mixture and combine well. Dip fillets in batter and deep-fry at 380 degrees for 3 to 4 minutes, or until golden brown.

—E. H. Hulsey, club member

FISH ALEXANDRIA

In this recipe the cream thickens as the fish bakes, creating a flavorful sauce.

1 or 2 bass or crappie fillets per person
Fresh lemon juice
Garlic, minced
Flour
Salt and pepper
Butter
1 quart whipping cream

Preheat oven to 350 degrees. Rub fish fillets with lemon juice and garlic. Generously season flour with salt and pepper. Generously grease a skillet with butter. Dredge fillets in seasoned flour and place in the prepared skillet. Pour cream over fillets, cover, and bake 30 minutes without removing lid. After 30 minutes, check fish for doneness (it is ready when it is no longer translucent and flakes easily with a fork). Serve immediately.

—E. H. Hulsey, club member

The feisty and delicious crappie

COON CREEK BROILED FISH

Crappie or bass fillets
Cooking oil
1 tablespoon fresh lemon juice per fillet
1 tablespoon melted butter per fillet
Seasoned salt
Paprika
Thyme
Lemon pepper
Chopped parsley

Preheat broiler to 500 degrees. Place fillets in a baking dish lined with foil. Lightly coat both sides of fillets with cooking oil. Pour lemon juice and melted butter over each fillet. Sprinkle with seasoned salt, paprika, thyme, lemon pepper, and parsley. Broil until fillets begin to crisp and brown on top. Do not turn.

—*Dorothy Adleta, club member*

SQUASH SOUFFLÉ

Serves 6

This dish can be assembled in advance and baked later in the day. It also doubles easily to fill a 9 × 13-inch baking dish.

5 small zucchini or yellow squash (about 2 pounds)
1 tablespoon salt
½ pound Longhorn cheese, grated
3 eggs, well beaten
½ cup half-and-half
Salt and pepper to taste

Preheat oven to 350 degrees. Slice squash and put in saucepan with water to cover. Add salt and bring to a boil. Cook until tender, about 10 minutes. Drain well and mash. Add cheese, eggs, and half-and-half and mix well. Adjust seasonings. Pour into a greased 8 × 8-inch baking dish and bake 1 hour.

—*Bill Richards, club cook*

DUCK AND WILD RICE CASSEROLE

Serves 6

This is a great dish that works well with any species of duck (or goose); it freezes very well.

  2 ducks, with skin on
  3 ribs celery
  1 onion, halved
  Salt and pepper to taste
  1 package (6-ounce) seasoned wild and long-grain rice
  ½ cup (1 stick) butter
  ½ cup chopped onion
  ¼ cup flour
  1 can (4-ounce) sliced mushrooms
  1½ cups half-and-half
  1 tablespoon finely chopped parsley
  1½ teaspoons salt
  ¼ teaspoon freshly ground pepper
  Slivered almonds, optional

Place ducks in a large stock pot; add celery, onion halves, salt, pepper, and water to cover. Bring to a boil and cook about 1 hour, or until ducks are tender. Remove ducks from broth and cool, reserving broth. Remove meat from bones and set aside.

Preheat oven to 350 degrees. Cook rice according to package directions. Melt butter and sauté onion until soft; stir in flour and cook 1 minute. Drain mushrooms, reserving juice, and add to onion mixture. Add enough duck broth to mushroom juice to measure 1½ cups liquid; stir into onion and mushroom mixture. Add remaining ingredients except almonds. Pour into a greased 2-quart baking dish. Sprinkle with almonds and bake, covered, 15 to 20 minutes. Uncover and bake an additional 5 to 10 minutes, or until very hot.

—*Friend of Coon Creek Club*

Opposite: Remnants of a bygone era in the Coon Creek boat yard (above). A deer blind and feeding station in the deep woods (below).
A respectable Henderson County buck.

THE BIG WOODS

⊞ **Tennessee Colony**

When the jeep rolled to a stop on a levee in the fading afternoon light, Dr. Robert "Doc" McFarlane closed the bolt on his rifle and reached for his binoculars. It was cold, gray, and still with flashes of lighting in the western sky. In front of us was a dark and glassy marsh pond, a remnant oxbow left behind eons ago when the nearby Trinity River abruptly changed its course. Two miles behind us, on slightly higher ground, was the Coffield Prison Unit.

Had Doc not explained that he was trying to discourage an importunate beaver from draining another one of his hard-claimed duck marshes, you could have easily painted us into one of those classic prison-break film scenes with baying hounds, shouting guards, and desperate escapees lunging through the marsh and breaking for a distant tree line.

After spending a weekend with Doc on his 7,500 acres of Trinity bottomland, near Tennessee Colony, I realized that I had never met a person who led a more divergent existence. During the week (doctor's hours) he dons pressed clothes and tends to his heart patients in his hometown of Palestine. In that role he's the Harvard Medical School graduate preaching the virtues of a healthy lifestyle. After hours, when he returns to his spacious hunting lodge on the Trinity, he abruptly transforms into the antithesis of his workaday persona. On the weekends Doc wears muddy boots and denim overalls over camo and admits that "once people get to know me, they figure out that I'm really nothing more than a dirtball."

Doc was born and raised in Anderson County and spent his youth hunting ducks, squirrels, and deer on his family farm and land that the prison owned in

The Big Woods, Dr. Robert McFarlane's lodge on the Trinity River

Opposite: Guide Woody hailing mallards in an oxbow lake at the Big Woods

Lab heading back to the blind with a gadwall hen (right). A buddy limit of mallards and gadwalls (below).

Opposite: Hunters, dogs, waders, and jackets drying by the wood stove in the barn

the Trinity bottom. He worked in Boston for a while after medical school, but he eventually realized that the gravitational pull of his upbringing was too strong to defy.

After moving his cardiology practice back home to Palestine in 1984, Doc began buying up parcels of land that adjoined his family acreage. At that point, a commercial hunting operation wasn't part of his long-term plan. What he really hoped to accomplish was a piecemeal restoration of the pristine hardwood bottomland that he remembered from his childhood. After he had spent several years planting trees, turning under old farm fields, and continually increasing the size of his landholding, Doc's wife suggested that a means of generating income from the property might at some point become necessary.

In 2002 Doc built a two-story stone lodge on the property with a commercial kitchen, a fully stocked bar, a game room with pool, poker, and shuffleboard tables, and a surround-sound movie room with leather recliners and a popcorn machine. Adjacent to the main lodge he installed sporting clay, trap, and rifle ranges as well as a fully functional game-processing facility with power wenches, walk-in coolers, duck pluckers, and butcher saws.

Today the Big Woods offers duck hunts in the oxbow marshes that Doc can pump full and drain as rainfall dictates or in flooded green timber alongside the Trinity River. Mallards, wood ducks, and gadwalls are the primary harvest, and if you've never stood in knee-deep water and watched them spiraling through the oak canopy into your decoys, then you are living deprived of one of our greatest waterfowling spectacles.

As much as Doc would like to base his entire program on duck hunting, he'll readily admit that it's the growing legion of hog hunters that's really keeping his bread buttered. "Last year we killed 400 of the bastards and didn't dent the population," Doc recounted. "I probably shot a hundred of them myself during the summer." Doc preaches the efficacy of the head shot, and he has no problem with a hunter who brandishes a rifle capable of a rapid-burst porcine serial killing. "There have been attempts to stock turkeys back into this area—and it would be nice to get the quail back," Doc says, "but these hogs will never allow anything that nests on the ground to get a start."

In Robert McFarlane's view, leaving the land better than you found it is a noble thing. His deer herd is thriving where deer were once nothing more than scarce. During the 2006 season he turned up a couple of 160-class bucks for his hunters, and it's only a matter of time before his fertile bottomland produces a legitimate, free-ranging, record-book deer.

Doc understands that bullets are just as valuable as a tractor when it comes to wildlife management, and he's a vocal and visible proponent of the "blood sports" as a means of preserving the delicate balance of habitat and inhabitants.

DUCK BREASTS WITH BLUEBERRY SAUCE

Serves 2–3

This recipe works best with larger ducks, such as mallards, gadwalls, and pintails. Try this one with late-season birds that have a good layer of fat over the breast. Demerara sugar is a raw cane sugar that can be purchased at gourmet shops and upscale grocery stores. Turbinado or light brown sugar can be substituted.

> *2 duck breasts with skin on, filleted (4 pieces)*
> *2 teaspoons sea salt*
> *2 teaspoons cinnamon*
> *4 teaspoons demerara sugar*
> *½ cup red wine*
> *¼ cup crème de cassis liqueur*
> *1 teaspoon cornstarch*
> *4 ounces fresh blueberries (½ cup)*

Preheat oven to broiler setting and line a baking sheet with foil. Use a fork to score the duck breast fillets through the skin and fat, but not into the meat. Heat a large, heavy skillet over medium-high heat. Quickly sear the fillets on both sides, skin side down first, about 1 minute per side. Transfer to prepared baking sheet. Mix salt, cinnamon, and sugar in a small bowl and sprinkle over the skin of the fillets. Place under broiler just long enough for sugar to begin to melt and form a glaze, about 2 minutes. Remove from oven and set aside.

Mix wine, liqueur, and cornstarch in a small bowl and whisk until smooth. Pour into the skillet with the duck drippings and simmer 3 minutes over medium heat, or until sauce thickens. Add blueberries and cook an additional 1 minute. Return the fillets to the skillet and simmer, covered, until an instant-read thermometer registers 135 to 140 degrees (medium rare), about 10 minutes. Do not overcook. Remove fillets from skillet, spoon extra sauce over them, and serve immediately.

—*Kay Fulford, lodge cook*

SQUIRREL AND DUMPLINGS

Serves 2

> *2 squirrels, skinned and cleaned*
> *Salt and pepper to taste*
> *1 cup all-purpose flour, sifted*
> *2 teaspoons baking powder*
> *½ teaspoon salt*
> *½ cup whole milk*
> *2 tablespoons vegetable oil*

Place squirrels in a large pot with water to cover; bring to a boil, reduce heat, and simmer until meat begins to come away from the bone, about 1 hour. When cool, remove squirrels and reserve broth. Pull meat from bones and set meat aside.

Season broth with salt and pepper and bring to a boil. In a medium bowl, combine remaining ingredients. Drop dumplings by tablespoonfuls into the boiling broth. Return to a boil, cover, and reduce heat to low. Simmer until dumplings are cooked, about 12 to 15 minutes. Add squirrel meat and simmer until heated through. Adjust seasonings and serve immediately.

—*Kay Fulford, lodge cook*

Unwrapping decoys at first light

DUCK AND SAUSAGE GUMBO

Serves 8

Goose or dove can be substituted for duck in this recipe. For a true "wild game gumbo" use smoked venison sausage instead of andouille. This recipe looks long and complicated, but the roux and the duck can be prepared a day ahead and refrigerated. The next day, allow them to come to room temperature and have all other ingredients chopped and ready before you start; the dish will come together quickly then.

⅓ cup vegetable oil
⅓ cup flour
2 or 3 wild ducks
1 large onion, quartered
Leafy tops from 1 bunch of celery
1 bay leaf
2 tablespoons kosher salt
¼ cup olive oil
1 cup diced green bell pepper
1 cup diced onion
1 cup diced celery
1 teaspoon red pepper flakes
½ teaspoon ground white pepper
½ teaspoon ground black pepper
¾ teaspoon gumbo filé powder
¾ teaspoon dried thyme
6 cloves garlic, minced
5 cups reserved stock
½ pound bacon, coarsely chopped
1 pound andouille sausage, cut into ¼-inch slices
1 can (16-ounce) tomato purée
1 pound large shrimp, peeled and deveined
1 pint oysters, drained, optional
½ pound crawfish meat, optional

Combine oil and flour in a small saucepan over medium heat. Cook, whisking constantly, until the mixture is the color of milk chocolate, about 15 minutes; be careful not to let the roux burn. Transfer to a small bowl, let cool to room temperature, and drain the excess oil. (The roux can be refrigerated at this point but for no more than 24 hours.)

Place the duck, onion, celery leaves, and bay leaf in a large stockpot. Cover with water and add salt. Bring to a boil, reduce heat, and simmer for 1 hour, or until meat is tender. Remove the duck and cool. Strain stock, reserving at least 5 cups; discard vegetables. When duck is cool enough to handle, remove meat from bones and shred into small pieces.

Heat the stockpot over medium-high heat and add olive oil. When oil is hot, add green pepper, diced onion, and diced celery. Cook, stirring occasionally, until the vegetables begin to brown lightly on the edges, about 12 to 15 minutes. In a small bowl, combine red pepper, white pepper, black pepper, filé powder, and thyme. Sprinkle over the vegetables and cook, stirring constantly, until the vegetables are thoroughly coated with the spices. Add the garlic and cook an additional 3 minutes.

Heat the reserved stock in a saucepan over medium heat. Whisk ¼ cup of the stock into the roux and mix well. Add the roux to the stockpot along with the duck meat and the remaining 4½ cups stock. Bring to a boil, lower the heat, and simmer 1 hour, stirring often.

Meanwhile, cook bacon in a large skillet until crisp. Add the sausage and cook 3 minutes. Drain and set aside.

After the gumbo has simmered 1 hour, add tomato purée and sausage mixture and simmer until slightly thickened, about 30 minutes. (At this point the gumbo can be refrigerated or frozen, then returned to a simmer before proceeding.)

Stir in shrimp, oysters, and crawfish and cook just until shrimp are pink, about 10 minutes. Serve in bowls over rice.

— *The Big Woods*

Dinnertime during duck and hog season

MASHED POTATOES WITH SAGE AND WHITE CHEDDAR CHEESE

Serves 10

4 pounds russet potatoes, peeled and cubed

4 tablespoons butter

2 tablespoons plus 1 teaspoon minced fresh sage

¾ cup whipping cream

¾ cup whole milk

9 ounces grated sharp white Cheddar cheese (2¼ cups)

Salt and pepper to taste

Preheat oven to 375 degrees. Butter an 8- to 10-cup baking dish. Cook potatoes in a large pot of boiling salted water until tender, about 12 minutes. While potatoes are cooking, melt butter in a medium saucepan over medium-high heat. Add 2 tablespoons of the sage and stir until butter begins to brown, about 3 minutes. Add cream and milk and bring to a simmer; do not allow to boil.

Drain potatoes and return to pot. Stir over medium heat until excess moisture has evaporated. Add cream mixture and mash potatoes. Stir in 1¾ cups of the cheese and season with salt and pepper. Transfer to prepared dish and sprinkle with the remaining ½ cup of the cheese and 1 teaspoon sage. Bake uncovered until heated through and golden brown on top, about 45 minutes.

—*Kay Fulford, lodge cook*

CATHEAD BISCUITS

Yield: about 12 biscuits

The name "cathead" refers to the shape and bulk of the biscuits; no kitties are harmed during the preparation of this recipe.

> 2 cups flour
> 1 tablespoon baking powder
> ½ teaspoon salt
> ¼ teaspoon baking soda
> 6 tablespoons butter plus 2 tablespoons melted butter
> ¾ cup buttermilk
> ¼ cup heavy cream

Preheat oven to 450 degrees. Combine flour, baking powder, soda, and salt; stir well. Cut in 6 tablespoons of the butter until mixture resembles coarse meal. Sprinkle buttermilk and cream evenly over flour mixture, stirring until dry ingredients are moistened.

Turn dough out onto a floured surface; knead 10 to 12 times. Shape dough into 2-inch balls and press with knuckles into ¾-inch-thick rounds. Place biscuits on a greased baking sheet. Bake 10 minutes. Brush tops of biscuits with melted butter and bake an additional 2 minutes, or until lightly browned.

— *The Big Woods*

Opposite: Now here's a guy who badly wants to go hog hunting.

Greenheads are the main attraction at the Big Woods, but pintails are also itinerant visitors.

East Texas • 321

SARTIN'S SEAFOOD

⊞ **Nassau Bay**

Making a bootstrap start in the restaurant business is a risky proposition, especially when your building sits a half mile from a temperate ocean body that frequently spawns killer hurricanes.

There wasn't much to the tiny town of Sabine Pass in the early 1970s when Charles Sartin worked a dual career as a freelance commercial fisherman–fur trapper and a pipe fitter for the Texaco refinery in Port Arthur. For years, Texas Highway 87 provided two different ways of reaching the true and absolute southeast corner of Texas. From Beaumont and Port Arthur you could head south on 87 into Sabine Pass, where the highway made a 90-degree right turn and then hugged the sand dunes all the way into High Island, Bolivar, and eventually Galveston.

Like most small settlements located at the end of the road, Sabine Pass has always attracted an eclectic mix of people. Shrimpers, crabbers, oil workers, beachcombers, and a few folks with nothing better to do made up the bulk of the town's tax roll when Charles's wife, Jerri, decided to act on the obvious demand for a decent place to eat in Sabine Pass.

With a couple of deep-fat fryers and four picnic tables, Sartin's Seafood officially opened for business in the front of their home in the summer of 1971. It didn't take long for word to spread of their all-you-can-eat barbecue crab platters, and within weeks the Sartins were adding on to their home and making the first of six hand-built additions to the restaurant. By 1980 the Sartins were on a roll with a sixteen-foot neon crab flashing over their restaurant and beckoning carloads of beachgoers and migratory diners from

Sartin's Nassau Bay location opened after Hurricane Rita destroyed the Beaumont restaurant in 2005.

Opposite: The appetizing and somewhat sporty blue crab

all over the Gulf Coast. Highway 87 was their lifeline, but over the next eight years the coast road would take a beating and their traffic would suffer terribly.

Hurricane Allen first chewed up the pavement from High Island to Sabine Pass in 1980, quickly followed by Alicia in 1983. The road was partially repaired in 1985, but hurricanes Gilbert and Jerry soon followed up with a double death blow to Sartin's primary tourist artery. In 1988, with Highway 87 indefinitely closed and with mounting utility bills facing them, the Sartins reluctantly pulled the plug on their seventeen-year history in Sabine Pass.

Convinced that the crowds would return if they had better access, the Sartin family moved the landmark crab sign into Beaumont and posted it over a new facility that would prosper until the fall of 2005, when massive Hurricane Rita roared in just east of Sabine Pass and spread chaos throughout Southeast Texas. With their family home destroyed and the roof collapsed on the restaurant, Charles and Jerri Sartin focused on rebuilding their home while their daughter, Kelli, started searching for another restaurant location.

Today Sartin's is back in business in Nassau Bay near the sprawling Johnson Space Center. A NASA engineer who moonlights as a crabber keeps Kelli stocked with her mainstay, and she's still offering the famed platter service along with fried catfish, oysters, and crab balls. "I'm even thinking about offering Maryland-style crabs," Kelli told me when I visited her in Nassau Bay. "We've learned to adapt after all we've been through, and at this point I'll do whatever it takes to keep this place packed."

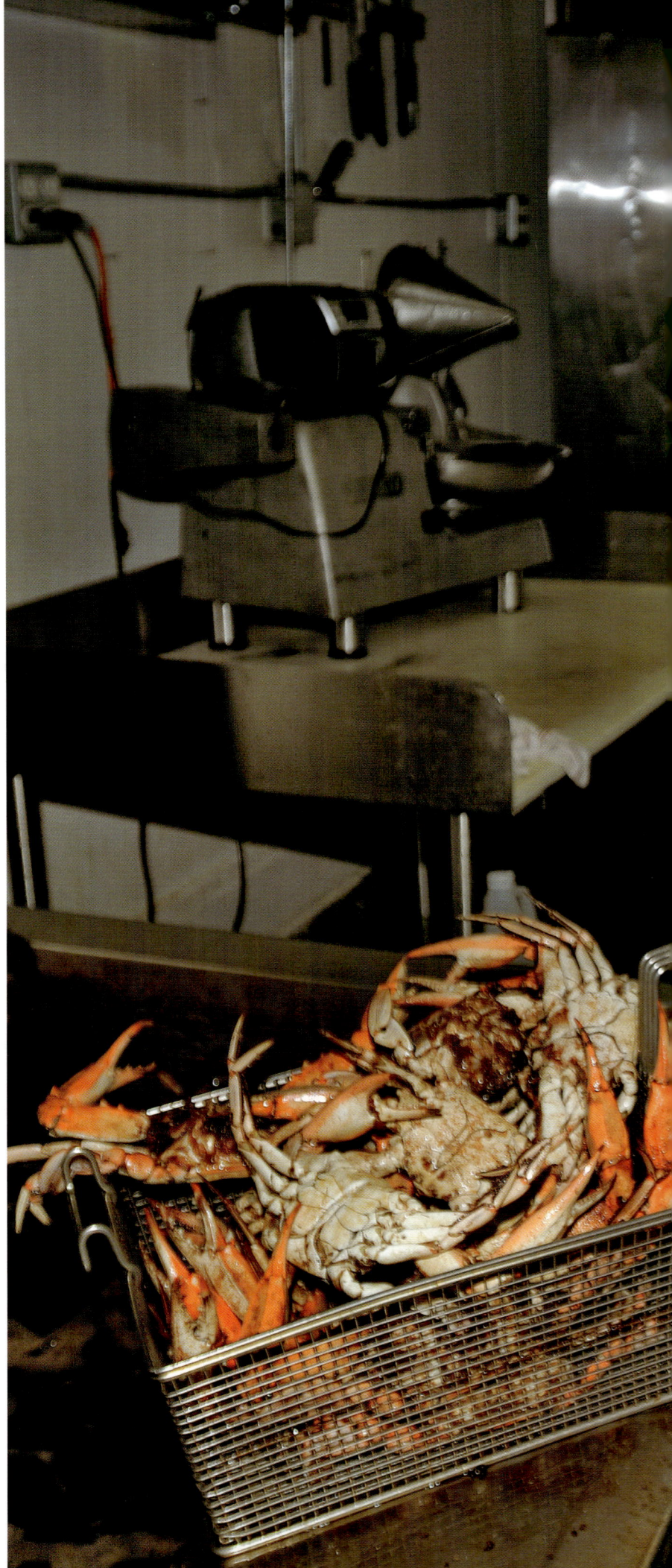

Serving mountains of barbecued crabs in Southeast Texas since 1971

SARTIN'S BBQ CRABS

While the Sartin family's recipe for dry crab seasoning remains a secret, you can purchase the prepared mix from the restaurant or from Bolner's Fiesta Products in San Antonio, which sells it as Fiesta Bar-B-Que Crab Seasoning through an online store (www.fiestaspices.com).

> *3 to 5 live blue crabs per person*
> *Sartin's Seafood Famous BBQ Crab Seasoning or Fiesta Bar-B-Que Crab Seasoning*
> Cooking oil

Place live blue crabs in ice water for 5 minutes to make them easier to handle. Remove the carapace (large top shell) of each crab by grasping the legs on one side of the body and prying and twisting away the carapace, using the pointed end of the shell for leverage. Turn the crab over and use a knife to lift and remove the crab's hard "apron shell" on the underside of its body. Turn the crab over again and remove the crab's mouth parts, entrails, and the spongy lung material. Rinse clean and drain.

Dredge each crab in the seasoning mixture and refrigerate for 1 to 2 hours to allow the mixture to penetrate into the meat.

Heat oil in a deep-fat fryer to 350 degrees. Fry the crabs until they turn red and float to the surface, approximately 5 to 7 minutes. Serve with lots of paper towels and lobster or crab pliers for opening the larger claws.

—*Sartin's Seafood*

East Texas • 325

UPLAND BIRD COUNTRY

⊞ Corsicana

When H. R. Stroube graduated from Corsicana High School in 1938, his father offered him the choice of a farm or a car as a graduation gift. At that time a used Model T Ford and a 300-acre patch of rural Navarro County land cost about the same: around $300. According to my recent spin through the on-line real estate listings for Navarro County, H. R. Stroube made the right choice for his graduation gift when he picked the farm. On a per-acre basis, his landholding has increased in value by about 3,000-fold. In perfectly restored mint condition, I seriously doubt that you could sell that Model T today for $900,000.

After fifty years of running registered Herefords on his farm and buying up surrounding parcels of land as they became available, H. R. showed his son, Steve, a magazine article that he had read about shooting preserves. Beef prices were down, and the Stroubes were looking for an alternate income source from their 640 acres. There were still a few scattered coveys of wild bobwhites in Navarro County in 1985, but everyone knew that their days were numbered.

"We're only an hour—straight down I-45—from Dallas," Steve Stroube pointed out. "We figured that those hunters could come down for a quality released-bird hunt and still make it home in time for dinner."

In 2005 Upland Bird Country celebrated the anniversary of its twentieth hunting season. H. R. Stroube passed away in 1998, but his original farm has since grown to 750 acres, and hunts are now based out of Steve's wonderfully appointed stone lodge. Overnight accommodations aren't available on the premises, but Steve does offer catered meals by request.

Field hunts for quail, chukars, and pheasants are a large part of Steve's business, but he also offers

Steve Stroube's lodge near Corsicana

Opposite: A staunch pointer and a respectable backup

tower shoots for released pheasants where shooters take up stations and then rotate around the tower. Open chokes and light loads are discouraged for tower pheasants as shots are typically forty to sixty yards high at birds that are traveling with a seventy-five-yard flying start.

The terrain at Upland Bird Country varies from open fields and mesquite flats to dense hardwood creek bottoms. Hunters have the choice of bringing their own dogs or booking one of Steve's staff guides and a string of pointing and flushing dogs.

A large portion of Steve's business comes from the Dallas–Fort Worth area, just as he and his dad presumed it would, but he has regular visitors from around the state as well. "This is a great setup for a guy who doesn't have a lot of time to go out and get a bird lease of his own," Steve explained. "We also have a lot of clients who bring their sons and daughters here for their first guided bird hunt."

Pushing a cline grass field at last light (left). An energetic pointer following his nose (above).

BARBECUED QUAIL

Serves 6

This recipe is also very good with dove. Instead of trying to stuff one small dove, put two breasts together, fill the cavity with the apple mixture, wrap with bacon, and secure with a toothpick. Baking the grilled birds keeps them from drying out while they finish cooking.

2 small Granny Smith apples, peeled and finely diced
1 can (4-ounce) chopped green chilies
12 quail, cleaned and skinned
12 slices bacon

Barbecue Sauce

½ cup (1 stick) butter, melted
1½ cups ketchup
2 tablespoons fresh lemon juice
1½ tablespoons molasses
1 tablespoon Creole mustard
1½ tablespoons Worcestershire sauce
½ teaspoon garlic salt

To make the barbecue sauce, whisk all ingredients together until thoroughly combined; set aside.

In a small bowl, combine apples and green chilies. Place 1 tablespoon of the apple mixture in the breast cavity of each quail. Wrap each with bacon and secure with a toothpick. Grill over medium-hot coals for 20 minutes, turning frequently and basting with the barbecue sauce.

Preheat oven to 300 degrees. Place grilled quail in a roasting pan and pour 1 cup of the sauce over the quail. Cover with foil and bake 1 hour. Serve immediately with remaining barbecue sauce.

—*Upland Bird Country*

Opposite: A beautifully plumed cock pheasant (above). Chukar partridge, the hard-flying import from Eurasia and popular stocker bird at shooting preserves around the country (below).

DOVE PÂTÉ

Serves 10–12

An excellent appetizer served with crackers, this is best if made a day ahead and refrigerated so that the flavors can blend. It also freezes well. The amount of mayonnaise is a matter of taste, but use enough to bind the pâté together without making it too creamy.

24 dove breasts, skinned
½ cup red wine vinegar
½ cup dry sherry
2 tablespoons Worcestershire sauce
2 teaspoons lemon juice
1 large onion, chopped
2 teaspoons celery seed
1 bay leaf
2 cloves garlic, chopped
2½ teaspoons seasoned salt
5 slices bacon
½ cup chopped celery
¼ cup chopped fresh cilantro
½ cup pine nuts
½ to 1 cup mayonnaise
¼ cup prepared horseradish
¼ teaspoon freshly ground pepper
Salt to taste

Place dove breasts in a large saucepan. Add vinegar, sherry, Worcestershire, lemon juice, onion, celery seed, bay leaf, garlic, and 2 teaspoons of the seasoned salt. Add enough water to just cover the doves. Bring to a boil, reduce heat, cover, and simmer 1 hour. Add bacon and simmer an additional 30 minutes, or until doves are fork-tender. Remove from heat and let stand 3 to 4 hours. Reserve bacon and remove dove meat from the bones.

In a food processor, combine dove meat, reserved bacon, the remaining ½ teaspoon of the seasoned salt, celery, and cilantro. Process mixture until it is finely chopped but not puréed, about 5 or 6 quick pulses. Add pine nuts and process until coarsely chopped.

Transfer mixture to a medium bowl and add mayonnaise, horseradish, pepper, and salt. Refrigerate before serving.

—*Upland Bird Country*

CORN PUDDING

....
Serves 12

1 can (15-ounce) cream-style corn
2 packages (10-ounce) frozen white shoepeg corn, thawed
½ cup flour
1 teaspoon salt
4 large eggs, beaten
1 cup whipping cream
½ cup sugar
½ cup (1 stick) butter, melted

Preheat oven to 350 degrees. Lightly coat a 9 × 13-inch baking dish with cooking spray. Combine all ingredients in a mixing bowl and mix thoroughly. Pour into prepared dish and bake, uncovered, for 1 hour. Serve warm.

—*Upland Bird Country*

GREEN BEAN BUNDLES

....
Serves 8

1½ pounds fresh green beans, trimmed
8 slices bacon
1 onion, chopped
2 tablespoons olive oil or bacon drippings
½ cup ketchup
1½ tablespoons fresh lemon juice
1 clove garlic, minced
1 tablespoon cider vinegar
2 tablespoons Worcestershire sauce

Cook the beans in boiling salted water for 8 minutes, or until crisp-tender. Drain and plunge into cold water to stop the cooking process.

Preheat oven to 300 degrees. Divide the beans into 8 equal portions and wrap each portion with a slice of bacon. Arrange the bundles in a 9 × 13-inch baking dish.

Heat oil in skillet and sauté onion until soft. Stir in ketchup, lemon juice, garlic, vinegar, and Worcestershire and mix thoroughly. Pour over green beans and bake, uncovered, for 45 minutes.

—*Upland Bird Country*

Guide John Kenner and Hunter and Jack Jernigan moving in on the point

LEMON BUNDT CAKE

Serves 16

This recipe uses the juice and zest of three lemons.

> 3 cups flour
> ¾ teaspoon salt
> ½ teaspoon baking soda
> 2 cups sugar
> 1 cup (2 sticks) butter, softened
> 4 large eggs
> 1 teaspoon vanilla
> 1 cup buttermilk
> 3 tablespoons fresh lemon juice
> 2 tablespoons lemon zest

Lemon Frosting

> 2 cups powdered sugar, sifted
> ½ cup (1 stick) butter, softened
> 4 ounces cream cheese, softened
> 2 tablespoons fresh lemon juice
> ½ teaspoon vanilla

Preheat oven to 325 degrees. Grease and flour a 12-cup Bundt pan. Sift together flour, salt, and baking soda; set aside. In a mixer, blend together sugar and butter at low speed until thoroughly mixed. Increase speed to high and beat for 3 minutes. Reduce speed to low and add eggs, one at a time, mixing thoroughly after each addition. Stir in vanilla. Beat in flour mixture, alternating with the buttermilk. Stir in lemon juice and lemon zest. Spoon into prepared pan and bake 60 to 70 minutes, or until cake tests done. Cool in pan 15 minutes and then invert onto a cake rack to cool completely.

To make the frosting, blend powdered sugar, butter, and cream cheese in a mixer at low speed until smooth. Add lemon juice and vanilla. Increase speed to high and beat until fluffy. Spread over the cooled cake.

—*Upland Bird Country*

EAST TEXAS À LA CARTE

Like the Plains and Panhandle section of our state, East Texas doesn't have many full-board lodges and restaurants that serve game and fish to their clientele. Ahead you'll find an eclectic mix of critters and cooking from a few solo acts that represent the home-style, Southern, and Cajun cooking cultures from the pine forests and hardwood bottoms of East Texas.

Larry Guilbeau grew up in Opelousas, Louisiana, and spent a good portion of his formative years hunting and fishing the marshes and lakes on both sides of the Sabine. After landing a cooking job in New Iberia, Louisiana, during college, Larry enrolled in culinary school in New York and formally launched his career after graduation. Since then, his cooking tour has taken him to New Orleans, Alaska, Telluride, and Dallas, where he cooked at the Mansion on Turtle Creek. Larry now lives in Austin and works as a chef at Central Market.

Nestled in the heart of the Angelina National Forest near Jasper, Sam Rayburn Reservoir is known for its fabulous fishing and 560 miles of sparsely developed shoreline. And since legendary lakes are often synonymous with the guide services that have contributed to their fame, it's hard to discuss the fishery on Rayburn without referencing Cathy and Mike Wheatley's combined forty years of fishing and guiding expertise. Cathy and Mike are widely known for their technique of sinking brush piles, marking them with a GPS, and then fishing them for crappie, bass, and bream.

Often operating in tandem with the Wheatleys, Jan and Bill Fondren (Tejas Guides) are also regulars

An osprey, or fish hawk, scans an East Texas lake for a surface-swimming meal.
Opposite: A fat Sam Rayburn crappie caught on a live minnow

on Sam Rayburn, where they guide anglers, arrange tournaments, and manage Beaumont attorney Walter Humphrey's private fishing lodge. In the following pages you'll find a couple of Cathy and Jan's favorite fish and game recipes.

Craig and Debbie Radley own Pincher's Boil'n Pot restaurant in El Campo. Their dining room may very well be closer to the Gulf of Mexico than the Sabine, but their cooking specialties are decidedly East Texas. Craig owned a crawfish farm before he got into the restaurant business, and many of his recipes came from a Cajun cook that he employed when the restaurant first opened.

Posturing to avoid the pot (above). Chef Larry Guilbeau at his annual Good Friday Crawfish Boil (right).

336 • GRAZING ACROSS TEXAS

GUILBEAU'S CAJUN SEASONING

This stout, flavorful mixture is very versatile. It can be used with practically any species of game or fish.

¼ cup salt
1 tablespoon onion powder
1 tablespoon garlic powder
1 tablespoon paprika
1 tablespoon cayenne pepper
1 tablespoon black pepper
1 tablespoon white pepper

Mix all ingredients together and store in an airtight container.

—Larry Guilbeau

CRAB CAKES

Serves 2

1 pound crabmeat
4 green onions, chopped
½ cup mayonnaise
Salt and pepper to taste
Old Bay seasoning or Guilbeau's Cajun Seasoning (page 337) to taste
1 tablespoon Worcestershire sauce
1 teaspoon Tabasco sauce or Louisiana-style hot sauce
1 egg
¼ cup milk
Flour
½ cup panko bread crumbs plus additional as needed
Olive oil

In a mixing bowl, gently combine crabmeat, onions, mayonnaise, salt, pepper, seasoning mix, Worcestershire, and Tabasco. Divide into equal portions and form into patties. In a small dish, whisk together egg and milk. Dredge each patty in flour, dip in egg mixture, and then roll in bread crumbs. Heat olive oil in a large skillet and sauté crab cakes until browned on both sides.

—Larry Guilbeau

CORN BREAD DRESSING WITH SHRIMP AND ANDOUILLE

Serves 12

4 tablespoons unsalted butter
2 medium onions, chopped
1 large bell pepper, finely diced
½ cup diced celery
2 tablespoons chopped garlic
1 pound andouille sausage
1 pound medium shrimp, peeled and deveined
¼ cup thinly sliced fresh basil
1 tablespoon fresh thyme
2 tablespoons Guilbeau's Cajun Seasoning (page 337)
12-inch pan corn bread, baked
1 cup chicken broth
1 can (13-ounce) evaporated milk
4 eggs

Preheat oven to 375 degrees. In a large sauté pan, melt butter and sauté onions 5 minutes; add bell pepper, celery, and garlic and sauté an additional 5 minutes. Add sausage and cook 5 minutes. Add shrimp, basil, thyme, and seasoning mix; cook 1 minute and remove from heat. In a large mixing bowl, break corn bread into pieces; add broth, milk, and eggs and mix well. Add sausage and shrimp mixture and mix well. Pour into a greased casserole dish and bake 30 minutes.

—Larry Guilbeau

CRAWFISH ÉTOUFFÉE

Now, before you call us out for including crawfish in a game and fish cookbook, we do fully understand that they're not really considered a sporting crustacean; but with two feet of string, a package of bacon, and a lot of idle time, one could conceivably dredge up enough of them to fill a good-sized pot.

- ¾ cup (1½ sticks) butter
- 1 pound crawfish tails, shells removed
- 1 tablespoon Guilbeau's Cajun Seasoning (page 337)
- 1 large onion, chopped
- 1 large bell pepper, chopped
- 1 stalk celery, chopped
- 1 clove garlic, minced
- 2 cups chicken stock
- ½ cup roux
- 1 medium tomato, diced
- ½ cup chopped fresh basil
- ¼ cup chopped green onion
- 4 tablespoons chopped fresh parsley

Roux

- ¼ cup vegetable oil
- ½ cup flour

To make the roux, heat oil in a heavy skillet until smoking, whisk in flour, and cook, stirring constantly, until dark brown. Set aside.

In a sauté pan, melt 6 tablespoons of the butter and sauté crawfish for 3 minutes. Add Cajun Seasoning and mix well; set aside. In a separate sauté pan, melt the remaining butter and sauté onion for 5 minutes. Add bell pepper, celery, and garlic and sauté an additional 5 minutes. Add chicken broth and bring to a simmer. Whisk in the roux and simmer 30 minutes. Add crawfish, tomato, basil, green onion, and parsley and bring to a simmer. Adjust seasonings. Finish with a dash of hot sauce and serve over white rice.

—*Larry Guilbeau*

WHOLE FRIED BREAM

This is a great way to cook fish for breakfast. The crisped tail and fins are excellent.

>   4 cups yellow corn meal
>   1 cup flour
>   3 tablespoons salt
>   1 tablespoon red pepper, or to taste
>   1 tablespoon ground black pepper
>   1 tablespoon Creole or Cajun seasoning
>   1 teaspoon garlic powder
>   10 bream, scaled and cleaned with heads removed
>   Peanut oil for frying

Mix together dry ingredients and pour into a paper bag. Add fish to the bag and shake to coat. Deep-fry in oil at 350 degrees until fish float to the top.

— Cathy Wheatley

Guide Cathy Wheatley working a brush pile on Sam Rayburn (left). This fish answers to a lot of names — bream, bluegill, perch . . . and breakfast. (below)

SQUIRREL JAMBALAYA

Serves 4

The secret to this recipe is a long, slow simmer that blends all of the flavors and produces almost creamy rice. The dish can be made early in the day and simmered again to reheat. Any game bird or animal can be substituted for the squirrel. Chopped andouille sausage can be added for extra kick. Use any commercial Cajun seasoning, or try the recipe for Guilbeau's Cajun Seasoning in this section.

3 or 4 squirrels, skinned and cleaned
Cajun seasoning to taste
3 tablespoons vegetable oil
2 large onions, chopped
3 celery stalks, chopped
1 large bell pepper, seeded and chopped
1 clove garlic, chopped
4 tablespoons chopped fresh parsley
1 can (14-ounce) diced tomatoes, undrained
1 can (8-ounce) tomato sauce
1 cup uncooked rice
1 cup chicken broth
Salt and pepper to taste

Cut squirrel into serving pieces and season well with Cajun seasoning. Heat oil in a large sauté pan, add squirrel, and cook until browned on all sides. Remove and drain on paper towels. Add onions, celery, bell pepper, garlic, and parsley and sauté until tender. Return squirrel pieces to the pan and add tomatoes and tomato sauce; cover and simmer at lowest setting for 30 minutes. Add rice, broth, salt, and pepper and simmer an additional 30 minutes, or until the meat is tender, the rice is cooked, and most of the juices have been absorbed. Adjust seasonings.

—*Cathy Wheatley*

HOT-WATER CORN BREAD

2 cups white cornmeal
½ cup flour
1 teaspoon salt
1 teaspoon sugar
1 to 2 cups boiling water
1 egg
1 tablespoon baking powder
Oil for frying

Combine cornmeal, flour, salt, and sugar in a mixing bowl. Stir in just enough hot water to make a thick batter; stir in egg and mix well. Add baking powder and mix well. Pour oil into a skillet to a depth of ½ inch and heat until very hot. Form patties by hand, making them as thin as possible; drop into hot oil and fry until golden brown. Drain on paper towels and serve hot.

—*Cathy Wheatley*

BAKED CRAPPIE

Serves 4–6

2 pounds crappie fillets
3 tablespoons butter
3 teaspoons fresh lemon juice
½ teaspoon basil
½ teaspoon dill
Salt and pepper to taste

Preheat oven to 350 degrees. Rub fillets with butter and place on a large piece of aluminum foil. Sprinkle with lemon juice, basil, dill, salt, and pepper to taste. Fold foil over fillets and tightly seal edges to form a pouch. Bake 15 to 20 minutes, or until fish is opaque and flaky.

—*Jan Fondren*

FRIED ALLIGATOR

Strips of meat cut from the alligator's tail are the tenderest.

> Strips of alligator tail
> Cajun seasoning (commercial or a favorite blend)
> Salt and pepper to taste
> Garlic powder to taste
> Flour
> Milk
> Oil for frying

Pound the strips of alligator meat with a tenderizing mallet to a uniform thickness. Season each strip with Cajun seasoning, salt, pepper, and garlic powder. Roll strips in flour, dip in milk, and roll in flour again. Fry in hot oil until golden brown.

—Craig and Debbie Radley

BLACKENED CATFISH

> 1 or 2 catfish fillets per person
> 3 tablespoons butter
> Fresh lemon juice
> Melted butter for basting

Blackened Seasoning Mix
> 2 teaspoons paprika
> 4 teaspoons dried thyme leaves
> 2 teaspoons onion powder
> 2 teaspoons garlic powder
> 1 tablespoon sugar
> 2 teaspoons salt
> 2 teaspoons ground black pepper
> 1 teaspoon cayenne pepper
> 1 teaspoon dried oregano leaves
> ¾ teaspoon ground cumin

To make the Blackened Seasoning Mix, combine all ingredients, mix well, and store in an airtight container.

Coat each fillet with the Blackened Seasoning Mix. In a large skillet, melt butter over high heat until it sizzles. Add fillets and baste with lemon juice and melted butter; cook approximately 2 minutes per side, or until fish is flaky. Serve over a bed of rice.

—Craig and Debbie Radley

Tough on bird feeders, tender in the skillet (left). If you're pining to cook an alligator, find one smaller than this (right).

CONTACT INFORMATION

Bayflats Lodge
391 Bayside Drive
Seadrift, TX 77983
888-677-4868
www.bayflatslodge.com

The Big Woods
14809 West FM 321
Tennessee Colony, TX 75861
903-391-1112
www.bigwoods.ws

Broken Arrow Ranch
3296 Junction Highway
Ingram, TX 78025
800-962-4263
www.brokenarrowranch.com

Bucksnag Hunting Club
P.O. Box 381
Garwood, TX 77442
979-758-3019
www.bucksnag.com

CF Ranch
P.O. Box 689
Alpine, TX 79831
432-364-2251
www.cfranch.com

Coon Creek Club*
Athens, TX

Copper Breaks Guide Service
Eric Guggenheim
4217 Snapdragon Drive
Keller, TX 76248
682-365-1273
www.copperbreaks.com

Executive Outfitters
629 PR 4221
Coleman, TX 76834
325-625-4111
www.txdovehunting.com

First Shot Outfitters
P.O. Box 974
Coleman, TX 76834
325-625-1671

Gage Hotel
101 Highway 90 West
Marathon, TX 79842
800-884-GAGE
www.gagehotel.com

Gaido's Restaurant
3802 Seawall Blvd
Galveston, TX 77550
800-525-0064
www.gaidosofgalveston.com

Hindes Ranch*
Charlotte, TX

Hudson's on the Bend
3509 Ranch Road 620 N
Austin, TX 78734
512-266-1369
www.hudsonsonthebend.com

Joshua Creek Ranch
P.O. Box 1946
Boerne, TX 78006
830-537-5090
www.joshuacreek.com

La Bandera Ranch
P.O. Box 1050
Carrizo Springs, TX 78834
830-876-8990
www.labandera.com

Lisabella's Bistro
224 East Cotter Street
Port Aransas, TX 78373
361-749-4222
www.lisabellasbistro.com

Lodge on the Arroyo
1629 Hunter Road
New Braunfels, TX 78130
888-477-3474
www.flyfishtx.com

Longfellow Ranch
P.O. Box 1603
Fort Stockton, TX 79735
432-290-3949
www.longfellowranch.com

McAllen Ranch
P.O. Box 1139
Edinburg, TX 78540-1139
956-383-1960
www.mcallenranch.com

Ocotillo Restaurant
HC 70 Box 400
Lajitas, TX 79852
432-424-5007
www.lajitas.com

Perlitz Ranch
P.O. Box 988
Uvalde, TX 78802
830-374-3200
www.perlitzranch.com

Perini Ranch Steakhouse
P.O. Box 728
Buffalo Gap, TX 79508
800-367-1721
www.periniranch.com

Pincher's Boil'n Pot
2911 Hwy. 59 East
El Campo, TX 77437
979-543-2645

Pitchfork Land & Cattle Company
c/o Mesquite Country Outfitters
P.O. Box 204
Roaring Springs, TX 79256
806-689-2302
www.mcohunts.com

Port "A" Seafood Company
108 Alister
Port Aransas, TX 78373
361-749-6456

Port Bay Hunting & Fishing Club
310 Port Bay Road
Rockport, TX 78382
361-729-6971
www.portbayclub.com

Reata Restaurant
203 North Fifth Street
Alpine, TX 79830
432-837-9232
www.reata.net

Redfish Lodge
P.O. Box 2295
Rockport, TX 78381-2295
800-392-9324
www.redfishlodge.com

Rough Creek Lodge & Resort
P.O. Box 2400
Glen Rose, TX 76043
800-864-4705
www.roughcreek.com

Salado Seco Ranch
P.O. Box 2099
Boerne, TX 78006
830-249-7063
www.saladoseco.com

Sandy Oaks Ranch
P.O. Box 641
Devine, TX 78016
830-663-5005
www.sandyoaksranch.com

Sartin's Seafood
18023 Upper Bay Drive
Houston, TX 77058
281-333-4040
www.sartins.com

Shells Pasta & Seafood
522 E. Avenue G
Port Aransas, TX 78373
361-749-7621

Stasney's Cook Ranch
P.O. Box 1826
Albany, TX 76430
888-762-2999
www.stasneyscookranch.com

Sunbelt Outdoors
Barry Batsell
1134 Belthair Street
Brownsville, TX 78520
888-353-2473
www.sunbeltoutdoors.com

Tejas Guide Service
Bill Fondren
Route 1, Box 674
Brookeland, TX 75931
409-698-3491

Tule Ranch Hunts
Box 658
Silverton, TX
806-847-2262
www.tuleranch.com

Upland Bird Country
P.O. Box 730
Corsicana, TX 75151
903-872-5663
www.uplandbird.com

U Ranch
c/o Tule Ranch Hunts
Box 658
Silverton, TX
806-847-2262
www.tuleranch.com

Mike and Cathy Wheatley
Route 3, Box 519-69
Jasper, TX 75951
409-489-1816
www.mikesfishingadventures.net

Wildlife Systems
P.O. Box 5121
San Angelo, TX 76902
325-655-0877
www.wildlifesystems.com

YO Ranch
1736 YO Ranch Road
Mountain Home, TX 78058
800-967-2624
www.yoranch.net

*Contact information withheld by request

INDEX

Number in bold type refer to illustrations.

A

Adamson, Bob *91*
Adleta, Dorothy *312*
alligator
    Fried Alligator *341*
Almond Bread Pudding with Amaretto Cream Sauce **38**, *39*
amberjack. *See* fish
Amundsen, Kris *284, 286*
Amundsen, Lisa *284, 286*
Amundsen, Luke *287*
Andrysiak, Thomas *151*
antelope
    Antelope Medallions with Mushroom Demi-Glace *120*
    Stuffed Antelope Tenderloin *104*
Antelope Medallions with Mushroom Demi-Glace *120*, **120**
appetizers. *See also* dips
    C. J.'s Shrimp Ceviche *275*
    Dove Pâté *330*
    Duck Cakes *263*
    Fresh Tuna Pâté *274*
    Lump Crab au Gratin *249*
    Quail Poppers *32*
    Texas Caviar *83*
    Trout-Mango Ceviche *270*

B

Bacardi Rum Blackened Trout *268*, **268**
Bacon-Wrapped Axis Backstrap *151*, **151**
Bacon-Wrapped Doves *172*
Baked Crappie *340*
Baked Doves *68*
Baked Pheasant *91*
Barbecued Doves *214, 215*
Barbecued Quail **16–17**, *330*
Barbecued Wild Turkey *207*
Barrington, Joe **56**
Batsell, Barry *91*
Bayflats Lodge *258–263*
beans
    Ranch Beans *218*
    Southwest Baked Beans *209*
Beer Batter Fish *311*
Beer Bread with Honey Butter *37*
Big Woods, The *314–321*
black drum. *See* fish

Blackened Catfish *341*
Blank, Jeffrey *110, 152, 155, 156, 157, 158, 159*
Blue Crab Enchiladas with Mango-Jalapeño Cream Sauce *288*, **288**
boar
    Chris's Almost Famous Chili *164*
    Pig in the Ground *57*
    Roasted Wild Boar Leg with Mustard-Caper Sauce *165*
    Wild Boar Schnitzel *159*
Boccafogli, Paul *186*
Bodecker, Brent **34**
Bouher, Cheryl *68, 70*
Bourbon Sweet Potatoes *173*
Box, Ray *296, 298*, **298**
breads
    Beer Bread with Honey Butter *37*
    Cathead Biscuits *321*
    Cheddar-Bacon Biscuits *190*
    Denver Biscuits *135*
    Hot-Water Corn Bread *340*
    Pepper and Cheese Beer Bread *107*
    Tule Ranch Corn Bread *62*
bream (perch, bluegill). *See* fish
Brister, Leigh Ann *293, 294, 295*
Broiled Redfish Parmesan on the Half Shell *300*
Broken Arrow Ranch *160–167*
Brothers, Al *201*
Brown, Blake **215**, *259*, **348**
Brown, Carolyn *215*
Brown, David *214*, **217**, *218*
Brown, Emily *282*
Bryan, J. P. *118*
Bryan, Mary Jon *118*
Bucksnag Goose *254*
Bucksnag Hunting Club *252–257*
Bunkhouse Meatloaf *164*
Bush, A. P., Jr. *65*
Buttermilk Pie *135*
Butterscotch Custard Pie *203*

C

C. J.'s Shrimp Ceviche *275*
Cajeta Pound Cake *141*
Caldwell, Cliff **44**, *45*
Caldwell, Lee *40*
Caldwell, Ruth *40*
Carmody, Jack *229*
Carpenter, Kent **44**, *58, 61*

Carpenter, Penny *58, 62*
Case, Jordan **206**
casseroles
    Corn Bread Dressing with Shrimp and Andouille *337*
    Dove Carne Guisada *224*
    Dove Pot Pie *217*
    Duck and Wild Rice Casserole *313*
    Pheasant Pot Pie *179*
    Squash Soufflé *312*
    Venison Sausage and Biscuit Casserole *233*
    Venison Sausage and Wild Rice Casserole *105*
    Wild Turkey Pie *80*
catfish. *See* fish
Cathead Biscuits *321*
Catto Gage Ranch *103*
Caudle, Pat *169*
Central Market *334*
CF Ranch *131–135*, **136**
Champagne Crab Dip *269*
Chapman Hotel. *See* Bucksnag Hunting Club
Cheddar-Bacon Biscuits *190*
Cheese and Bacon Grits *140*
Chicken-Fried Venison with Wild Boar Sausage Gravy *122*
chili. *See* stews
Chris's Almost Famous Chili *164*
Christensen, T. J. **260**
Coffee Rub Duck Breasts *269*
Cogdell, D. M. *58*
Colbert, Mike *43, 45, 46*, **46**, *49*
Coleman, David *234*, **236**
Coleman, Youngs O. *149*
Conklin, Jim *264*
Cook, Matilda "Dude" Nail *51, 54*
Cook Children's Medical Center *54*
Cook Ranch. *See* Stasney's Cook Ranch
Coon Creek Broiled Fish *312*
Coon Creek Club *308–313*
Corn Bread Dressing with Shrimp and Andouille *337*
Corn Pudding *331*
Cotton, Paula *135*
Cowan, Trey *104, 105, 107*
Cowboy Potatoes *83*
crab
    Blue Crab Enchiladas with Mango-Jalapeño Cream Sauce *288*
    Champagne Crab Dip *269*

Crab Cakes *337*
Crab Finger Dressing *281*
Lump Crab au Gratin *249*
Sartin's BBQ Crabs *325*
Crab Cakes *337*
Crab Finger Dressing *281*
crane, sandhill
    Sandhill Crane in Port Cream Sauce *94*
crappie. *See* fish
Crappie-Stuffed Chayote Squash *311*
crawfish
    Crawfish Étouffée *338*
Crawfish Étouffée *338*

D

Dain, Daniel **289**
Dallas Airomotive *169*
Denver Biscuits *135*
desserts
    Almond Bread Pudding with Amaretto Cream Sauce *39*
    Buttermilk Pie *135*
    Butterscotch Custard Pie *203*
    Cajeta Pound Cake *141*
    Flan *239*
    Grilled Peaches with Spicy Lemon Honey *156*
    Hot Cocoa Cake *70*
    Kahlua Pecan Pie *183*
    Lemon Bundt Cake *333*
    Oatmeal Apple Crisp *129*
    Peach Cobbler *49*
    Praline Bars *203*
    Turtle Cheesecake *38*
    Warm Apple Tart *191*
dips
    Champagne Crab Dip *269*
    Salsa Roja *219*
    Tomatillo Sauce *219*
    Venison Sausage Dip *62*
dove
    Bacon-Wrapped Doves *172*
    Baked Doves *68*
    Barbecued Doves *214, 215*
    Doves and Dumplings *202*
    Dove Carne Guisada *224*
    Dove Empanadas *216*
    Dove Pâté *330*
    Dove Pot Pie *217*
    Fried Doves *172*
Doves and Dumplings *202*
Dove Carne Guisada *224*
Dove Empanadas *216*

Dove Pâté 330
Dove Pot Pie 217
duck
　Coffee Rub Duck Breasts 269
　Duck and Black Bean Chili 187
　Duck and Sausage Gumbo 319
　Duck and Wild Rice Casserole 313
　Duck Breasts with Blueberry Sauce 318
　Duck Breast with Red Chili Glaze 114
　Duck Cakes 263
　Grilled Duck Breast 263
　Grilled Orange Duck 180
　Maple Syrup and Apple Cider Brined Duck 88–89
　Roast Duck with Currant Sauce 218
Duck and Black Bean Chili 187
Duck and Sausage Gumbo 319
Duck and Wild Rice Casserole 313
Duck Breasts with Blueberry Sauce 318
Duck Breast with Red Chili Glaze 114, **114**
Duck Cakes 263
Durham, Donnie 169
Dworaczyk, Harold **260**

E

Ellis, Delbert 20
El Capitan 116
El Paisano 116
Espresso-Rubbed Venison Backstrap with Shiner Bock Beer Blanc 156, **157**
Evans, Mike 136
Executive Hunts. See Executive Outfitters
Executive Outfitters 169–173

F

Fairmont Hotel 152
Faith Ranch 230
Fidel (dog) **201**
First Shot Outfitters 25–39
fish
　Bacardi Rum Blackened Trout 268
　Baked Crappie 340
　Beer Batter Fish 311
　Blackened Catfish 341
　Broiled Redfish Parmesan on the Half Shell 300
　Coon Creek Broiled Fish 312
　Crappie-Stuffed Chayote Squash 311
　Fish Alexandria 311
　Fresh Tuna Pâté 274
　Grilled Amberjack with Tomatillo Sauce 280
　Grilled Red Snapper with Cilantro-Lime Butter 289
　Grilled Redfish Veracruz 300
　Grilled Speckled Trout 262
　Grilled Wahoo with Coconut Curry Sauce 287
　Hot and Spicy Speck Po' Boy 295
　Mahi Sapporito 251
　Maria's Sautéed Trout with Cilantro 300
　Redfish Cakes 293
　Stuffed Whole Flounder 294
　Trout-Mango Ceviche 270
　Tuna Steak with Japanese Mayonnaise 281
　Whole Fried Bream 339
Fish Alexandria 311
Flan 239
flounder. See fish
Fondren, Bill 334
Fondren, Jan 334, 336, 340
Fort Concho 52
Fort Griffin 51, 52
Foster Ranch 20
Fox, James 264
French, S. L. 308
Fresh Tuna Pâté 274
Fried Alligator 341
Fried Corn and Peppers 107
Fried Doves 172
Fried Green Beans 227
Fried Quail 34
Fried Wild Turkey Fingers 46
Fulford, Kay 318, 320

G

Gage, Alfred 116
Gage Hotel 116–123, 136
Gaido, Michael 248
Gaido, Rick 248
Gaido, San Jacinto (S. J.) 246
Gaido's Restaurant 246–251
Gates, Jay **65**
Gilley, Buddy 272
Gilley, Colby 272, 275
Gilley, Linda 272, **272**
Gilley's Flounder Run. See Port "A" Seafood Company
Gomez, Jose Manuel 234
Gonzalez, Blas 108–109, **112,** 113, 114, 115
goose
　Bucksnag Goose 254
　Goose Breast in Cognac Gravy 91
Goose Breast in Cognac Gravy 91
Greene, Kenny 272
Green Bean Bundles 331
Green Chili and Mexican Crème Smashed Potatoes 115
Green Chili Twice-Baked Potatoes 107
Grilled Amberjack with Tomatillo Sauce 280
Grilled Duck Breast 263
Grilled Orange Duck 180
Grilled Peaches with Spicy Lemon Honey 156, **157**
Grilled Redfish Veracruz 300
Grilled Red Snapper with Cilantro-Lime Butter 289
Grilled Speckled Trout 262, **262**
Grilled Venison Backstrap with Apricot Glaze 140
Grilled Venison with Green Peppercorn Sauce 183
Grilled Wahoo with Coconut Curry Sauce 287
Gruene Outfitters 296
Guerra, Melissa 237, 238, 239
Guerra, Melissa McAllen 236
Guggenheim, Erik 88, 89, 94
Guilbeau, Larry 334, **336,** 337, 338
Guilbeau's Cajun Seasoning 337
Gustafson, Jim **104–105**
Gus (dog) **201**

H

Hamilton, Paul **70**
Hindes, David 198
Hindes, George 198
Hindes, Leroy 198
Hindes, Moses 198
Hindes, Pam 198, 202, 203
Hindes, Roy, V 198
Hindes, Roy "Big Roy," II 198, 201
Hindes, Roy "Cuatro," IV 198, 201
Hindes, Roy "Little Roy," III 198, 201, **201,** 203, **203**
Hindes Ranch 198–203
Hixson, Bob 229, 230
Hoet, Franklin, Jr. **131**
Holden, Brian 264
Gomez, Jose Manuel 234
Honey Creek Sporting Clays 25
Hot-Water Corn Bread 340
Hot and Spicy Speck Po' Boy 295
Hot Cocoa Cake 70
Houston, Foard 220, 223, **225**
Hudman, Debbe 51
Hudman, Johnny 51, 52, **56,** 57
Hudson's on the Bend 108, 152–159
Huff, Don 169
Hughes, Chris 160, **160,** 162
Hughes, Elizabeth 160
Hughes, Mike 160
Hulsey, E. H. 311

J

Jamison, Harwin **184,** 185
Jernigan, Hunter 332–333
Jernigan, Jack 332–333
Joshua Creek Ranch 174–183

K

Kahlua Pecan Pie 183
Kenner, John 332–333
Kercheville, Ann 174, 176
Kercheville, Joe 174
Koffee Kup 25
Koster, Lars **280**

L

Lakeway Inn 152
Lambshead Ranch 75
Land, Dale **43,** 46
La Bandera Ranch 229–233
Lee, Bernice 170
Lee, Chris 268, **269,** 270
Lee, Richard 169, 170
Leigh Ann's Seafood Seasoning 293
Lemon Bundt Cake 333
Lewis, Sandra 135
Lisabella's Bistro 284–289
Lodge on the Arroyo 296–301
Longfellow Ranch 124–129
Lorio, Vince **134**
Lump Crab au Gratin 249

M

mahi-mahi (dolphin). See fish
Mahi Sapporito 251
Mansion on Turtle Creek, The 334
Maple Syrup and Apple Cider Brined Duck 88–89

Maria's Sautéed Trout with Cilantro 300
marinades
  Crab Finger Dressing 281
Martin, Chris 258, 260
Martin, Deb 258
Mashed Potatoes with Sage and White Cheddar Cheese 320
Matthews, Watt 75
McAllen, Jim 234, 236
McAllen, John 234
McAllen Ranch 234–239
McCoy, Colt 76–77
McEntire, William Randolph 40
McFarlane, Robert "Doc" 314, 317
McKeown, Chris 212–213
McKeown, Ellen 216
McKeown, Russell 218
Micallef, Al 131, 132, 136
Micallef, Mike 131, 132
Miller, J. H. 308
Mitchell, Malone 126
Mize, Mike 25
Moore, Rodney 185, **186**
Myers, Will 289

N

Nail, James H. 51
Nellie (dog) **216**
Novack, Ben **30–31**
Novel, Martha 218, 219

O, P

Oatmeal Apple Crisp 129
Ocotillo Restaurant 108–115
Peach Cobbler 49
Peacock, Pat 126
Pepper and Cheese Beer Bread 107
Perini, Lisa 77
Perini, Tom 75–77, **78**
Perini Ranch Steakhouse 75–83
Perini Ranch Steak Rub 78
Perlitz, Jimmy 204, 206
Perlitz Ranch 204–209
Petersen, Paul 120, 122
pheasant
  Baked Pheasant 91
  Pheasant Pot Pie 179
  Pheasant Royale 178
  Pheasant Salad 187
  Roast Pheasant 188
Pheasant Pot Pie 179
Pheasant Royale 178
Pheasant Salad 187
Pickens, Bryan **309**
pig, feral. See boar
Pig in the Ground 57
Pincher's Boil'n Pot 336

Pineapple-Rum Shrimp **15**, 269
Pitchfork Land and Cattle Company 65–71
Pondren, J. A. 308
Port "A" Seafood Company 272–277
Port Bay Hunting & Fishing Club 290–295
Potato-Mushroom Hash 122
Praline Bars 203
Pyle, Buck 124

Q

quail
  Barbecued Quail 330
  Fried Quail 34
  Quail and Spinach Salad with Honey Mustard and Bacon Dressing 158
  Quail in Wine Sauce 233
  Quail Poppers 32
  Smothered Quail 70
  Tailgate Quail 224
  Tamale Cheese and Quail Pie with Chipotle Mexican Crème 115
Quail and Spinach Salad with Honey Mustard and Bacon Dressing 158, **158**
Quail in Wine Sauce 233
Quail Poppers 32, **32**

R

Radley, Coy **287**
Radley, Craig 336, 341
Radley, Debbie 336, 341
Ranch Beans 218
rattlesnake
  Rattlesnake Cakes in a Pistachio Nut Crust 112–113, **113**
Rattlesnake Cakes in a Pistachio Nut Crust 112–113, **113**
Ray, Murphy 201
Reata Grill Blend 140
Reata Restaurant 131, 136–141
red snapper. See fish
redfish. See fish
Redfish Cakes 293
Redfish Lodge 264–271
Reel, Jimmy 252
Remoulade Sauce 276
Richards, Bill 312
Richard Lee Recreational Area 170
Roasted Wild Boar Leg with Mustard-Caper Sauce 165
Roast Duck with Currant Sauce 218
Roast Pheasant 188
Rogers, Melissa 264

Rogers, Phil 264
Rough Creek Lodge & Resort 185–191
Ruiz, Maria 300

S

Salado Seco Ranch 210–219
salads
  Pheasant Salad 187
  Quail and Spinach Salad with Honey Mustard and Bacon Dressing 158
salad dressings
  Crab Finger Dressing 281
  Honey Mustard and Bacon Dressing 158
  Vinaigrette 187
Salsa Roja 219, **219**
Sandhill Crane in Port Cream Sauce 94
sandwiches
  Hot and Spicy Speck Po' Boy 295
Sandy Oaks Ranch 220–227
Santa Anita Ranch. See McAllen Ranch
Sartin, Charles 322, 324
Sartin, Jerri 322, 324
Sartin, Kelli 324
Sartin's BBQ Crabs 325
Sartin's Seafood 322–325
sauces
  Amaretto Cream Sauce 39
  Apple Cider Brandy Sauce 159
  Barbecue Sauce 180, 215, 330
  Cajeta Sauce 141
  Chipotle Mexican Crème 115
  Chipotle Sauce 112–113
  Cilantro-Lime Butter 289
  Coconut Curry Sauce 287
  Cream Sauce 178
  Currant Sauce 218
  Green Peppercorn Sauce 183
  Honey-Cilantro Ginger Glaze 158
  Japanese Mayonnaise 281
  Mango-Jalapeño Cream Sauce 288
  Mushroom Demi-Glace 120
  Mustard-Caper Sauce 165
  Port Cream Sauce 94
  Red Chili Glaze 114
  Red Remoulade Sauce 295
  Remoulade Sauce 276
  Roasted Garlic–Horseradish Cream Sauce 82
  Sauce (for Venison Henry) 238
  Shiner Bock Beer Blanc 156
  Tomatillo Sauce 280
  Veracruz Sauce 300
  Wild Boar Sausage Gravy 122

Yakitori Sauce 274
Savory Venison Stew 165
Scallops of Venison 214
Scates, Chuck 264
Scates, Lynn 264
Schreiner, Charles 149
Schreiner, Myrtle 149
seasonings
  Blackened Seasoning Mix 341
  Blackened Spice Mix 268
  Coffee Rub 269
  Espresso Rub 156
  Guilbeau's Cajun Seasoning 337
  Leigh Ann's Seafood Seasoning 293
  Perini Ranch Steak Rub 78
  Reata Grill Blend 140
  Smoke Rub 159
Shells Pasta & Seafood 278–283
shrimp
  C. J.'s Shrimp Ceviche 275
  Corn Bread Dressing with Shrimp and Andouille 337
  Pineapple-Rum Shrimp 269
  Shrimp Pegues with Brown Sugar Glaze 249, **249**
side dishes
  Bourbon Sweet Potatoes 173
  Cheese and Bacon Grits 140
  Corn Pudding 331
  Cowboy Potatoes 83
  Fried Corn and Peppers 107
  Fried Green Beans 227
  Green Bean Bundles 331
  Green Chili and Mexican Crème Smashed Potatoes 115
  Green Chili Twice-Baked Potatoes 107
  Grilled Peaches with Spicy Lemon Honey 156
  Mashed Potatoes with Sage and White Cheddar Cheese 320
  Potato-Mushroom Hash 122
  Ranch Beans 218
  Smashed Ranch Potatoes 68
  Southwest Baked Beans 209
  Squash Soufflé 312
  Texas Caviar 83
  Wild Mushroom and Sweet Garlic Bread Pudding 189
  Yogurt-Fried Red Onion Rings 295
Siegman, Mike **285**
Simons, Greg 103–104, **104–105**
Smashed Ranch Potatoes 68
Smith, Allyson **282**
Smothered Quail 70
Sorenson, Andrew 290
Southwest Baked Beans 209
Spears, Grady 136, 138

speckled trout. *See* fish
Squash Soufflé   312
squirrel
   Squirrel and Dumplings   318
   Squirrel Jambalaya   340
Squirrel and Dumplings   318
Squirrel Jambalaya   340
Stasney, Dick   51
Stasney, Eska Gage   51
Stasney's Cook Ranch   51–57
Stephens, James   **66**
Stephenson, M. B.   40
stews
   Chris's Almost Famous Chili   164
   Duck and Black Bean Chili   187
   Duck and Sausage Gumbo   319
   Savory Venison Stew   165
   Squirrel Jambalaya   340
   Venison Carne Guisada   202
   Venison Chili   231
   Venison Cortadillo   238
   Venison Posole   45
   Venison Stew   34
Stokes, Harold   129
Stokes, Pat   129
Stone, Heber, IV   278
Stone, Heber, V   278
Stroube, H. R.   326
Stroube, Steve   326, 329
Stuart, Jesse   204
Stuffed Antelope Tenderloin   104
Stuffed Whole Flounder   294
Sugar-Cured Smoked Venison Ham   129
Swiss Venison   202

T

Tailgate Quail   224
Tamale Cheese and Quail Pie with Chipotle Mexican Crème   115
Tarpon Inn   286
Taylor, Ben   169
Taylor, Meredith   169
Taylor, Sonya   169, *172, 173*

Taylor, Ted   169, 170
Tejas Guides   334
Texas 4-H Conference Center   169, 170
Texas Caviar   83, **83**
Texas Wild Game Cooperative   160
Thompson, Gerard   187, 188, 189, 190
Tomatillo Sauce   219, **219**
trout. *See* fish
Trout-Mango Ceviche   270, **270**
Tule Ranch Corn Bread   62
Tule Ranch Hunts   58–63
tuna. *See* fish
Tuna Steak with Japanese Mayonnaise   281
turkey
   Barbecued Wild Turkey   207
   Fried Wild Turkey Fingers   46
   Wild Turkey Pie   80
Turtle Cheesecake   38

U, V

Upland Bird Country   326–333
Urbanczyk, Brad   132
U Ranch   40–49, 61
venison
   Bacon-Wrapped Axis Backstrap   151
   Bunkhouse Meatloaf   164
   Chicken-Fried Venison with Wild Boar Sausage Gravy   122
   Chris's Almost Famous Chili   164
   Espresso-Rubbed Venison Backstrap with Shiner Bock Beer Blanc   156
   Grilled Venison Backstrap with Apricot Glaze   140
   Grilled Venison with Green Peppercorn Sauce   183
   Savory Venison Stew   165
   Scallops of Venison   214
   Sugar-Cured Smoked Venison Ham   129

Swiss Venison   202
Venison-Stuffed Peppers   135
Venison and Sweet Potato Hash   190
Venison Backstrap with Roasted Garlic–Horseradish Cream Sauce   82
Venison Carne Guisada   202
Venison Chili   231
Venison Cortadillo   238
Venison Henry   238
Venison Jerky   **128,** 129
Venison Kabobs   167
Venison Piccata   207
Venison Posole   45
Venison Sausage and Biscuit Casserole   233
Venison Sausage and Wild Rice Casserole   105
Venison Sausage Dip   62
Venison Steak with Mushroom Gravy   62
Venison Stew   34
Venison Tampiqueña   237
Venison-Stuffed Peppers   135
Venison and Sweet Potato Hash   190
Venison Backstrap with Roasted Garlic–Horseradish Cream Sauce   82
Venison Carne Guisada   202
Venison Chili   231
Venison Cortadillo   238
Venison Henry   238
Venison Jerky   **128,** 129
Venison Kabobs   167
Venison Piccata   207
Venison Posole   45
Venison Sausage and Biscuit Casserole   233
Venison Sausage and Wild Rice Casserole   105
Venison Sausage Dip   62
Venison Steak with Mushroom Gravy   62
Venison Stew   34
Venison Tampiqueña   237

W

Wagster, John   **281**
wahoo. *See* fish
Warm Apple Tart   191
Watson, Ambrose   **217**
Watson, Bea McCall   311
Weaver, Josh "Treebark"   **172**
West, James "Silver Dollar Jim" Marion, Jr.   124
West-Pyle Cattle Company   124
Wheatley, Cathy   334, 336, **338–339,** *339,* 340
Wheatley, Mike   334
Whole Fried Bream   339
Wildlife Systems   103–107
Wild Boar Schnitzel   159
wild game, handling and preparing   162
Wild Mushroom and Sweet Garlic Bread Pudding   189
Wild Turkey Pie   80
Williams, Eugene F.   65
Wolff, David   254
Woodward, Bob   **176, 177**
Woody (guide)   315
Wyatt, Mike   25, **28,** 29, **34, 35**
Wyatt, Monica   25, 29, 32, 34, 37, 38, 39
Wyndam, Jack   ***154–155***
Wyndam, Jimmy   ***154–155***

Y, Z

Yakitori Sauce   274
Yankee and Betty's Seafood Galley. *See* Port "A" Seafood Company
Yogurt-Fried Red Onion Rings   295
Young, Salomé Ballí Dominguez   234
YO Ranch   149–151
Zachry, H. B.   201
Zipprian, James   132

GRAZING ACROSS TEXAS
Rod, Gun, and Ranch Cooking

Editor:
Alison Tartt

Food Editor:
Ellen McKeown

Book Designer:
Barbara Jezek

Food styling for cover, pages 7, 16–17, and 83:
Julie Hettiger and Sharon Kuhner

Type:
Boton and Palatino Linotype

Paper:
128 GSM Japanese Matte

Production:
Asia Pacific representing Phoenix Offset

Blake Brown with a sunrise redfish